Crossfires

Crossfires

Nationalism, Racism and Gender in Europe

Edited by
Helma Lutz, Ann Phoenix
and Nira Yuval-Davis

Pluto Press
LONDON • EAST HAVEN, CT
for the European Forum of Left Feminists

First published 1995 by Pluto Press
345 Archway Road, London N6 5AA, UK
and 140 Commerce Street,
East Haven, CT 06512, USA

99 98 97 96 95   5 4 3 2 1

British Library Cataloguing in Publication Data
A catalogue record for this book is available from the British
Library

ISBN 0 7453 0994 1

Library of Congress Cataloging in Publication Data
Applied for.

Designed and produced for Pluto Press by
Chase Production Services, Chipping Norton, OX7 5QR
Typeset from disk by Stanford DTP Services
Printed in the EC by T J Press, Padstow, England

Contents

Preface

This volume originated in the eighth annual conference of the European Forum of Left Feminists (EFLF), held in November 1993 in Amsterdam. The European Forum is an international network of individual feminist activists and scholars which has a European focus. It develops and encourages discussions on gender-related issues by linking them to other aspects of social division.

The first conference of the Forum took place in Copenhagen in 1985. The original objective of its organisers was the urgent need for a Europe-wide meeting of socialist feminists in order to insert a feminist voice into the new Left in Western Europe. The discussion at that time aimed to highlight the dangers for women of a Europe based on exclusion of the Third World and the poorer countries of Southern Europe. Since then, the Forum has met annually in different European countries, with an expanding network of feminist activists and a developing political agenda.

With perestroika and the collapse of the Soviet Bloc and the Cold War, the Forum has been enriched by the joining of feminists from Eastern and Central European countries. One of the results of their coming to the Forum, together with the growing voice of feminists from Southern Europe, has been the decision to change, after a lengthy debate, the name of the Forum from the European Forum of Socialist Feminists to the European Forum of Left Feminists. In spite of the fact that most of the members of the Forum continue to define themselves as socialists, it was decided to respect the feelings of the newcomers in whose countries the word 'socialism' was appropriated by the ruling governments and the parties they opposed.

The shift in Europe's boundaries has also alerted women in the Forum to the constructed character of Europe and the need to engage more with intra-European exclusions and racisms rather than just in relation to the Third World. Thus the sixth conference of the Forum in Norwich was dedicated to questions of the differential positioning of women and citizenship in Europe. This resulted in a book edited by Anna Ward, Jeanne Gregory and Nira Yuval-Davis, which was called *Women and Citizenship in Europe: Borders, Rights and Duties* and published by Trentham Books in 1992. The eighth Forum conference in Amsterdam from which the chapters in this book were developed was, in many ways, a continuation of the Norwich conference.

While discussions of racism and gender as well as racism in the feminist movement have been on the feminist agenda since the beginning of the 1980s, it is only very recently that nationalism has been discussed as a gendered dimension of social division. The emergence of this is closely linked to the emergence of 'Fortress Europe' and to the war in the former Yugoslavia. This book, emerging as it does from EFLF concerns, addresses the intertwining of both nationalism and racism with gender. If we take into consideration the dramatic changes occurring in the European social landscape with, in many cases, devastating results, it is clearly timely that this volume analyses new forms of social exclusion and their ideological legitimation. The book which follows is particularly concerned to highlight the ways in which women are affected by, and at the same time are involved in, the (re)production of these divisions.

Helma Lutz, Ann Phoenix and Nira Yuval-Davis
Amsterdam and London

Acknowledgements

Many individuals and organisations helped to make the Amsterdam conference successful. In particular we would like to thank the students and volunteers who did the administration for the conference, who womanned the desks throughout the conference and helped to make it the friendly and stimulating event that it was. They were: Marinella Vermaas; Pauline van Gelder; Ans Zwerver; Jacqueline van Loon; Ciska Pattipilohy; Hetty Greuter; Til van Maurik and Rianne Esseboom.

We would like to thank the following organisations for their financial support of the conference: Commission of the European Communities – Directorate General of Employment, Industrial Relations and Social Affairs; De Nationale Commissie Voorlichting en Bewustwording Ontwikkelingssamenwerking (NCO); Het Ministerie van Sociale Zaken en Werkgelegenheid, Directie Coordinatie Emancipatiebeleid (DCE); Ministerie voor Buitenlandse Zaken, Speerpunt programma Vrouwen en Ontwikkeling; Vrouwenbond FNV and Emancipatiebureau Amsterdam.

The volume itself would not, of course, have been possible without the efforts of the contributors who were unfailingly cheerful as they turned their conference presentations into chapters. Their achievements are particularly impressive given that, for many, English was a second (or third) language. Our grateful thanks to them.

Thanks are also due to Maria Harrison, whose word-processing skills contributed to the production of the book. Last but not least, we would like to express our appreciation of the wonderful electronic mail and fax machines, without which the coordinated international work on editing the book would probably not have been possible, but which also encouraged many telephone conversations when, for whatever reason, connections failed.

Notes on Contributors

Tatjana Djuric (University of Novi Sad, Yugoslavia) completed her Ph.D in Economics in 1992 at the University of Beograd. She has published extensively on issues of alternative development and on socialism and the economy. She lives and teaches in Novi Sad, Federal Republic of Yugoslavia.

Philomena Essed (University of Amsterdam, the Netherlands) is a cultural anthropologist. She has researched and written widely on gender, 'race' and ethnic relations, including *Everyday Racism* (Hunter House, 1990) *Understanding Everyday Racism* (Sage, London 1991) and *Diversity: Gender, Color and Culture* (University of Massachusetts Press – in press).

Natalya Kosmarskaya (Moscow, Russia) is a sociologist at the Russian Academy of Sciences and the Center for Gender Studies. She is working on the issue of migration and gender.

Helma Lutz (University of Utrecht, the Netherlands) is a sociologist. She has published widely on migration, gender relations and migrant identity. Her publications include *Welten Verbinden. Türkische Sozialarbeiterinnen in den Niederlanden und der Bundesrepublik Deutschland* (IKO-Verlag, Frankfurt aM 1991).

Ann Phoenix (Birkbeck College, University of London, Great Britain) is a psychologist. She has published extensively in the field of gender and race relations. Her main publications include *Young Mothers?* (Polity Press, Cambridge 1991) and *Black, White or Mixed Race? Race and Racism in the Lives of Young People of Mixed Parentage* (with B. Tizard) (Routledge, London 1993).

Nora Räthzel (Hamburg, Germany) is an educational scientist. She is the co-founder of the Hamburg Institute for Migration and Racism Research and has published extensively on issues of racism, nationalism and gender issues. Her main publications include *Rassismus und Migration in Europa* (Argumentsonderband, Hamburg/Berlin 1992) (co-editor with Annita Kalpaka).

Gloria Wekker (University of Utrecht, the Netherlands) is a cultural anthropologist. She has published in the fields of Caribbean studies and gender relations. Her publications include *Ik Ben een Gouden Munt. Subjectiviteit en Seksualiteit van Creoolse Volksklassevrouwen in Paramaribo* (Feministische uitgeverij VITA, Amsterdam 1994) (which translates as: *I Am Gold Money. The Construction of Selves, Gender and Sexualities in a Female Working Class Afro-Surinamese Setting*, Dissertation UCLA, 1992).

Theresa Wobbe (Free University of Berlin, Germany) is an historian and sociologist. She has published in the fields of gender relations and sociology of knowledge and National Socialism. Her publications include *Gleichheit und Differenz. Politische Strategien von Frauenrechtlerinnen um die Jahrhundertwende* (Campus, Frankfurt aM/New York 1989) and she is the editor of *Nach Osten. Verdeckte Spuren nationalsozialistischer Verbrechen* (Verlag Neue Kritik, Frankfurt a.M. 1992).

Nira Yuval-Davis (Greenwich University, London, Great Britain) is a sociologist. She has published extensively in the fields of gender relations, ethnic studies and nationalism. Her most recent books are *Racialized Boundaries. Race, Nation, Gender, Colour and Class and the Anti-Racist Struggle* (co-authored with Floya Anthias) (Routledge, London/New York 1992); *Refusing Holy Orders: Women and Fundamentalism in Britain* (co-editor with Gita Sahgal) (Virago, London 1992) and *Unsettling Settler Societies: Articulations of Gender, Ethnicity, Race and Class* (co-edited with Daiva Stasiulis), (Sage, London and Newbury Park, CA, 1995).

Dubravka Zarkov (University of Nijmegen, the Netherlands) is a cultural anthropologist who studied sociology, anthropology and development in the former Yugoslavia (Beograd) and the Netherlands. She has published in the areas of gender relations and socialist discourse and is currently working on her Ph.D thesis 'From "media war" to "civil war": the female body and nationalist processes in the former Yugoslavia (1986–1992)' at the Centre for Women's Studies, University of Nijmegen.

Introduction
Nationalism, Racism and Gender – European Crossfires

Helma Lutz, Ann Phoenix and Nira Yuval-Davis

In recent years, there has been increasing concern about 'new nationalism' among scholars in Europe and elsewhere. Rapid, dramatic and (in some cases) bloody developments within Europe have fuelled these concerns. In particular, increases in attacks from right-wing nationalist groups, the consolidation of 'Fortress Europe' with the finalising of the European Union (EU), 'ethnic' wars designed to change the constitution of nation states in Eastern Europe, and the opening up of the 'Irish question' with the ceasefire in Northern Ireland, have all served to bring to international attention questions of nationalism and racism in Europe. Less visible and less discussed, however, is the fact that nationalism and racism (however and wherever expressed in Europe) have gender dimensions. Thus, while there are some common experiences for men and women from the same racialised, ethnic and religious groups, an understanding of the differences and specificities in the ways in which women and men are positioned within these issues is crucial to the understanding of and, hence, action against them.

This book is designed to shed some light on these issues. The chapters in the book provide insights into the ways in which nationalism, racism and gender intersect in Europe. Together they make a contribution to the understanding of these issues in particular European countries (Britain, Germany, the Netherlands, Russia and the former Yugoslavia) and to illustrating the importance of understanding how current situations are socially located and that Europe is not hermetically sealed but, rather, part of the process of globalisation. Thus the question of where Europe starts and ends has ramifications for the ways in which Europeans are socially constructed (see chapters by Djuric and Wobbe). In addition, a consideration of other countries can clarify helpful and unhelpful processes within

Europe (see chapters by Wekker and Wobbe). All the chapters consider the gender dimension of the situations they discuss so that, overall, gender is foregrounded within the volume.

This introduction firstly interrogates the notion of nationalism. It asks whether what has been identified as 'new nationalism' is really so and argues that, like the concept of 'new racism', it is comprised of both new and old themes. It then explores the ways in which gender is central to processes of racism and nationalism, and women's resistance to some of the ways in which they are inserted into both racism and nationalism. The final section of the introduction discusses some of the themes which emerge from the chapters which follow. It thus provides one possible perspective from which the book can be viewed and, hopefully, points the way forward for feminist struggles against racisms and nationalist exclusions.

The Ghost of Nationalism

The Dutch writer Harry Mulisch opened his lecture at the Frankfurt Book Fair in October 1993 by claiming that 'The ghost of nationalism is roaming over Europe.' This paraphrase of Karl Marx's famous introduction to the 'Kommunistisches Manifest' – 'The ghost of communism is roaming over Europe' – can be seen at first as countering the meaning of Marx's words. Marx's comment was meant as a demand for demystification of the ghost of communism and an invitation for politicians and social scientists to face the positive aspects of what then was a powerful social movement as well as a political programme for social equality. Mulisch, on the other hand, was referring to the threatening aspects of a new nationalism and of nationalist movements which he saw as dangerous to democracy and human rights in Europe. Thus, whereas Marx wanted to 'promote' his 'ghost', Mulisch's aim was the negation of what Marx was describing through the rejection of the ghost of nationalism.

Nevertheless, the two 'ghosts', when understood as historical constructs, also correspond with each other. They can each be seen as Janus-headed concepts, embodying both positive and negative social forces. On the one hand, each provides enlightened (symbolic) meanings of belonging to a community, and on the other hand each stands for the oppression and murder of those groups which resist adjustment or submission to dominant ideologies. Just as, originally, communism was a response to social inequality and to the exploitation of the capitalist economy, nationalism in eighteenth and nineteenth-century Europe was a liberating power, a reaction to the aristocratic despotism of hundreds of small feudal states. In the twentieth century it became a liberating force in the fight for state-independence of colonised peoples all over the world. Authors like Benedict Anderson (1983) and W.F. Wertheim (1964) have focused on the unifying forces of anti-colonialist nationalist ideas. Anderson, in particular, in *Imagined Communities* (1983) has pointed out that nationalism, using a whole set of constructed symbols and tools like a shared history, a common language, slogans, newspapers and anthems, has provided a feeling of belonging, self-confidence and 'the dream of immortality' to the citizens of modern time. According to Anderson, nationalism is fundamentally a positive force which is transcending social class and which has replaced the religious beliefs of pre-modern times. While Anderson reminds us of the beautiful face of the Janus-head, others, like Eric Hobsbawm (1990, 1994), have warned against the ugliness of the opposite face. According to Hobsbawm, nationalism was once a political enterprise which aimed to establish nation states by broadening and transforming elitism into universalism, based on common (national) education. However, it completely moved away from its traditional function, becoming a forceful and destructive ideology, 'filling up the emptiness which has been left by the breakdown of other states and ideologies' (1994: 14). Hobsbawm refers particularly to the Eastern European situation after the collapse of communist state-ideologies, a development which has also had repercussions in other continents. His main concern is that in 'new' nationalism, violent exclusion is prevailing over universalism. In the search for unifying elements and common ground, the newly emerging states maintain and reinvent ethnic symbols, often borrowing symbols from the Middle Ages which comprise archaic attitudes against other ethnic groups who are defined as 'not belonging'. The evolving definitions draw upon 'Blut und Boden' (blood and soil) arguments, claiming that entitlement to a particular territory is by inheritance and being of the same 'stock'. The requirement to be of the same 'stock', however, makes living in a particular place for generations irrelevant to the national status of some groups of people. For not everyone who has lived for a certain period of the past on a certain territory is seen as a 'lawful' inheritor. The Rom-peoples (Gypsies) in Hungary, for example, have recently been deprived of their nationality, their citizenship, their Hungarian passports, despite the fact that they have lived on that soil for centuries.

The (re)organisation of national states along ethnic or 'racial' lines highlights the interconnections between nationalism and racism. Anderson (1983), for example, constructs nationalism and racism as mutually exclusive. He views nationalism as a positive sentiment, 'which thinks in terms of historical destinies, while racism dreams of eternal contaminations, transmitted from the origins of time through an endless sequence of loathsome copulations: outside history ... On the whole, racism and anti-Semitism manifest themselves, not across national boundaries but within them' (Anderson, 1983: 136). While it is clear that not all nationalist ideologies are equally racist, this complete separation is highly problematic. Wherever a delineation of boundaries takes place – as is the case with every ethnic and national collectivity – processes of exclusion and inclusion are in operation. These can take place with varying degrees of intensity and with a variety of cultural, religious and state mechanisms. But exclusions of 'the Other' can become an inherent part of national ethnicities and an obsessive preoccupation of the national culture and of the national political project. It is not just a question of nationalism and racism finding common ground, as Miles (1993: 59) has put it, but that racist exclusions become central to the national symbolic order.

Nationalist projects have different dimensions, such as origin, culture and citizenship (Anthias and Yuval-Davis, 1992; Yuval-Davis, 1993), which in different historical situations can be emphasised by different historical agents in specific nationalist projects. Although the link between nationalism and racism is especially strong when the national collectivity is constructed purely in terms of origin, racist exclusions, inferiorisations and exploitations can be linked to all these dimensions. Civic (non-aggressive, civilised) nationalism is, unfortunately, not the automatic antidote to racism as, for example, Michael Ignatieff (1993) and Julia Kristeva (1993) would have us believe. This becomes clear when, for example, policies of immigration and settlement in 'Fortress Europe' are examined. Since the main elements of the European Union have been completed, in theory, freedom of movement within the community and of trade between community members have made national boundaries within Europe less important and more permeable than they had been. Yet in practice the right to freedom of movement between

European countries without a passport is reserved for those Europeans who are majority members and equipped with fully fledged citizenship rights. For many minority members ('immigrants') the European Union has not removed the obstacles to travel within Europe. In fact, the requirement of carrying some form of identification has affected majority members as well. In Britain, for example, passport controls at ports and airports have been reinforced with Union membership since there are more penalties than before for airlines which carry passengers without legal rights of entry to the countries to which they are bound. Thus, in order to keep out minorities, majority members are denied some of the freedom they might otherwise have. Countries such as Britain continue to resist any EU attempts to relax internal European border controls.

The boundaries between Europe and the rest of the world are constantly being fortified. Never before has Europe been concerned so much with legitimising measures designed to keep out the 'alien flood'. Since measures to exclude 'Others' go together with the construction of cultural, religious or 'racial' otherness, racialised minorities within the European Union have gradually become the targets of this 'othering'. With these developments, the metaphor of nationalism as a 'ghost' seems slightly inappropriate since it certainly has material consequences.

'New' Nationalism?

If theorists such as Hobsbawm (1994) are correct, the question arises about what is 'new' in the 'new European nationalism'. It is certainly debatable whether, in effect, 'old nationalisms' have been more multiethnic, tolerant and/or non-exclusive than the 'new' ones. Most nation states, in the name of maintaining and creating internal cohesion, have been and are dominated by one ethnic group with other ethnic groups being restricted to minority positions by virtue of being marginalised, rather than because their numbers are small. Moreover, if we take Europe as the cradle of the nation state, even before massive and visible immigration, in many Western European nations ethnic and/or regional minority groups have long fought for cultural if not political autonomy (the Irish, the Basques, the Frisians, and many others). National states have always had to deal with internal ethnic divisions. For this reason Robert Miles, referring

to the case of Great Britain and France, calls the nationalisation
endeavour an 'uncompleted project' (1993: 207).

It seems reasonable to assume, therefore, that the seeds of ethnic
division have always been part of nationalism and are not new.
Nevertheless, on the basis of the universal and humanist claims of
Western democracy, ethnic minority groups have had, to a certain
extent, rights to demand legal protection and recognition of their
cultural practices. In the newly emerged states of Eastern Europe,
however, rights and protection are in many cases withheld from
ethnic minorities. In Latvia and Estonia, for instance, large numbers
of the countries' inhabitants, Russians, are excluded from eligibil-
ity for citizenship.

In view of the fact that the former Yugoslavia, the former Soviet
Union, the Baltic states and other Eastern European states all belonged
to the former socialist/communist bloc, one can certainly speak about
a 'new nationalism' in those states. The Yugoslavian case, in particular,
has consequences for the rest of Europe. Since the drama of the war
in the former Yugoslavia, the illusion that had been cherished for
more than 40 years that political conflicts ending in war would never
again be a European issue, melted away within a couple of months.
Although some Yugoslav social scientists and economists had
predicted the menace of war – even the economic necessity of the
war for the stabilisation and retention of hegemonic power by the
central Yugoslav army (see the chapter by Djuric in this volume) –
many European citizens were astounded by the events which
unfolded in front of them when the war literally spread out into their
living-rooms. Millions of television spectators found themselves
restricted to the role of voyeur of war atrocities. For the first time
since the trials of Nazi Germany in Nuremberg, Europe 'witnessed'
war crimes committed in Europe, better documented than ever before,
while little was done to stop the cruelty.

Events in the former Yugoslavia were all the more shocking given
the contrast with the 'cleanness' of the portrayal of the Gulf War, a
contrast which made the Gulf War mesmerising. The war in the former
Yugoslavia has become part of daily news-life and it has developed
a certain 'normality'. Only a little while ago a term like 'ethnic
cleansing' was hardly used in public discussion. Yet the term itself
has now become so normal that in many accounts it is not even put
in quotation marks. One effect of the various unsuccessful attempts
to sign and enforce peace treaties in Bosnia has been the legitimation of 'ethnic cleansing' as a successful strategy of new state building.

These dramatic changes have all happened within a very short period. From our perspective today it is quite remarkable that in her 'country-report on Yugoslavia', written in 1991 for the European Forum of Left Feminists (EFLF) conference on the eve of the outbreak of civil war, Zarana Papic expressed her hope for a 'reasonable solution for shaping a new and different Yugoslavia' (1992: 58) – a wish which, since then, few would dare to articulate. In the meantime, language has been adjusted to political realities: one either speaks of the former Yugoslavia or of the separate states of Croatia, Bosnia, Slovenia and Serbia. At the same time political reality has been adjusted to the language of those nationalist ideologists who, through their writing, had already circumscribed and prepared for the 'new nations' in poetry and novels (as for example in the writings by current political leaders such as Seselj, Draskovic, Tudjman and Karadžić).

In considering the question of whether it makes sense to talk of 'new nationalism', a look at debates on 'new racism' might help. Like 'new racism', current nationalism is plural and is fundamentally old in the sense that forms of old nationalism have sedimented into common sense. Like racism, current nationalism is shaped by both commonalities and differences with its predecessors. In many cases 'new nationalism' is more exclusive than former nationalisms in as far as it coincides more than ever before with forms of racist exclusion. This development is not restricted to Eastern Europe or specifically to the Balkans but includes political shifts in the West. A consideration of discussions about how Europe has to be redefined elucidates this.

Exclusions From the Nation: Europism, Welfare-Chauvinism and Racisms

Etienne Balibar (1990) suggests that the fall of the Soviet Bloc and the end of the Cold War have brought into focus questions of 'what is Europe' and what are its boundaries. Before 1989, 'Europe' was assumed to be those countries of Europe included in the then European Economic Community (EEC) and the other parliamentary democracies of Western Europe. Since then, there has been a search for alternative organising principles which could unify Europe, often focusing around the elusive concept of 'European civilisation'. (The former Yugoslavia has largely been excluded from this construction of Europe – see Dubravka Zarkov's chapter in this volume.)

Discourses of culture, politics and space thus become closely
intermeshed with discourses of nationalism and racism, home
('*Heimat*') and otherness ('*Ausländer*' – see Nora Räthzel's chapter
in this volume). The new racist nationalism which is gathering
force in contemporary Europe is much concerned with notions of
defending 'our' home, space, territory. Philomena Essed (in this
volume) points out that there has been a shift from Eurocentrism
into what she calls 'Europism'. Eurocentrism is the discourse of
European superiority and domination over the South. Europism is
the defensive discourse of constructing a 'pure Europe' which is
cleansed of all foreign and 'uncivilised elements' in its territory.
Although Eurocentrism and Europism are constructed around the
same key elements, the clear territorial delimitation of the outside
and the homogenising pressure on the inside certainly indicate a
current development from Eurocentrism towards Europism.

Others, like the German philosopher Jürgen Habermas (1992),
have called this 'welfare-chauvinism', thereby focusing on the
current process of European self-definition through defending the
institutions of the welfare state – seen as proof of self-achievement
through suffering and hardship – against greedy, indigent 'outsiders'
(see also Leiprecht, 1991). Both 'Europism' and 'welfare-chauvinism'
can serve as theoretical concepts for the analysis of racist nationalism. Related discourses – of culture, religion, history and democracy
– are being used in different ways for reinforcing and 'embodying'
ethnic and nationalist boundaries in different countries in Europe.
This often happens in such a way that non-Christian and former Soviet
bloc countries are marginalised, politically and economically. It is
also important to recognise that this construction of 'pure Europe'
is not just an ideological construction but that a wide range of laws
and regulations of the European Union have come together to
structure what is known as 'Fortress Europe' in which the more than
14 million 'non-nationals', non-Europeans constitute second-class
citizens (see Lutz, 1994b). Ideological, legal, economic and political
constructions of racism in Europe have used both the other side of
the 'Iron Curtain' as well as post-colonial and migrant labour positionings to promote images of demonic 'Others'. The former have
been transformed by the developments in Europe since 1989 but
have not disappeared. The latter continue to exist (see Nora Räthzel's
chapter in this volume; Lutz, 1991; Yuval-Davis, 1995b)

It is important to emphasise that there is more than one kind of
'racism'. Racism can be constructed around any signifier of ethnic

boundaries and not just when constructions of 'race' are present (see Cohen, 1988; Anthias and Yuval-Davis, 1992; Brah, 1993). Colour, culture, religion, origin etc. can all be used to exclude, inferiorise and/or exploit the 'Other'. In contemporary Europe a variety of groupings – from colonies, former colonies as well as from the margins of Europe itself and from the 'old European minorities' (such as Gypsies and Jews), migrants, refugees and those who have been living in the country for many generations – can all become targets for these different racisms. Some of these racialised minorities are at the bottom of the class structure of the societies in which they live and many are unemployed or even 'unemployable'; others occupy vulnerable entrepreneurial positions or have even managed to become part of the 'established' middle classes. They all are, however, excluded at least to some degree from the boundaries of 'the nation' (see the chapter by Ann Phoenix in this volume; also Lutz, 1994a).

As Michel Wieviorka (1994) has argued, both exclusion and exploitation, the cultural and the social, need to be present in the process of racialisation. By itself, exclusion might just lead to separation rather than to racialisation which requires social relations. Exploitation on its own could as easily refer to class relations as to racialisation, which involves the construction of fixed boundaries between collectivities. The relative emphasis of each of these elements as well as their specific constructions vary from situation to situation.

The Gender Dimension

Racialised minorities, however, are not homogeneous. Class, sexuality, stage of the life-course and intra-ethnic divisions are, of course, also relevant. Gender is important in understanding the positionings of specific individuals and groupings in contemporary Europe. In this volume we are concentrating on issues which are of particular relevance to the positioning of racialised and ethnicised women in Europe.

Women often play important symbolic roles in nationalist and racialised narratives, carrying in their bodies the collective love and honour of 'the nation' (Anthias and Yuval-Davis, 1989). In many ways women's membership in their national collectivities is similar to that of men, and women are often active participants in national and ethnic struggles. However, in general, women are symbols of the nation while men are its agents (*Feminist Review*, 1993). It is not surprising, given that women symbolise the nation and men act to represent it, that it is generally particular sorts of men who are 'ethnic agents'. Yuval-Davis (1994a) illustrates the ways in which ethnic agents are constructed to be men with fundamentalist religious beliefs in communities constructed as authentic 'Other'. In confirmation of this, Margaret Wetherell and Jonathan Potter (1992) have demonstrated how, outside Europe, in the New Zealand context, old traditional Maori men are those who are constructed as the repositories of ethnic authenticity for all Maoris. However, in other cases, as for example in the case of Muslim immigrants, it is veiled women who are considered to be the most authentic symbols of their group (for a discussion of veils and headscarfs see Lutz, 1991; Bhavnani, 1993). The construction of men as the representatives and agents and women as symbols for ethnicised and racialised collectivities is detrimental to women in that it allows existing gender oppression to be legitimated to some extent, suppresses intragroup differences and thus has an essentialising effect (Yuval-Davis, 1994b). It also has a silencing effect in that it gives only men legitimate voice. In addition, constituting men as the mouthpieces of an ethnic or racial collectivity has another contradictory consequence. Since it constructs men as the ethnic agents, it constitutes women as marking the boundaries between groups: the 'guardians of the "race"' (Bland, 1982; Anthias and Yuval-Davis, 1989).

As such, issues of protection/violation for women are key themes (Anthias and Yuval-Davis, 1989; Brah, 1993) in discourses of the nation. As many feminists have pointed out, both sides of the protection/exploitation couplet are exploitive in that each silence women and uses assumed vulnerability to attempt to deny women access to power. Clearly, women are positioned differently from each other according to whether they are constructed as to be protected or to be violated (see Wobbe, Zarkov and Djuric in this volume). This construction varies by geography and is racialised and ethnicised.

Women affect and are affected by racisms and nationalisms in several specific ways. They are, for example, sometimes used to legitimise war. 'Womenandchildren' (as it is put by Cynthia Enloe, 1990), the 'mourning mother' or 'the rape victim' are common symbolic constructs in nationalist discourses prior to war and during wars which are used to mobilise the indignation of the masses. At the same time these constructs can also retain or reinforce sexual divisions of labour during war time, 'naturalising' both men's and women's roles. Controlling women's reproduction, by pressurising or encouraging them to produce more or less children is also often a major tool in national and ethnic conflicts (see Zarkov and Djuric in this volume; Yuval-Davis, 1995a). In the former Yugoslavia, forcing women, through rape, to bear children from their enemy's ethnic group was used as a deliberate strategy. The control of female sexuality and the female body can be used as a 'natural strategic weapon' to increase or reduce numbers in ethnic groups in situations where 'demographic races', the relative size of the competing collectivities, achieve prime political importance in claims for land and independence. Anti-abortion policies can also become, as in Poland, primary signifiers of new nationalist agendas and the adoption of religious discourse as a nationalist symbolic border guard (Armstrong, 1982). Systematic rape can be used as a means of damaging the honour of the 'Other' (in the Geneva convention, for example, rape is defined as a 'crime against honour' rather than as a mode of torture). On the other hand, constructing the enemy as 'the rapist' can also be used as a way to demonise the 'primitive Other'. This is a common phenomenon in racist discourses where the black (or, in Germany, as Theresa Wobbe describes in this volume, the Turkish) man is constructed as a threat from which 'our' women have to be defended. The women of the collectivity who dare to have relationships with men from minorities are seen as traitors. Terms like 'nigger-prostitutes' convey the derogatory manner in which such women are constructed as threats to the honour of the group.

The fact that it is women who produce children, and that 'recalcitrant' women are often constituted as if they reproduce alone, and are solely responsible for doing so, produces an elision of discourses on motherhood and nation. One consequence of this is the differentiation of women from majority ethnic groups in Europe and those from minority ethnic groups (whether or not they are migrants). For example, in various European countries there has been a consistent linking of 'race', nation and reproduction. Mothers who fall outside (white) majority ethnic groups have often been constructed as having too many children and, as a result, being 'drains' on state welfare provision (Phoenix, 1990). Far from their motherhood being romanticised and celebrated (as it is for majority ethnic groups) it serves to further their construction outside the norm, outside good citizenry and hence outside the 'imagined community' of the nation state (Phoenix and Woollett, 1991). It demonstrates one of the ways in which national ideologies are cultural resources that nationalists bring to the creation of common national identities (see *Feminist Review*, 1993).

Since 'race', ethnicity and national ideologies are always gendered, there are specific, rather than general, constructions and positionings of women of particular collectivities. They might differ in their rate of participation in the labour market, and within it they might cluster in different occupations or different positions within the same occupation. For example, figures from the 1991 British census show that black women of African Caribbean descent are still more likely to be in nursing than in any other professional occupation and that they are the 'race'/gender group most likely to be in those occupations (Owen, 1994). Overall, black women and women from other minority ethnic groups are more likely than white, majority women to be in marginal sectors of employment, like cleaning and sewing. Minority ethnic women are heavily represented in 'sweatshop industries' which provide cheap, disposable labour in circumstances where labour markets are simultaneously gender differentiated and racialised. They have little opportunity of finding well-paid, attractive jobs by moving around the European Union (see also Lutz, 1994a). The free market of the European Union does not, therefore, produce as many benefits for them as for middle-class women from the majority ethnic group. The fact that minority women tend to be in occupations where they have marginal status and little job security makes them vulnerable within Europe and is one of the reasons that they are unlikely to be among those taking advantage of free movement in Europe to secure better living conditions (including employment).

Attempts to exclude women from minority ethnic groups from European nation states have meant that, for a long time, there have been more restrictions on the free movement of minority women's male partners. In Britain, Avtar Brah (1992) points out that between 1969 and 1983 the British rules governing the entry of foreign husbands or fiancés to join their black and other minority ethnic group partners were changed five times in an ever more restrictive direction. White, majority women continued to be allowed this right. Immigration officials, acting on behalf of the British state, can also use their own interpretations of 'ethnicity as cultural practice' differentially to treat women from different ethnic groups. Thus, in the 1970s, women from the Indian subcontinent who went to Britain to join their fiancés were subjected to 'virginity tests', justified on the grounds that, culturally, they have to be virgins when they marry (see WING, 1985; Bhabha and Shutter, 1994; Lutz, 1994b). There are also differences between black and minority women from different groups which relate to claims on the British state and formal inclusion in the British nation.

About one million black and other minority women in Britain are not full British citizens, but have 'Third Country' national status which allows them access to employment, housing, education, health care and pensions, but which are not transferable to other countries in Europe. The two million black and other minority women who have full citizenship do, theoretically at least, have full rights to free movement in the EU although this cannot protect them from infringements of that freedom which result from the difficulty of distinguishing them from people who are not full citizens (Brah, 1992). Altogether, there are 6.4 million women in the EU who live in these conditions (classified as denizens rather than citizens) and whose situation clearly differs from that of European women who are constructed as 'indigenous' (see Lutz, 1994b).

It is thus clear that although women are differentiated by 'race' and nation, they are centrally positioned within the inclusions and exclusions of nationalism and racism. Not surprisingly, given long histories of women's resistance to oppression, many women within Europe have actively struggled, in a variety of ways, against both nationalism and racism.

Women's Resistance to Racism and Nationalism

Racism and nationalism are troublesome and annoying phenomena for feminist activities and/or theorists. The slogans and ideals of the 1970s, announcing that 'sisterhood' is global and that women's solidarity is able to bridge or solve all conflicts of whatever nature, have long been demystified. The slogan that 'the personal is political', once a powerful and empowering strategy to bring feminist issues onto the political agenda, has recently been criticised (Anthias and Yuval-Davis, 1992; Yuval-Davis, 1994a). Although it is true that this strategy has been successful in bonding those who were not part of the hegemonic structure by problematising 'naturalised' arenas of life (like the family, sexual violence etc.) and thereby deconstructing these notions, there are also considerable weaknesses. Theorising 'the personal' as if it was an objective reality rather than itself being a construction, essentialises the reality, a reality which is assumed to be shared by all members of the social category (in this case women) which is then perceived to constitute a basically homogeneous social grouping with shared interests. This essentialising view (all women share the 'personal') was first challenged by lesbians during the anti-abortion campaign ('why should we campaign for abortion as undesired pregnancy is not our paramount problem?'). This was also forcefully challenged by black feminists who argued that forced sterilisation and unsafe contraceptives like Depo-Provera injections (rather than abortions) were the main threat to their reproductive freedom. This was seen by black feminists as just one instance of the overall tunnel-vision ethnocentrism of white feminists and their blindness to forms of oppression other than gender-based ones (see the chapters by Philomena Essed and Gloria Wekker in this volume). These discussions led to the separate organisation of different groups within the women's movement, each on the basis of their own 'personal', sexual difference, skin colour and/or ethnic origin, religion and culture, class status and/or age difference. Whereas the claim of these identity politics for (discursive) space and entitlement in the hegemonic structure is of course legitimate, one of its negative consequences is fragmentation. In the words of Jenny Bourne, identity politics are 'separatist, individualistic and inward looking. The organic relationship we tried to forge between the personal and the political has been so degraded that now the only area deemed to be legitimate is the personal' (Bourne, 1987: 2). However, the uncontested merit of the slogan 'the personal is political' and of the identity politics to which it gives rise, is its importance for the development of notions of subjectivity and agency. Not only has it fuelled explanations of all the different ways in which subjectivity is experienced, constructed and used, the very fact that women's movements and anti-racist movements have become motors of major social changes can be seen as a confirmation of the positive aspects of the shift to theorising the ways in which the personal is political. Feminists are still arguing about this notion (Griffin and Phoenix, 1994). Nora Räthzel, for example, argues that the understanding of constructions of '*Heimat*' (home) and '*Ausländer*' ('foreigners') is important for the understanding of (German) racism (Räthzel, 1994 and in this volume). Thus, any attempt to disrupt racism has to take into account the ways in which people construct their imagined 'homelands' or 'communities' and how they position themselves in relation to others.

Whether the re-examination and questioning of subjective boundary construction has to lead automatically to reconciliation with identity politics is an open question. The proponents of the antithesis of identity politics, pursuing a 'politics of issues' (rainbow coalitions), have so far not answered the question of why the mere credo for a society which is not divided by social inequality would be a sufficient basis for mass campaigning for solutions to 'other people's problems'. Those who hold on to feminist identity politics have stressed the necessity for a common denominator expressed in the multifaceted concept of 'unity in diversity' (Brunt, 1990: 150). However, the lesson to be learned from feminist disillusionment is more usefully expressed in the notion of 'universality in diversity' (Yuval-Davis, 1994b: 422), emphasising that political struggles do not have to be uniform, nor do they have to be united. If the differences of interest and the foci of struggles is not given recognition, then the notion of sisterhood by feminists who initially challenged the universal applicability of sisterhood would continue to be inherently racist (classist, ageist etc.). Viewed in this light, sisterhood becomes a goal rather than a pre-condition of political agency: instead of anticipating solidarity among women, solidarity has to be achieved through dialogue (see also Hill-Collins,1990).

In this volume Dubravka Zarkov emphasises that in the current situation in Serbia, women's groups are still active in dialogue with their 'sisters' in the other former Yugoslav republics. One of these groups participated in the 1993 European Forum of Left Feminists conference in Amsterdam, where they tried to communicate their engagement in anti-nationalist, peace-making processes to women from other European countries. They emphasised that they are still crossing the borders, using the shared resources of all women's groups in the former Yugoslavia, their former networks. Moreover, by the very existence of a peace group, the women from Serbia are challenging the demonising image the western media paints of Serbs: women's peace groups do not fit the imagery of monster-Serbs. It is for this reason that they simply do not appear in media reports. Although it was not an easy task, the Serbian women were successful in communicating this complex reality to the EFLF audience, emphasising that 'sisterhood' even in their situation is meaningful, not as a given, but as an aim.

Both the notion of sisterhood and the concept of 'the personal is political' have long been linked to the concept of 'consciousness-raising'. In this volume Gloria Wekker speaks of the necessity of raising awareness of the complexities of racism for both black and white women. Interrogation of the unspoken privileges of 'whiteness', for Gloria Wekker, is a prerequisite of coalition building. It should be noted, however, that this is a very complicated process. It avoids the quest of invoking notions of 'false' consciousness as a fixed unitary phenomenon which has to be erased and replaced by a more 'real' consciousness. Yet consciousness itself is contradictory. In order to avoid essentialism, it is rather the process, the creation of discursive dialogue, the constant reflection and re-formulation of the taken-for-granted which lie at the heart of awareness. Thus, consciousness-raising aims to be boundary transcending rather than boundary building. Furthermore, this whole issue cannot be separated from the understanding of new state policies which often coincide with gender and ethnic divisions. In other words, where the state regulates society by subsidising different groups on the basis of their claimed different 'identity' (for example by giving grants to 'ethnic' community projects), fragmentation and conflicts of interest become logical consequences. Coalition building becomes even more difficult under those circumstances.

The Book

The chapters in this book reflect the wide range of backgrounds and disciplines from which the authors, and the EFLF membership, come. The book is thus truly multidisciplinary, combining contributions from historians, sociologists, economists, social psychologists, anthropologists and community activists. The contributions in this volume focus on the European countries which have been the stage for ethnic and national conflicts: Britain, the Netherlands, Germany, the former Yugoslavia and Russia. Many of the authors of these chapters are members of racialised minorities in these countries.

In one way the conference on nationalism, racism and gender which inspired the production of this book, held in Amsterdam in November 1993, was a follow-up to the 1991 conference in Norwich, England on women and citizenship (see Ward, Gregory and Yuval-Davis, 1992). In 1991, at the doorstep of the European unification of 1992, the question of what citizenship in the 'New Europe' would be like and what it would mean – legally and economically – for migrant women in particular, was the nexus of the debate. The 1993 conference, reflecting the recent developments in the former

Yugoslavia, as well as in Germany and other parts of Europe, focused much more on the impact of physical and discursive violence on women. This shift from the legal and economic aspects towards the violation of citizens' rights in everyday reality can be seen as a mirror of the dramatic changes which the contemporary European landscape is undergoing. The concept of nationalism lies at the very heart of these developments.

Crossfires

We have called this volume *Crossfires* because this metaphor expresses several positions and positionings which women convey in nations and nationalist struggles. Women are and have been caught physically and symbolically in the angry crossfires produced by ethnic, national and racist conflicts in Europe. Women are also at cross-purposes in these fires, positioned on different sides and thereby divided. Their involvement in such conflicts reflects their membership of different collectivities while (at the same time) these positionings can make them targets of gendered racism and nationalism. Women can be warriors, actively fighting in the frontline or rear of a 'real' war. They can 'fire' verbally (rhetorically) through participation in the (media)-war-machinery or they can physically and psychologically support their male partners/warriors. Women can also suffer from the atrocities of war and propaganda offences. They can organise and secure their children's and families' survival in war. They can be silent 'watchers', trying not to offend either side and just keeping quiet until everything is over. This last image is probably suitable for many women in peace-time as well as in war. The anger of women can also set up cross-currents which sometimes influence aspects of war. Those who speak up against involvement in war, whether in active participation and/or passive endurance, dare to risk their lives. They are accused of being traitors to their collectives as they resist the demands of loyalty. This, again, is not only true for interventions in war-conflicts, but also for interventions against racist violence in peace-time Western Europe (for example the burning of the house of a woman-deputy of the Greens in Germany who was an active leader of anti-racist campaigns). Countless examples emphasise women's active opposition to nationalisms and racisms.

This is why we see the necessity of intervention, of producing crossfires to counter some of the current problems. The project of EFLF, through facilitating communication between women from

all groups throughout Europe, has been trying to offer the possibility of dialogue and coalition building. We hope that this book
will make an intervention in as far as it demonstrates the diversity
of the ways in which women are positioned with respect to 'race'
and nation. The argument of this introduction and the chapters which
follow is that, however we look at it, nationalisms need to be
disrupted.

The Thematic Framework

The chapters in this volume illustrate the plurality of issues and perspectives relevant to the consideration of nationalism, racism and gender
in Europe. Together, the stories they tell illustrate the widespread
nature of nationalism, even in circumstances where the embracing
of processes of 'modernisation' lead to its denial (see the chapter on
the former Yugoslavia by Djuric). In the same way, racism is also
common, even in countries like the Netherlands, where it is denied
(see Essed and Wekker). It is also clear from the chapters which follow,
that the last decade has been a period of dramatic change within Europe.
In the former Yugoslavia, 'nationalist hysteria' and 'ethnic war' has
divided states into warring nations (see Djuric and Zarkov). In
Russia, there has been a 'collapse of empire' (Kosmarskaya) and, by
way of contrast, Germany has been reunified across its east–west divide,
necessitating a process of reconstruction of the nation (Räthzel).

    Despite the current ubiquity of discussions on nationalism, one
theme which emerges from this book is that nationalism is difficult
to define (see the chapters by Räthzel and Wekker and the discussion
above). This difficulty is partly because nationalism can appear to
be very simple; inhering in and expressed through binary, either/or,
oppositional identities such as 'foreigners' or 'allochtonous' people
in opposition to white, Christian, Dutch 'auchtononous' people (Essed
and Wekker); white English/black British (Phoenix); '*Heimat*' (home
or homeland)/'*Ausländer*' (foreigners) (Räthzel); those who are
related by 'blood' and 'others' (Djuric). Yet, in fact, nationalisms
comprise a complex of inclusions and exclusions which partly result
from the fact that nationalisms are dynamic, shifting form over time
as well as being geographically differentiated (Djuric) and exist at
the intersections of 'race', ethnicity, gender and nation (Essed, Kosmarskaya, Phoenix, Wekker). The fact that there are commonalities
and differences between the expression of nationalism in different
countries sometimes makes it difficult for those outside a country

to understand the situation within it (Kosmarskaya). There is clearly a need for the continued analysis of such similarities and differences between European countries.

These articulations of 'race', ethnicity, nation, gender and history raise questions about both 'what' and 'who' is Europe? Indeed, how can Europe be bounded when those considered to be at the margins ('foreigners', black people, Turkish people etc.) are at the centre of Europe and thus make arbitrary differentiations between 'insiders' and 'outsiders' both meaningless and difficult to enforce? Perhaps it is not surprising then that ideological constructions of 'primitive Others' (Zarkov) and 'the history of ethnic hatred' and 'orientalisation' (Djuric) are so powerful in nationalist discourses. Processes of ethnicisation and ethnic exclusions are crucial to nationalist discourses (Kosmarskaya). Thus, while black/white differences continue to be central to nationalist exclusions (Essed, Phoenix, Wekker, Wobbe), there are, as indeed there have always been, nationalist exclusions which are not racialised through colour (Djuric, Kosmarskaya, Zarkov). In the case of the former Soviet Union, population movements make the concept of 'diaspora' as relevant to Russia as to the rest of Europe (Kosmarskaya) – one indication of the ways in which historical changes lead to commonalities as well as differences within the broad, geographical region of Europe. The very use of terms such as 'unified Germany', 'the former Soviet Union' and 'the former Yugoslavia' as well as 'the near abroad' (Kosmarskaya) demonstrates one reason why the terminology of nation, 'race' and ethnicity needs to be dynamic, namely that there are historical shifts in what constitutes nation states and that these have far reaching consequences for 'who is Europe'.

The examination of the gender dimension in the chapters of this book indicates that men are often active in the production and reproduction of constructions of the nation, while women are used as national symbols (Zarkov, discussion above). In the former Yugoslavia (as elsewhere), sexist ideology converges with increased militarisation of everyday life to construct men as the 'defenders' of the nation and women as both the ones to be defended and the 'guardians of the "race"' (see discussion above).

Gender differentiation is also relevant to racialised definitions of belonging to the nation and to immigration and asylum policies (see discussion above and in the chapters by Essed and Kosmarskaya). However, it is also the case that women can be 'active and influential agents of inter-ethnic relations' (Kosmarskaya) since their daily household and childcare responsibilities often give them a mediating role, something which can be taken for granted as natural to women (see also the chapters by Essed and Djuric).

Since 'ethnic groups' are defined through natural norms of purity, the sexualised body is important in delineating the boundary between 'us' and 'them', 'insiders' and 'outsiders' in the nation (Zarkov). Thus, the sexuality (and positioning) of the women of the European nation is differentiated from that of women who are 'Other' (Wobbe, Zarkov), a disparity which prevents some women from recognising that they themselves perpetuate or collude in the oppression of other women (Djuric, Essed, Wekker). The significance of women's bodies to the construction of the nation and the prosecution of 'ethnic/national wars' is partly responsible for the naturalising of both ethnic violence and violence against women, making rape a strategy in an 'ethnic war' (Zarkov) and making women vulnerable to sexual violence (Wobbe).

Overall, women continue to be positioned less favourably than men within nations, even as political systems shift. This is particularly the case since economic shifts often favour the employment of young men rather than women and changes in definitions of citizenship have also been detrimental to women (Djuric, Kosmarskaya). While women are generally badly affected, 'race' and ethnicity differentiate the impact of these effects (see the discussion above). Thus, women from national minorities have been particularly badly affected by changes in Russia (Kosmarskaya) and 'women of colour' continue to fare badly in comparison with white, majority ethnic women, in Europe and the United States (Essed, Wekker).

What often seems to be a bleak and dispiriting picture when nationalism is addressed becomes clearer and more hopeful when the resistance of some women to the ways in which they and other women are oppressed is considered (see chapters by Essed, Wobbe, Zarkov). While there are contradictory pressures on women, for example, to accept nationalist discourses (Kosmarskaya) and to resist them, Essed argues that one positive outcome of women's exclusion from positions of power in 'ethnic organisations' is that they are less vulnerable to governmental 'divide and rule' tactics.

In her chapter, Räthzel argues that there is no simple good/bad binary opposition between notions of multiplicity and diversity as progressive and notions of unity as backward or racist. Räthzel also points out that it is easy for solutions proposed to stay within the logic of the 'fears expressed', for example about *Ausländer*, rather than to move debates away from the frameworks established by nationalists. In this context, it is heartening that none of the authors argue for either the ignoring of differences between women or for narrow identity politics. Instead, they take forward feminist debates by arguing for an inclusive politics of coalition building (Essed, Wekker); solidarity and networking (Zarkov); broader, more inclusive ways of theorising identities (Phoenix, Wekker) and for recognition that nations and nationalisms are not static, but are continually constructed and reconstructed (discussed in the chapters by Djuric, Räthzel and Zarkov) so that oppositional strategies also need to be fluid, plural and well-informed.

The coining of the term 'Europism' by Philomena Essed (this volume) is helpful to the recognition of changes in the ways in which nationalisms are expressed (see also the discussion above). Gloria Wekker (this volume) also makes it clear that it is not strategically useful for women to renounce and rise above claims of nation as Virginia Woolf suggested in the 1930s, since the very ability to stand aloof from issues of nationalism takes for granted the privileged status of belonging. For feminists, therefore, it is important to engage critically with, and in opposition to, the nationalist exclusions of minority groups.

While academic institutions of higher education are often thought to be bastions of equality and egalitarian ideologies, the chapters by Kosmarskaya and by Wekker indicate that the intersection of nationalism, ethnicism, racism and gender inequality need to be combated within, as well as outside, the academy. Thus, while the chapters point the way forward to possible political action, they do not do so in a simplistic way.

The chapters in this book are unified by the themes they address. However, one of the strengths of the book lies in the differences between the chapters, the main ones being that they cover issues from a range of European countries in a multidisciplinary way. Thus authors are variously concerned with issues and methodologies which come from different theoretical locations. For example, material and economic gender inequalities, patriarchal relationships, social constructionism, post-modern positionings, the uses of case studies, cultural analysis and survey data are all represented within the chapters which follow. Since there are overlapping themes in the book, the use of different theoretical frameworks and methodologies allows consideration of the ways in which diverse frameworks allow fresh insights. The importance of this lies in the fact that one of our aims in producing this volume is to make a small contribution towards understandings which can help to elucidate the ways in which the plurality of the intersections of nationalisms, racisms and gender can be disrupted.

References

Anderson, Benedict (1983) *Imagined Communities* (London and New York: Verso).

Anthias, Floya and Yuval-Davis, Nira (1989) 'Introduction'. In N. Yuval-Davis and F. Anthias (eds) *Woman–Nation–State* (London: Macmillan).

Anthias, Floya and Yuval-Davis, Nira (1992) *Racialized Boundaries. Race, Nation, Gender, Colour and Class and the Anti-Racist Struggle* (London and New York: Routledge).

Armstrong, Jill (1982) *Nations Before Nationalism* (Chapel Hill: University of North Carolina Press).

Balibar, Etienne (1990) 'The Nation Form – History and Ideology', *Review*, vol. XIII, no. 3 (Summer 1990) pp. 329–61.

Bhabha, Jacqueline and Shutter, Sue (1994) *Women's Movement: Women under Immigration, Nationality and Refugee Law* (Stoke-on-Trent: Trentham Books).

Bhavnani, Kum-Kum (1993) 'Towards a Multicultural Europe? "Race" Nation and Identity in 1992 and Beyond', *Feminist Review*, vol. 45 (Autumn 1993) pp. 30–45.

Bland, Lucy (1982) '"Guardians of the Race" or "Vampires upon the Nation's Health"? Female Sexuality and its Regulation in Early Twentieth-Century Britain'. In E. Whitelegg, M. Arnot, E. Bartels, V. Beechey, L. Birke, S. Himmelweit, D. Leonard, S. Ruehl and M. Speakman (eds) *The Changing Experience of Women* (Oxford: Blackwell).

Bourne, Jenny (1987) 'Homelands of the Mind: Jewish Feminism and Identity Politics', Race & Class, Pamphlet number 11 (London: Institute of Race Relations).

Brah, Avtar (1992) 'Black Women and 1992'. In A. Ward, J. Gregory and N. Yuval-Davis (eds) *Women and Citizenship in Europe: Borders, Rights and Duties* (Stoke-on-Trent: Trentham Books).

Brah, Avtar (1993) 'Re-framing Europe: En-gendered Racisms, Ethnicities and Nationalisms in Contemporary Western Europe', *Feminist Review*, vol. 45 (Autumn 1993) pp. 9–28.

Brunt, Rosalind (1990) 'The Politics of Identity'. In S. Hall and M. Jacques (eds) *New Times. The Changing Face of Politics in the 1990s* (London: Lawrence and Wishart).

Cohen, Phil (1988) 'The perversion of inheritance'. In P. Cohen and H.S. Bains (eds) *Multi-racist Britain* (London: Macmillan Education).

Enloe, Cynthia (1990), 'Womenandchildren: Making Feminist Sense of the Persian Gulf Crisis', *The Village Voice* (25 September 1990).

Evans, David T. (1993) *Sexual Citizenship: The Material Construction of Sexualities* (London: Routledge).

Feminist Review Editorial (1993) 'Thinking through Ethnicities', *Feminist Review,* vol. 45 (Autumn 1993) pp. 1–3.

Griffin, Chris and Phoenix, Ann (1994) 'The Relationship between Qualitative and Quantitative Research: Lessons from Feminist Psychology', *Journal of Community and Applied Social Psychology*, vol. 4 (December 1994) pp. 287–98.

Habermas, Jürgen (1992) *Faktizität und Geltung* (Frankfurt a.M.: Suhrkamp).

Hill-Collins, Patricia (1990) *Black Feminist Thought* (London: Harper Collins Academic).

Hobsbawm, Eric (1990) *Nations and Nationalism since 1780: Programmes, Myth and Reality* (Cambridge: Cambridge University Press).

Hobsbawm, Eric (1994) 'Today's Nationalism is a Completely New Phenomenon', interview with Max Arian in *De Groene Amsterdammer,* 6 April 1994.

Ignatieff, Michael (1993) *Blood and Belonging: Journeys into the New Nationalism* (London: BBC Books and Chatto and Windus).

Kristeva, Julia (1993) *Nations without Nationalism* (New York: Columbia University Press).

Leiprecht, Rudolf (1991) 'Rassismus und Ethnozentrismus bei Jugendlichen', *DISS-Texte,* 19, (Duisburg: Duisburger Institut für Sprach-und Sozialforschung [DISS]).

Lutz, Helma (1991) 'Migrant Women of "Islamic Background". Images and Self-Images', Occasional Paper no. 11 (Amsterdam: Middle East Research Associates).

Lutz, Helma (1994a) 'The Tension between Ethnicity and Work. Immigrant Women in the Netherlands'. In H. Afshar and M. Maynard (eds) *The Dynamics of 'Race' and Gender* (London: Taylor and Francis) pp. 182–95.

Lutz, Helma (1994b) *Obstacles to Equal Opportunities in Society by Immigrant Women with Particular Reference to the Netherlands, the United Kingdom, Germany and the Nordic Countries,* report written on behalf of the Council of Europe, Strasbourg, October 1994.

Miles, Robert (1993) *Racism after 'Race Relations'* (London and New York: Routledge).

Owen, David (1994) *Ethnic Minority Women and the Labour Market: Analysis of the 1991 Census* (Manchester: Equal Opportunities Commission).

Papic, Zarana (1992) 'Women as Citizens in Yugoslavia'. In A. Ward, J. Gregory and N. Yuval-Davis (eds) *Women and Citizenship in Europe. Borders, Rights and Duties* (London: Trentham Books and EFSF) pp. 58–61.

Phoenix, Ann (1990) 'Black Women and the Maternity Services'. In J. Garcia, R. Kilpatrick and M. Richards (eds) *The Politics of Maternity Care: Services for Childbearing Women in Twentieth-Century Britain* (Oxford: Clarendon Press).

Phoenix, Ann and Woollett, Anne (1991) 'Motherhood: Social Construction, Politics and Psychology'. In A. Phoenix, A. Woollett and E. Lloyd (eds) *Motherhood: Meanings, Practices and Ideologies* (London: Sage).

Räthzel, Nora (1994) 'Harmonious "Heimat" and Disturbing "Ausländer"', *Feminism and Psychology,* vol. 4, no. 1 (February 1994) pp. 81–98.

Ward, Anna, Gregory, Jeanne and Yuval-Davis, Nira (1992) *Women and Citizenship in Europe. Borders, Rights and Duties* (Stoke-on Trent: Trentham Books and EFSF).

Wertheim,W.F. (1964) *East–West Parallels* (The Hague: Van Hoeve).

Wetherell, Margaret and Potter, Jonathan (1992) *Mapping the Language of Racism* (Hemel Hempstead: Harvester Wheatsheaf).

Wieviorka, Michel (1994) 'Racism in Europe: Unity and Diversity'. In A. Rattansi and S. Westwood (eds) *Racism, Modernity & Identity on the Western Front* (Cambridge: Polity Press).

WING (Women, Immigration and Nationality Group) (1985) *Worlds Apart: Women under Immigration and Nationality Laws* (London: Pluto Press).

Yuval-Davis, Nira (1993) 'Gender and Nation', *Ethnic and Racial Studies,* vol. 16, no. 4 (October 1993) pp. 621–32.

Yuval-Davis, Nira (1994a) 'Women, Ethnicity and Empowerment'. In K-K. Bhavnani and A. Phoenix (eds) *Shifting Identities Shifting Racisms* (London: Sage).

Yuval-Davis, Nira (1994b) 'Identity Politics and Women's Ethnicity'. In Valentine Moghadam (ed.) *Identity Politics and Women* (Boulder, San Francisco and Oxford: Westview Press).

Yuval-Davis, Nira (1995a), 'Women and the Biologial Reproduction of the Nation', *Women's Studies International Forum* (forthcoming).

Yuval-Davis, Nira (1995b) 'Colour, Culture and Anti-Racism'. In F. Anthias, C. Lloyd and N. Yuval-Davis (eds) *Rethinking Racism and Anti-Racism in Europe* (London: Macmillan – forthcoming).

1 Young People: Nationalism, Racism and Gender

Ann Phoenix

Issues of race, ethnicity, religion and nationalism have forced themselves onto the European stage in new ways in the last decade as they have become increasingly problematic within Europe and the European Union. For many of those interested in countering racism and xenophobia in Europe, the millennium and the twenty-first century seem foreboding.

In the early 1990s, ethnic conflicts in the former Yugoslavia pushed issues of ethnicity into public consciousness as the neologism 'ethnic cleansing' entered popular consciousness as a term for genocide but became sanitised, to some extent, by its use in less calamitous contexts (Gamman et al., 1993). In various European countries (Germany, France, Italy and Britain) attacks on minority ethnic groups by extreme right-wing groups and resistance by anti-racist alliances have received widespread media coverage.

The beginning of 1993 (when the main elements of the European Union were completed) marked a turning point, at least in theory, for nations and states within the newly created European Union. Freedom of movement within the community and of trade between community members made national boundaries within Europe less important and more permeable than they had been. At the same time it fortified those boundaries between Europe and the rest of the world against those constructed as 'outsiders' who have been portrayed as an 'alien flood' in many EU countries. This has potential consequences for those constructed as 'outsiders', particularly since those rendered marginal are generally excluded on the basis of characteristics (such as country of parents' or grandparents' origin) which, in Britain, are often considered to be colour-coded and which take no account of nationality or connection with a country (Brah, 1993).

Although there is no clear collective European identity (Schlesinger, 1991) or even the desire for one in some countries, the creation of

26

'Fortress Europe' potentially has an impact on the ways in which national identities are constructed and reconstructed in individual countries. Constructions of who is excluded and who is included as nationals of the European Union have, so far, served to solidify existing centre-periphery relations (Brah, 1993). Within Europe, Schlesinger (1991) suggests that European Commission publications on national and cultural identity within the EU have attempted to create collective identities by stressing that there is 'unity in diversity' and hence creating an 'imagined community'. Since Britain is a plural society, it is, at least theoretically, possible for people to have hyphenated identities (as in the United States) such as Asian British or black British. There is also the possibility of a dynamic and negotiated consensus to reconcile the demands of uniformity (a unitary British identity) and plurality. However, British national identity has assumed racist overtones because it has come to be associated with 'race':

> We increasingly face a racism which avoids being recognized as such because it is able to link 'race' with nationhood, patriotism and nationalism, a racism which has taken a necessary distance from crude ideas of biological inferiority and superiority, and now seeks to present an imaginary definition of the nation as a unified *cultural* community. It constructs and defends an image of national culture – homogeneous in its whiteness yet precarious and perpetually vulnerable to attack from enemies within and without. (Gilroy, 1990, reproduced 1992: 53)

> ... ethnicity, in the form of a culturally constructed sense of Englishness and a particularly closed, exclusive and regressive form of English national identity, is one of the core characteristics of British racism today. (Hall, 1992: 256)

From Racism in the EU to National Identities

The issues discussed above are large-scale and complex ones. The enormity, for example, of the ways in which 'race', ethnicities, nationalisms and religions intersect to produce the killing of thousands of citizens and the systematic rape of women in the former Yugoslavia is plain to all. In attempting to understand such momentous issues, however, it is also important to consider issues which are apparently more trivial but which potentially contribute to sudden, unexpected tragedies like those in the former Yugoslavia and in the Second World War. In order to comprehend how antagonisms can be mobilised quickly and systematically, it is important to give some attention to the construction of national identities in a situation where issues of nation are not as urgent or as deadly. Although women engage in neo-Nazi movements, it is frequently young men who are its visible face, attacking minority ethnic groups on European streets. Relatively little is known about how young people who do not publicly belong to neo-Nazi movements construct their national identities. Yet, in order to oppose European racism effectively, it is important to be informed about the criteria used by young people (the citizens of the future) to include or exclude themselves or others in the nation. Are their discourses differentiated by gender, 'race' and ethnicity or are young people more egalitarian than older Europeans?

Insights into the processes that construct the national identities of young British people can hopefully give indications of the factors that help to constitute and differentiate the national identities of young people who have attended the same secondary schools (from 11 years to either 16 or 18 years).

This chapter is concerned with whether, and if so, how, young people's discourses of national identities are differentiated by majority/minority ethnic status as well as by gender. It examines some ways in which gender, 'race' and ethnicity intersect to produce a complex of inclusions and exclusions in the construction of the 'imagined community' (Anderson, 1983) of the British nation for British young people attending schools in London. The final part of the chapter uses the analysis of the young people's accounts to make a few suggestions of possible strategies for disrupting racialised exclusions from, and inclusions in, the nation. The ways in which people construct their 'imagined communities' have an impact on how they position themselves in relation to other people and where they place the boundaries between national groups.

The argument of the chapter is that young people's constructions of their national identities are not merely discursive constructions divorced from reality. Instead, they have wider consequences. In many European countries, vociferous denunciations of 'foreigners' and 'immigrants' from extreme right-wing groups have affected the policies supported by mainstream politicians. Political constructions of popular racism have helped to push mainstream politics to the right which, in turn, has provided a space for more right-wing reaction.

Consideration of British young people's national identities is interesting since the British state maintains an ambivalent position to membership of the EU. While racism permeates all of Europe, 'race' has often been considered by other Europeans to be a 'British problem' and preoccupation, particularly associated with black people. It is thus worth asking the question of whether minorities in Britain are any more accepted as part of the nation than minorities anywhere else in Europe. In addition, the election, in 1993, of an extreme right-wing councillor from the British National Party (BNP) demonstrates the ease with which it is possible to interpolate 'race' into social concerns for ordinary white, working-class people in Britain as in France and Germany (albeit on a smaller scale). Since the BNP councillor was defeated at the next election, it also demonstrates the fact that it is possible to counter racism within the political process.

It is perhaps particularly illuminating to consider young people's national identities since they are often considered to be less racist than their parents' generation and, in addition, have had more opportunities to mix in large British cities with a variety of ethnic groups. This chapter discusses issues important to a consideration of whether young Londoners can be said to be nationalist.

'English is if you are White': the Intersection of 'Race', Ethnicity and Nation

The study from which the young people's accounts discussed here were taken was of 'Social Identities in Adolescence' where 248 14–18-year-old black, white and mixed-parentage Londoners (more of whom were young women than young men) were interviewed at the beginning of the 1990s about their racialised, gendered and social class as well as more personal identities (see Phoenix and Tizard, in prep; Tizard and Phoenix, 1993). In this instance, the black sample were of African Caribbean descent; the sample of mixed parentage had one black parent of either Caribbean or African descent and one of white European descent; and the white sample had parents from the United Kingdom. The interviewers were both black and white and were often (but not always) matched with black or white interviewees. The mixed parentage sample were interviewed by either black or white interviewers. The analysis of the young people's discursive constructions of 'race' and nation was one part of the study.

The young people whom we interviewed are not at the margins of the European Union. Almost all were British born and all had British nationality. Studying them thus gives a picture of how gender, 'race' and ethnicity have an impact on the inclusions/ exclusions of national identities. It became clear in the study that racialised identities intersected with national identities for many young people, so that some black and some white young people saw Englishness (and sometimes Britishness) as synonymous with whiteness. In Anthony Smith's (1984) terms, they had a 'primordial' view of ethnicity, perceiving the symbolic boundaries of 'English-ness' to be predicated on colour and descent. 'English is if you are white and you are born and raised here and everything. If you are British now your parents can be of a different colour ...' (black young woman).

Accounts such as the one presented above indicate that some young people's national identities are such that black people, born in Britain and possessing British passports, are constructed as, and sometimes consider themselves to be, 'Others' – outsiders in the British nation. This is even while the vast majority of the young people eschew racism and racialised exclusions, maintaining an egalitarian ideology to do with 'race', social class and gender which is particu-larly marked for those of mixed parentage. Gender had relatively little differentiating effect on the accounts of their national identities given by the young people.

Asked whether they thought of themselves as being English, British or neither, white and mixed-parentage young people were more likely than were black young people to define themselves as English. Nearly half the white and the mixed-parentage young people said this, while only just over a quarter of the black young people did. Black young people were as likely to say that they are British as that they are English whereas the mixed-parentage and white young people were less likely to say that they define themselves *only* as British than that they define themselves only as English. There was a slight gender difference here in that young women were slightly more likely than young men to say that they considered themselves to be English (44 per cent, N = 63 cf. 34 per cent, N = 33). For many Europeans, this distinction between being English and being British is a difficult one to understand, although with the reunification of Germany it is perhaps easier to see the distinctions that potentially arise when one nation is more powerful than others within the state.

Not many of the black young people thought of themselves as being of the nationality of their parents or grandparents. Not surprisingly, given that we selected the white sample to be of United Kingdom origin, few white young people had grandparents who had come from somewhere other than Britain. Six white young people who said that they thought of themselves as being of the nationality of their parents or grandparents were mainly of Irish origin. Black young people were as likely to think of themselves as being of the nationality of the Caribbean country from which their parents and grandparents came as they were to report themselves to be British. Mixed-parentage young people, who all had one parent of Caribbean or African descent as well as a white British parent, were much more like the white young people than the black young people in that several did consider themselves to be English.

A handful of the young people (of all colours) said that they refused to think of themselves as being of any nationality (6 per cent of the whole sample) and simply said that people should not place importance on national categories. Their refusal to do so was because they considered nationalism to be a potential cause of strife.

In order to gain some insight into the young people's reasons for either affiliating themselves with or 'vacating' Englishness or Britishness, we asked them what they considered to be the differences between being English and being British, who they considered were English and whether they considered that English people were white. The question of whether English people were white (and hence that blackness necessarily precluded Englishness) was specifically prompted if necessary with the question 'Do you think that English people are white?' This was partly to overcome the possibility that young people (particularly white young people for fear of being thought racist) may have been reticent to mention colour when asked about nationality.

Young black people were more likely than the other young people interviewed to mention colour and birth in England (either for parents or for self) as things that differentiate the English and the British. Some 45 per cent of black young people, 9 per cent of white young people and 29 per cent of mixed-parentage young people gave these reasons. Young people of mixed parentage fell in between those who were white and those who were black. Few of the young white people said that they did think that colour (4 per cent) and place of birth (4 per cent) differentiated Englishness and Britishness.

When asked who they considered to be English, the young people gave slightly different answers to those they gave when asked what they thought were the differences between being English and being British. The two most frequently occurring responses to the question of who the young people considered to be English were white people (50 per cent of the overall sample) and people born in Britain (40 per cent). Only 9 per cent said that parents had to have been born in England for their children to be English. Young women were more likely than young men to say that residence was a sufficient condition for someone to claim Englishness. A fifth of them said this (21 per cent, 29 cf. 13 per cent, 12). They were also slightly less likely to say that Englishness necessitated whiteness.

It seems that many young black people were actively 'vacating' a claim on Englishness because they considered that their colour signified exclusion from the category 'English'. Therefore, they did not want to make Englishness their main national allegiance.

Q. Do you think of yourself as English or British, or neither?
A. Well I guess now I think I'm British because I was signing up like – not signing up for a Saturday job – and I wrote, I think I wrote English and then the lady crossed it out and wrote British. (black young woman).

Some white young people who had been born in England also 'vacated' Englishness for reasons akin to those given by young black people – their parents or grandparents had been born in another country and hence they had access to affiliations that most of the white young people did not.

Q. Do you think of yourself as English or British, or neither?
A. Well I'm not English because my grandad is part German and my nan's part Irish I think, so I've got German, Irish and Scottish … so I mean I'm a bit of a mixture so I don't know. British I suppose, even though I've lived in England all my life. (white young woman)

A. I class myself as English, but if anybody asks what I am, I always say I am Irish for some reason. Always do. (white young woman)

In a study of young people's Irish ethnicity, Philip Ullah found that those young people who reported that they considered themselves to be Irish or partly Irish were those who retained other aspects of Irish identity (Ullah, 1985). The discourses that the young people in the study reported here produced fit with Hall's (1992) and Gilroy's (1992) contention that the symbolic boundaries of 'English-ness' are perceived, in Smith's primordial terms, to be predicated on colour and descent.

While many of the black young people's accounts indicated that they could not be fully English because they were black, the black parents that we interviewed perceived their children to be different from them in being English born and brought up. If some black young people's accounts are followed to their logical conclusion, then the young people's children cannot be English because they will not be born to white, English parents. Other black young people said that parental place of birth was more important than colour. Theoreti-cally, therefore, their children could be English in their terms. The fact that the mixed-parentage young people, although also not white, were more likely than black young people to consider themselves English indicates that some may disrupt the link between 'race' and nation. However, for many of the young people, the issue of colour was too intertwined with the question of nationality for place of birth to override it.

'There's no Such Thing as Pure, Pure English': Resisting Exclusion

Although many of the black young people reported that their colour excluded them from full claims to the nation in which they had been born and reared, they did not necessarily decry Britain.

Q. Do you feel that Britain is your country?
A. No. I live in this country ... I can't really cuss the country I live in, cos I live in it, but I don't – I'm not English though. (black young man)

In addition, although two-thirds of the black young people said that they thought that English people were white, they did not homo-geneously accept that Englishness and whiteness necessarily had to intersect. Some acknowledged that many people see Englishness in

terms which exclude black people, but they themselves resisted
such notions. As such, they resisted notions that their colour automatically excluded them from belonging to the English nation. The
first person quoted below rejected the primordial notion of the purity
of an English 'race' constituted through descent.

A. I'd say a lot of people think of English as being white, but I
don't think of English as being white.
Q. What do you think of English as being?
A. Multicultural I suppose. There's no such thing as pure, pure
British or pure English because if you trace it back to their
ancestors there's no way they're pure. (black young man)

A further way for black young people to resist other people's definitions of the inclusions and exclusions to do with Englishness or
Britishness was simply to consider themselves beyond national
categories by focusing only on colour.

Q. Do you think of yourself as English or British, or neither?
A. I usually say I am black. (black young man)

Such accounts allowed young people simultaneously to give
recognition to discourses which exclude them from full membership
of the nation and to resist those discourses.

Dilemmas of Whiteness

There sometimes seemed to be some embarrassment for white
young people about appearing to be 'racist' or jingoistic when
discussing the intersections of 'race' and nation. The following
example illustrates Billig's (1990) 'dilemmatic' notion of ideology,
in that the young man quoted reported himself to be experiencing
a dilemma about how to express his views while not appearing racist.

Q. ... And what sort of people do you think of as being English?
A. Um [pause]
Q. ... Do you think of English people as being white?
A. Yes, probably yes I do ... I know I shouldn't but I probably
do.
Q. Why do you think you shouldn't?

A. Because I think that's probably racist.

Q. Why ...?

A. Um because I think it's discriminating. It's saying that people who are not white are not like fully a part of this country ... which is wrong. It's kind of a subconscious thing ... like the stereotyped English man. (white young man)

The fact that the equation of 'race', nation and culture poses dilemmas for some of the young people leads them to use rhetorical devices which are 'two-sided', in which 'two contrary themes are expressed simultaneously ...' (Billig et al., 1988: 109). In the above instance, the young man indicates that he recognises that it is racist and exclusionary to equate Englishness and whiteness. He thus expresses reluctance to espouse the idea and indeed does not do so until expressly asked.

Discomfort on the part of white young people could be warded off by viewing ethnicity and nationality as optional and voluntary. From this perspective young black people were perceived as having more choice than young white people about opting into or out of Englishness. As such ethnic and national differences could be a focus of resentment in a similar way to that described in the Burnage report (Macdonald et al., 1989).

They *can* call themselves English, but some of them choose to call themselves West Indian. They can still do that. (white young man)

White young people's dilemma about appearing nationalist was particularly evident when it came to talking about allegiance to the British Flag (Union Jack). We asked a series of questions about whether or not the young people felt patriotic to any country. It is striking that, on the whole, the sample really did not consider themselves to be patriotic. Some 69 per cent of them overall reported that they were either not patriotic or were not sure if they were. This may have been because many were not really familiar with the concept, did not recognise the word 'patriotic' and had to ask for clarification. However, colour differences were apparent in their answers. White young people were the most likely to say that they were patriotic to Britain and only to Britain. The middle classes also expressed more patriotism than did the working classes. Nonetheless, on the basis of their discourses about patriotism, it appears that it is a minority of white young people who could be mobilised to any nationalistic activity.

Colour differences were also apparent in young people's discourses about the Union Jack as the national flag. Sixteen white young people who answered this question, two black young people and five mixed-parentage young people were unequivocally positive about the Union Jack. Similarly, 20 young white people were unequivocally positive about the royal family, while only three black young people and eight mixed-parentage young people said that they were. There were slight gender differences in that young women were slightly more likely to be positive about the royal family than were young men (19 per cent, 21 cf. 13 per cent, 10). They were also, however, more likely to express negative feelings about the royal family (36 per cent, 39 cf. 27 per cent, 21) and less likely to express indifference to it (28 per cent, 30 cf. 44 per cent, 34). This is perhaps not surprising given that much attention focused on the royal family is about the appearance and dress of its young women (ex-)members.

The following quotes illustrate how difficult it is for some young white people unreservedly to pledge allegiance to the Union Jack. The first young white man, who considers himself patriotic, seems unable to bring himself to say anything about the Union Jack to the interviewer (although it is possible that he really had no feelings about the Union Jack).

Q. Would you call yourself patriotic or not really?
A. Yes, patriotic.
Q. How do you feel about the royal family?
A. I love them.
Q. Can I ask what you mean when you say you are patriotic?
A. Well I love my country. I am right behind them, whatever.
Q. How do you feel about the Union Jack?
A. How do I feel? [pause] Nothing.
Q. Do you feel loyal to Britain?
A. Yes. (white young man)

The second quote is from a young white woman who clearly experiences dilemmas in expressing allegiance to the Union Jack. She thus uses the discursive device of qualifying what she has to say so that, while her allegiance to the Union Jack is not diluted, she claims it as a non-racist, non-exclusionary national symbol.

Q. Would you call yourself patriotic or not really?

A. Yes I am.

Q. What do you mean by that?

A. ... There are things like sort of cricket and the proms and traditional Christmases and things that are special that I don't really think you get anywhere else in a particular way. They are really just a British thing ...

Q. How do you feel about the royal family?

A. I am pro-royalist.

Q. And the Union Jack?

A. Yes, but I think not to use it to the extent that it should be used to guard off everybody else.

Q. Do you feel loyal to Britain?

A. Yes. (white young woman)

To some extent English and British national pride have come to be seen by many people as the prerogative of the National Front and other nationalist groups and, for some, the Union Jack is the ultimate symbol of this. It is partly for this reason that the young people we interviewed were not, on the whole, very enthusiastic about the Union Jack. Only 13 per cent of the young people were positive about the Union Jack. Most of those who expressed positive feelings were white, with black young people being most likely to express negative feelings about it. The following quotes are all from black young women.

Q. How about the Union Jack? How do you feel about the Union Jack?

A. Ah, there is a song about that: There ain't no black in the Union Jack so send the niggers back. We learnt that in sociology.

Q. So how do you feel about it?

A. The Union Jack? ... I don't know what to feel about it. It's only blue, white and red. I don't know about the Union Jack because I don't actually look at it as a big thing, the flag. I just think of it as England and that's it. (black young woman)

Q. And how about the Union Jack?

A. Um, sometimes I think that it's no worse than having the um flag for America. But um the thing that always worries me about patriotism is that it's er, a mild form of racism, it's like we're better than anyone else. Especially with England you know. Rule

Britannia … Britannia rules the waves … so that's one of the reasons why I don't really describe myself as patriotic. And also the Union Jack reminds me, makes me think of skinheads. (black young woman)

A. Nowadays I am opposed to it because a lot of kids who use it, they tend not only to be patriotic but they really go to extremes, 'There'll always be an England'. They usually sing that song. More to the National Front. (black young woman)

Similarly negative feelings to those expressed about the Union Jack by the above black young people were sometimes expressed by white young people as ambivalence about being British. This was because of the contradictions perceived in being part of a colonial power that had not always behaved well, but which was still attractively powerful.

Q. Do you feel that Britain is your country?
A. Unfortunately it does belong, but I don't think I'm actually very proud to be British or English whatever. I suppose yes. I am proud to be British in that it's a very important country … It's a universal language English so, yes I'm proud sometimes. But then I think the English have caused so many problems around the world that I – I wish I wasn't sometimes. (white young woman)

Expressed ambivalence about national discourses should not be overstated, however, since 69 per cent (59) of the white young people and 58 per cent (30) of the mixed-parentage young people said that they considered that Britain was their country. By way of comparison, only 30 per cent (23) of young black people said this. Asked whether they felt loyal to Britain 51 per cent (44) of young white people, 31 per cent (16) of mixed-parentage young people and only 19 per cent (14) of black people said that they were loyal to Britain. By way of contrast, 46 per cent (25) of black young people and 33 per cent (13) of mixed-parentage young people said that they felt loyalty to the countries (other than Britain) that their parents came from. Not surprisingly, only six (8 per cent) white people expressed such allegiances. Young women were less likely to say that they felt loyal either to Britain (29 per cent, 37 cf. 43 per cent, 37) or, where relevant, to their parents' country (18 per cent, 17 cf. 34 per cent, 27).

Young Europeans?

When asked whether they thought they would live in Britain for the rest of their lives, less than half the young people said that they would. Black young people were the least likely to say that they would definitely do so. The figures were 33 per cent (27) black, 44 per cent (24) mixed-parentage, and 59 per cent (55) white. Some 63 per cent (39) of those black young people who said that they wanted to live abroad said that they would like to go to live in the United States and/or the Caribbean. This compares with 39 per cent (12) of those mixed-parentage young people who said that they wanted to live in the United States and/or the Caribbean. Almost a third (31 per cent, 11) of the young white people who wanted to live abroad also wanted to live in the United States. However, exactly a quarter (9) said that they would like to live in Europe, whereas no black young people said this and only 13 per cent (4) of the mixed-parentage young people considered Europe a possible home.

Thus, while young people from all the three groups included in the study who said that they wanted to live abroad were most likely to say that they wished to live in the United States, more young white people reported themselves to be attracted to living in European countries than did mixed-parentage young people. Young black people were more likely to see the United States as the land of opportunity and to feel links to the Caribbean. None expressed any desire to live in European countries other than Britain. Young women were less likely to express an attraction to the United States as a home (25 per cent, 18 cf. 42 per cent, 20) and slightly more likely to be attracted to Europe (only white and mixed-parentage young people) (13 per cent, 9 cf. 8 per cent, 4).

Q. Do you feel that Britain is your country?
A. No.
Q. Which country do you think is your country?
A. A country in the Caribbean ... where there's more black people. (black young woman)

Q. Do you think that you will live in England for the rest of your life?
A. I hope not.
Q. Where do you think you would like to live?
A. Jamaica [visited once]. (black young woman)

A. … America simply because of money, economic reasons. You
know, once you've got your qualifications America … and Canada
are good places to go and use them. (black young woman)

Q. Do you see yourself living in England for the rest of your life?
A. Um, probably, but I'd like to go and live in France for a bit
… Nowhere hot because I can't stand the heat. Perhaps Australia.
(white young woman)

Ranking of National Identities

We asked the young people to rank the identities we had asked them
about throughout the interview by sorting into order cards on
which each was written. We were slightly sceptical initially that this
procedure would produce any useful data. However, it did differentiate the sample by colour on a number of factors, including
nationality. White young people were the least likely to say that
nationality was important to their sense of identity. Some 70 per
cent of them left it out of their rankings as not important. However,
61 per cent of young people of mixed parentage also considered it
not important while only 39 per cent of black young people did.
The explanation for this may be that the racialisation of nationality
makes it more important to black young people's identities than to
white young people's, in much the same way that colour was more
important in the rankings to black young people's social identities
than to white young people's. For young people of mixed parentage,
having one white British parent gave them a stake in Britain and in
Europe that black young people did not have.

Young women were more likely not to rank nationality as
important than were young men. No young women ranked it as
the most important area of their social identities (four young men
did) and only eight young women (6 per cent) ranked it in the first
three compared with 17 young men (19 per cent). Altogether 60
per cent (77) of young women and 52 per cent (47) of young men
did not rank nationality as important.

The Impact of These National Identities

There was thus a complex pattern of inclusions/exclusions with regard
to national identities. Many black young people who were not

constructed as English by white young people, recognised that other white people did not accept them as such and defined themselves in different terms. It might be argued that this is irrelevant because Britain contains many nations and the English, Welsh, Irish and Scots are also ambiguously positioned with regard to the dominant ethnicity of Englishness (Brah, 1993). Yet these young people are almost all English born and, within Europe, they have no other legitimating national identity on which to draw since only to be British is to belong to the state, but not a nation within it. The young people's accounts of nation were often built on exclusion, not choice. There have, in the past, been fairly concerted resistances to the notion that black people are automatically excluded from Britishness. It may be that claims to Englishness matter more within the European context than has previously been the case.

The ambiguity caused by the recognition that national status involves inclusions and exclusions also had an impact on young white people. Some felt unable to claim Englishness because they perceive that the symbols of Englishness have been hijacked by the extreme Right. This raises the issue of whether positive features of nationalism (if one accepts that there are some) can be maintained when symbols of Englishness/Britishness are perceived to be predicated on racism. For many of the young people we interviewed, the Union Jack has been 'vacated' because its symbolism is seen to have been appropriated by far Right groups.

It is, however, important to remember that few young people in this study espoused nationalistic or racist ideas. Clearly, such discourses exist and can be mobilised even for young people who consider that they are egalitarian (Billig, 1991), but nationalist discourses were not widespread in this study. Primordial notions of biological descent and 'race' were important to the construction of national identities. The inclusions/exclusions they set up also have an impact on which groups of young people consider Europe to be open to them and to be a desirable place in which to live. Although young people in general reported themselves to be more attracted to living in the United States than to living in other countries in Europe, white young people were much more likely than black young people to consider that Europe is the place in which they will eventually choose to live, whereas black young people were more likely to say that they would prefer to go to the United States or to Canada.

In general, there were few gender differences with regard to young people's accounts of national identities. However, the differences that can be found generally were in the direction of young women being less exclusionary in setting boundaries between British people, English people and others. However, experiences of racism and exclusion from the British nation appears, to some extent, to have had a differential impact on black young women and black young men. For example, black young women were less likely than any other 'race'/gender group that we interviewed to say that they would be prepared to marry or cohabit with people of other colours, even while such black–white relationships are increasing in Britain. Their accounts serve to construct them as 'guardians' of the artificially produced boundaries between racial/ethnic groups. In the young people's accounts (as in society in general) black young men are constructed as violent, lawless and undesirable, but conversely and contradictorily they are also admired by white young men and some of their qualities desired (as setters of style, as tough and truly masculine). As a result, they are seen both as the most authentic black people and as most outside the nation and hence, Other.

Possible Political Strategies?

From the young people's accounts of their national identities, a few possible political strategies can be suggested for disrupting the linkages between 'race', ethnicity and nation. It seems, for example, important to air discourses of nationality which are inclusive of those constructed as Other (even though they are part of the nation) so that there are positive alternatives available to young people. Possibilities for change lie as much with understanding white young people's 'imagined communities' as with understanding black young people's constructions and imaginings.

The British incorporation into the European Union indicates that mobilisation around chosen identifications needs to shift to encompass new situations. Defining oneself as African Caribbean is sometimes useful in the British context where it speaks to a shared history and (mythic) shared cultural origins. However, it provides no clear point of political mobilisation or political clout in the rest of Europe where the relationship of European states to Caribbean former colonies or colonies is different or non-existent. It may be that 'black British' proves more useful on the European stage if Britishness is arrived at through claims on one of the constituent British nations, England, Scotland or Wales. The issue of self-definition also affects the political struggles that are waged. The slogan 'Come what may, we are here to stay' was, in the 1970s, a key mobilising slogan against threats to exclusion from black Britishness. Given that exclusions are still a feature of British life, there need to be fresh considerations of how to disrupt the intersection of 'race' and nation with regard to the British in Europe.

One way in which such considerations may be furthered is for young people (from any groups) to be able to claim and allow multiple national affiliations. Thus, blackness, whiteness, Englishness and Britishness all need to be invoked without being considered the provenance of extreme right-wing groups or mutually exclusive. For this system of exclusions and inclusions from the nation was as potentially damaging to white as to black young people. In addition, it is possibly damaging to the nation state that all except the minority of young people who consider themselves nationalist feel reluctant to locate themselves within the nation. In other words, it is important to shift the inclusions/exclusions couplet with regard to national identities and to promote alliances between those whose claims to national belonging within Europe are differentially accepted. In this, feminism can lead the way, since the promotion of such allegiances is a key feature of some modern feminisms.

The parents (mainly mothers) who were interviewed as part of this study were under the illusion that things were 'different' for their children because their children were genuinely English while they themselves were British, but not English. This was not, however, the case in that the black young people did not necessarily consider themselves to be English or any more part of Britain than their parents did. Unlike the situation in the United States, birth in the country and possession of a passport was not sufficient to the discursive construction of children as nationals.

Conclusions

The young people that we interviewed did not have unitary views or unitary identities in relation to nationality. In Smith's (1984) terms they had both primordial and instrumental views about national identity. Primordial views were most evident in statements which showed that young people from each of the colour groups that we studied equated being English with being white. The data from the study indicate that, for many of the young people we interviewed, nationality is racialised in such a way that Englishness is symbolically predicated on notions of colour and 'racial' and cultural purity through descent. Instrumental views were most evident in the accounts of the minority of young people who said that residence or birth were sufficient to confer Englishness or Britishness. Some of the young people simultaneously used both primordial and instrumental discourses of national identity. The young people's simultaneous commitments to 'primordial' and 'instrumental' views of nationality, illustrate Billig's (1991) concept of the 'dilemmatic' nature of ideology which has its own contradictions inherent in it. For black young people there was sometimes resistance to the primordial view evident in statements such as 'They say it [Englishness] is white, but I don't think so.' For white young people, there was sometimes reluctant admission that they did hold a primordial view. 'I know it ought not to, but I think it [Englishness] does [equal whiteness].' However, some young people were aware that the primordial view of nationality was an imagined one, involving a mythic past and, as a result, rejected it.

In general, the young people did not assert hyphenated identities. The black and mixed-parentage young people mostly had at least one parent who came from a country other than Britain, whereas the white young people mostly did not. However, many of the black young people were more likely to express themselves as both the nationality of their parents and as British. They thus had cross-cutting allegiances to Britain and to the Caribbean. Those white young people who also had other allegiances were those who had parents or grandparents who came from another country. In this study, it was particularly young people of Irish descent who had such cross-cutting allegiances.

A few white young people appeared to be resentful about the fact that black young people could, as they saw it, 'choose' to identify either with the countries from which their parents came or with Britain. However, the assertion of those Caribbean or hyphenated identities was extremely important to many of the black young people interviewed because of the intersecting exclusions of 'race' and nationality. These differences suggest that there is, as yet, no negotiated consensus between these young people about how to reconcile the demands of uniformity and plurality within British society. Despite the fact that the young people saw colour as differentiating the nationality of people born and bred in Britain, most of the young people interviewed (both black and white) said that they had some loyalty (however grudging) to Britain as the place in which they had grown up and been educated. We did not get any accounts which indicated support for nationalist groups such as the far Right. Similarly, patriotism was not commonly reported. Those young people who considered themselves to be patriotic and expressed passionate commitment to their country were more likely to be white. For most of the British young people in the study reported here, Europe did not figure in their future plans about where they would live. While no black young people expressed a desire ever to live in any European country other than Britain, few white or mixed-parentage young people did so.

There were relatively few gender differences in young people's accounts of 'race' and nation. Where differences were expressed, young women's accounts were less exclusionary than young men's. Thus, young women were less likely than young men to report themselves to be loyal either to Britain or to the countries in which their parents were born. In addition, they were more likely than young men to report that residence was a sufficient condition for people to be considered English. However, when asked about relationships with, and marriage to, people of other colours, young black women were the 'race'/gender group who were least likely to say that they would be prepared to have such 'mixed' relationships. This may well fit with work which argues that women are 'guardians of the "race"' (Bland, 1982; Anthias and Yuval-Davis, 1989, 1992).

The accounts given by the young people in this study were, obviously, expressed through discourse constructed in an interview situation. This may have raised dilemmas for some of the young people interviewed in that they may have felt reluctance to voice some discourses (for example, strongly nationalist ones) in circumstances where they assumed that interviewers (who were older than they were and, sometimes, of a different colour) would not approve of such sentiments. In addition, as Billig et al. (1988) indicate, the young people probably did not see themselves as racist or want to be associated with racism. It was probably for reasons such as this that they presented justifications of discourses which equated 'race', nation, ethnicity and insider/outsider status. The fact that they did not uncritically accept such equations, in itself, raises hopeful possibilities for forging new and more positive national identities and policies.

References

Anderson, Benedict (1983) *Imagined Communities* (London and New York: Verso).

Anthias, Floya and Yuval-Davis, Nira (1989) 'Introduction'. In N. Yuval-Davis and F. Anthias (eds) *Woman–Nation–State* (London: Macmillan).

Anthias, Floya and Yuval-Davis, Nira (1992) *Racialized Boundaries. Race, Nation, Gender, Colour and Class and the Anti-Racist Struggle* (London and New York: Routledge).

Billig, Michael, Condor, Susan, Edwards, Derek, Gane, Mike, Middleton, David and Radley, Alan (1988) *Ideological Dilemmas: A Social Psychology of Everyday Thinking* (London: Sage).

Billig, Michael (1990) 'Stacking the Cards of Ideology: The History of the *Sun Souvenir Royal Album*'. *Discourse and Society*, vol. 1, no.1, pp. 17–38.

Billig, Michael (1991) *Ideology and Opinion* (London: Sage).

Bland, Lucy (1982) '"Guardians of the Race" or "Vampires upon the Nation's Health"? Female Sexuality and its Regulation in Early Twentieth-Century Britain'. In E. Whitelegg, M. Arnot, E. Bartels, V. Beechey, L. Birke, S. Himmelweit, D. Leonard, S. Ruehl and M. Speakman (eds) *The Changing Experience of Women* (Oxford: Blackwell).

Brah, Avtar (1993) 'Re-framing Europe: En-gendered Racisms, Ethnicities and Nationalisms in Contemporary Western Europe', *Feminist Review,* vol. 45 (Autumn 1993) pp. 9–28.

Gamman, Lorraine, Hall, Catherine, Lewis, Gail, Phoenix, Ann and Whitehead, Annie (1993) 'Thinking Through Ethnicities', *Feminist Review*, vol. 45 (Autumn 1993).

Gilroy, Paul (1992) 'The End Of Antiracism'. In J. Donald and A. Rattansi (eds) *'Race', Culture and Difference* (London: Sage).

Hall, Stuart (1992) 'New Ethnicities'. In J. Donald and A. Rattansi (eds) *'Race', Culture and Difference* (London: Sage).

Macdonald, Ian, Bhavnani, Reena, Khan, Lily and John, Gus (1989) *Murder in the Playground* (London: Longsight Press).

Phoenix, Ann and Tizard, Barbara (in prep.) *The Social Identities of Young Londoners* (London: Routledge).

Schlesinger, Philip (1991) *Media, State and Nation: Political Violence and Collective Identities* (London: Sage).

Smith, Anthony (1984) 'Ethnic Myths and Ethnic revivals', *Archives Europeenes de Sociologie*, vol. 24, no. 3, pp. 283–303.

Tizard, Barbara and Phoenix, Ann (1993) *Black, White or Mixed Race? Race and Racism in the Lives of Young People of Mixed Parentage* (London: Routledge).

Ullah, Philip (1985) 'Second Generation Irish Youth: Identity and Ethnicity', *New Community*, vol. 12, pp. 310–20.

Ullah, Philip (1990) 'Rhetoric and Ideology in Social Identification: The Case of Second Generation Irish Youths', *Discourse and Society*, vol. 1, pp. 167–88.

2   Gender, Migration and Cross-Ethnic Coalition Building

Philomena Essed

Recently, I had the opportunity to participate in a workshop organised by a women's group among Iranian refugees, the majority of whom had been in the Netherlands for less than five years. The discussion, on the theme of integration in a context of racism, was significant for two reasons. First, it is always a learning experience to exchange information and experiences with refugee women. My own family had migrated to the Netherlands more than 25 years ago, under very different circumstances. Second, the experiences of refugee women are unique in their particular details, but many of their stories, as migrants in the Netherlands, are also similar to those of first- and second-generation women of the so-called established black and migrant groups (Essed, 1991; Lutz, 1991).

The majority of the group of Iranian women, numbering 20, has been to college. But apart from two, none of them has been able to get a job in the Netherlands. In everyday life, they are constantly reminded of the fact that they are non-European and that they do not belong in the Netherlands. To give a few examples:

> One woman, I shall call her Farah, lives with her 10-year-old daughter in a small Dutch village, where they are terrorised by a group of four youngsters: phone calls in the middle of the night, banging on the front door, harassment in the street, and abusive language. The other day, the tyres of their bicycles were cut and they got faeces thrown into her mail box. Farah knows the reason why. The social worker she has turned to for help knows. The medical doctor she went to see, because she developed sleeping problems, knows. The local housing agency who has offered assistance in finding another place also knows. Even the local policeman knows; one of the youngsters is his nephew. But the

taboo against naming the problem is so strong that it does not get to be voiced. Racism.

Farah has not even completed her first five years in the Netherlands, but she has already learnt about the strong defensive tone of Dutch non-racism (Essed, 1991; van Dijk, 1993). She feels repressed when she finds that the dominant consensus shows more understanding and tolerance for racial prejudice and discrimination than for individuals who pinpoint the act, who name the problem, and who object to racism in everyday life. Despite the discouragement to pursue further the racism she experiences, she refuses to be silenced.

The seven-year-old daughter of another woman – Soraya, I will call her – is being harassed by her peer group in school. The daughter is ridiculed for being a 'darkie'. Pupils spit at her and they pull at her hair. At first, Soraya did not know what to do. But then she thought of explaining to her daughter that white children are only jealous of her beautiful dark eyes and her abundant black hair. According to Soraya this has helped. Her daughter has been able to keep her self-confidence.

These Iranian women had hoped to find safety in the Netherlands. However, like other European countries, Dutch society is increasingly tolerant of racism, including its blatant manifestations. Everyday racism is also expressed in more implicit ways. Institutions involved with refugee care tend to patronise refugee women, whom they consider pitiful, traditional and backward. Yet it takes courage, will power and an enormous amount of internal strength to flee from one's country, let alone to undertake the journey on your own, like Farah and Soraya did. In the media refugees are criminalised and accused of entering the country under false pretences. Once refugees have obtained permits to stay, it is expected that they will adapt to the Dutch way of life, but the government provides little protection against racism and xenophobia in return.

These and other factors indicate that earlier distinctions between refugees from the South and other migrant groups are diluting and that similarities between people of colour in an otherwise white Europe are gaining prominence. Indications of this development can be found in the emergence of cross-ethnic networks on local and inter-European levels. Defying the boundaries determined by nation-

ality, ethnicity and migrational history, women search for a common
ground of struggle for human rights and dignity, as women in an
increasingly hostile Europe. The background and political implications of cross-ethnic coalition building among women are the
subject of this chapter.

Changing Patterns of Migration

In the first few decades after the end of the Second World War two
main types of migration led to the formation of new ethnically distinct
populations in Western European countries: migration of workers
from the poorer and less industrialised European periphery, often
through the 'guestworker systems', to the more highly developed
parts; and migration of colonised populations to the colonial
'motherland'. The period since the 1980s has seen the emergence
of new patterns of migration and settlement. Chain reactions to
previous migrations, growing economic disparities, environmental
disasters, wars, political instability and the threat of genocide have
produced a growing number of refugees and asylum seekers from
the South to the North, and within Europe, from the East to the
West (Castles, 1993; Castles and Miller, 1993). The extent of displacement is such that the issue of refugees is high on the political
agenda of many European countries (Wrench and Solomos, 1993).
    Influx control of immigrants represents one dimension of population
politics; another dimension appeals to the issue of population growth.
The European Union is suffering from a declining birth rate and a
rapidly ageing population which, in the near future, will be detrimental to the EU's ability to have a viable workforce. Despite these
developments, the EU nations do not have a commitment to utilising
effectively their diverse populations. European governments react
with increasingly restrictive and exclusionary moves to maintain the
myth that Europe is not a continent of immigration.
    The constitution of new minorities in Europe is, however, an
irreversible process. At the beginning of the post-1945 population
movements, the emphasis in the receiving countries was on labour
supply and control of migrant workers. There was a widespread belief
that migrations were of a temporary nature, and that the migrants
would return to their countries of origin. Following the oil crisis
of the mid-1970s, labour migration to Western Europe declined
and state responses shifted to immigration control and repatriation.

Despite these state interventions to prevent immigrant populations from gaining permanence, however, the majority of the migrants settled. During the 1980s family reunions followed and children of migrant families were sent to schools in the new country. The emphasis shifted to the long-term position of minorities, a stabilisation which facilitated gradual improvement in the civil and political rights of immigrants and of their socioeconomic situations (Castles, 1993).

In the 1990s, migration has become a central issue in international relations and a burning question in many countries. Never before have so many people been on the move, due to the collapse of communism in Eastern Europe, the explosion of violent conflict in many parts of the world, economic deprivation, ecological catastrophe, violence of war, or persecution. An increasing number of people face semi-permanent or permanent displacement. The large majority of the people who are forced to leave their country, in search of safety and a better quality of life, remain in the same regions. During the past decade, an increasing number of migrants and refugees from the South, however, have sought entry to the rich countries of the North. In the course of this process former distinctions between different types of migration, such as economic migration, family reunion, refugees and illegal workers, are collapsing (Castles, 1993). This has consequences for the way the so-called established black and ethnic minority groups perceive themselves in relation to refugees and other newly arriving migrants.

Migration and Racism

The formation of ethnic minorities, often a result of migration, has led to a growing ethnic diversity in the countries in the North, which is affecting institutions and cultures. To many in the developed countries the economic restructuring of the world order, the increasing international cultural exchange, the settlement of populations from the South and the ongoing global migrations have been experienced as a threat to their social and economic security and their sense of national identity. Increasingly the vision of 'being swamped' by masses from the South is being constructed in exclusionary and discriminatory terms.

There is ample documentation of the exclusion and marginalisation of immigrants from the former colonies and immigrant workers from Southern European countries during the first three decades of the post-Second World War period. It has been pointed out that racism does not only refer to a system of biological determinism, a remnant of the nineteenth-century pseudo-theory of race hierarchy, but also to deterministic constructions of culture and ethnicity (Barker, 1981; Essed, 1990, 1991; Lutz, 1991; Anthias and Yuval-Davis, 1992). By the late 1980s there appeared to be a much higher degree of social acceptance of intra-European immigrants than of immigrants from the South and minorities who were phenotypically different (Castles, 1993). These indications announced the emergence of another strand of racism, which has surfaced in connection with the problematic of refugees (Feteke and Webber, 1994).

The increase of populations on the move in search of safe regions has activated the idea that white, Western European prosperity must be protected against asylum seekers, refugees and immigrants from the South. Refugee and immigration regulations, by treating people as sheer numbers, often dehumanise migrants and refugees. At the same time fascism is gaining respectability, while European governments passively tolerate violence motivated by racism and xenophobia. On national and European agendas the issue of refugees has gained momentum. Standard clichés are that the 'boat is full'. The rapid spread of Western European anti-foreigner sentiment in governmental debates and in popular thinking applies not only to refugees but also to the so-called established immigrants.

The Construction of 'Otherness'

The slogan of a 'united Europe' to face the rest of the world stands in sharp contrast to racial and ethnic politics within the various Western European countries. The construction of 'outsiders' on the basis of such characteristics as colour, origin of parents or grandparents, justifies second-class citizenship for a few million minority people. The construction of 'Otherness' is reflected, among other things, in names, words or concepts used to refer to minority groups. Names or labels attached to minority groups often reflect current and changing politics of oppression and of resistance, examples of which can also be found in the Netherlands.

The first considerable immigrant group of colour arrived in the Netherlands in the 1950s and 1960s from the then newly independent Indonesia. Many of these immigrants were of racially mixed background and used to be called 'half-blood' people. Although this particular 'race conscious' term is disappearing from Dutch popular discourse, another word 'Negro', a racist term used to refer to people of African descent from the Dutch (former) colonies of Surinam and the Dutch Antilles, is still common. Southern European and North African migrant workers who came in the 1970s were initially called by the German adopted name of *Gastarbeiter* (guest-worker). Later, policy-makers and academics popularised the term of 'ethnic minority', to refer to people from the former colonies as well as to Turkish and Moroccan workers and their families.

During the 1980s, emerging oppositional groups claimed the term 'black', in order to acknowledge the common experience of all groups who are the target of racism. In late 1980s, Dutch policy-makers came back with a term which in effect strips all political presuppositions from discourses on minority–majority relations from associations or implications having to do with power relations. Instead of 'ethnic minorities' the concept of '*allochtoon*' is now prominent in popular discourse. The Dutch word *Allochtoon* is the equivalent of 'non-native'. The notion of *allochtoon* is not used for just any 'non-native', such as US, British, or German immigrants, but explicitly for 'non-natives of colour' and for immigrants with real or attributed Muslim identity. The term *allochtoon* is functional in setting apart people from the South, both the newly arriving refugees and the established black and ethnic minority groups, from a constructed image in which 'genuine' Dutch or European identity is a white identity.

The contemporary search for a European identity is not a new phenomenon, but the particular constellation of global forces in which this process takes place is specific. With respect to Europe's self-centredness it seems relevant to make a distinction between the concept of Eurocentrism and 'Europism'. Eurocentrism was a product of the history of conquest and colonisation, of the Age of Europe (Amin, 1988; West, 1993). Ideologies of European superiority, and in particular the idea that Europe is the cradle and the norm for human civilisation, typify an extrovert mode of European assertion. Today, a more introvert process of Europe-centrism is taking place. This I will call 'Europism', a form of European introspection. Whereas Euro-centrism emerged from the victory of conquest, Europism is based in the defeat of Europe, first by the United States, now gradually being followed by the far East. The 'Fortress Europe' ideology and the bureaucratic machinery operating to create legal, economic and political boundaries to protect Europe against the rest of the world, in particular the South, can be considered part of the phenomenon of Europism. Economic decline and internal decomposition are giving way to identity crises and the construction of new enemies, both within and on the doorstep. Enemies within include: first, second and third generation racial and ethnic minorities; and enemies on the doorstep are refugees who are supposedly pouring in by the million in order to take advantage of Western European welfare.

The trend, within Europe, for relatively small nations to seek statehood on the basis of shared ethnic identity, whether as a response to colonialism or as a response to a perceived threat of incursion, goes hand in hand with the resurgence of nationalism and neo-Nazi groups within Europe and an emphasis on 'quasi-natural' notions of biological descent. Although this issue cannot be dealt with here, it should be noted that it is imperative to investigate the politics through which national and ethnic identities are created. The invention, strategic use and political manipulation of nation–ethnic–race identities by political leaders have specific gender implications. Nationalism nourishes and is nourished by the subordination of women, whether it concerns racial, religious, ethnic or political fundamentalisms (Cock, 1992; Yuval-Davis and Anthias, 1992; Yuval-Davis, 1994; Moghadam, 1994). Relevant gender questions in this respect are: is nationalism a 'natural' product of patriarchy? Is the strategic use of national or ethnic identities characteristic of male leadership or of male styles of leadership? If so, what conclusions and which consequences can we draw from this, as women? The answering of these specific questions would be a study in itself, but it seems feasible to outline below some of the general gender implications of migration, racism and ethnic leadership in Western Europe.

Refugees and Immigration Policies in the Netherlands

The majority of refugees (from the South) who manage to reach (Western) Europe are men, even when, globally, the majority of people who are seeking refuge from civil wars, ethnic and other conflicts are women (Vickers, 1993; see also Schrijvers, 1993). Further, the majority of those who propagate and organise ethnic violence are men, yet in international politics few have questioned the gender dimension in the production of wars (Enloe, 1983; Elshtain, 1987; Cooke and Woollacott, 1993). For the sake of clarity, it must be emphasised that I do not mean to suggest that men are the aggressors and that women are passive victims only. There are conflicting images of women in war situations (Vrouwenberaad Ontwikkelingssamenwerking, 1994). Among the innocent victims are millions of women: mothers, daughters, sisters and wives. But some mothers are proud to send their sons to fight ethnic wars, and some women are active agents of violence, for instance in the former Yugoslavia and in Rwanda. Women are among the cheering crowd when men violate, torture and abuse individual members of the perceived enemy group. Despite these conflicting images it seems relevant to recognise gender as an important factor in conflict situations, in migrant and refugee situations as well as in the integration of refugees in new countries and/or in the rebuilding of societies in post-conflict situations.

About 30 per cent of the yearly requests for asylum in the Netherlands are submitted by women (Desta, 1994). Dutch asylum policy makes a distinction between those who have a chance to obtain refugee status and those who do not comply with the refugee Convention of Geneva. Decisions used to be made within one year, but recently the time has been reduced to 30 days and a policy is in the making to cut it down even further to 24 hours.[1]

Time pressure works to the disadvantage, in particular, of refugees who suffer from trauma and other serious psychological distress, probably including a high number of women who have been sexually abused before or during their flight. Further, the Dutch law acknowledges the so-called 'toleration rule', meaning that some of the asylum seekers who will not be accepted eventually, but who cannot return back to their countries for safety reasons, are allowed to stay in the Netherlands for a maximum period of three years. In return they must withdraw their request for asylum. Those who fall under this rule are only tolerated in the Netherlands. They have little or no rights: no rights to be reunited with family members, they are unable to travel to any of the other European Union states, they have no facilities for further education, and they are not allowed to engage in any form of employment. As Desta (1994) points out, it is difficult enough for refugee women with an 'A-status', that is with full rights and obligations recognised by the UN convention, to cope in the Netherlands, let alone for anyone with a less secure status. She continues to explain that refugee policies reinforce traditional gender roles. In the short term, taking care of the usual family and household responsibilities may ease the transition to a new situation, because at least in this respect there is some continuity. In the long run, however, disconnection from the world outside of the home contributes to the further isolation of refugee women.

Restrictive migrant, refugee and remigration policies have gender specific effects. Women who enter with their husbands, or in order to join them, are seen as dependants, not as migrants or refugees in their own right. Therefore, they are refused an independent residence permit. The consequences are that they face deportation in the case of divorce from their husband. The dependent status of women who migrate or flee with their families is particularly unfair, also, considering that hardship or life-threatening conditions experienced in the home country, the experience of fleeing, lack of employment opportunities in the new country, and concomitant tensions and frustration, put marriages and peaceful family life severely to the test. The almost complete dependence upon their partner impedes women from benefiting from equal opportunity regulations and from participating in women's activities.

Refugee women often find themselves in a vulnerable social situation. Social networks and structures, for instance with respect to childcare, are no longer available in the Netherlands, where overall childcare provisions for working women are largely insufficient. Further, refugee women are often isolated from or being denied access to resources in the economic, political and social sphere (Desta, 1994). One way for women to break through the isolation of family life is by organising women's groups. The organising of women's groups can be empowering, because it is a means of breaking the silence of lost hopes and frustrations. Together women can voice wishes and discuss problems and needs that would otherwise remain unspoken.

Gender, Leadership and Community Struggle

Within the European Union, black, ethnic minority groups and refugees are divided by national, cultural and language boundaries. They have to learn the languages of the countries in which they reside, in addition to one or more of the languages of the countries from which they originate. The so-called European unification, which is putting into effect the idea of 'Fortress Europe', reinforces the need for more effective ways of organising among black, ethnic minority and refugee groups, in order to bridge the gaps of language and culture. The imperative to organise also on cross-ethnic and cross-European levels forms a new challenge to ethnic leadership.

Leadership of ethnic organisations reflects the level of consciousness of the target group as well as the changing circumstances of migration and settlement. Initially many organisations concentrated on issues related to the country of origin, with the view in mind that migrants would return to their countries. Later, emphasis shifted to social, economic and political issues in the country of residence. Initially, leaders were often individuals who, owing to their class background and level of education, could play the role of intermediaries between migrants and the receiving society. Their position became strengthened by the authorities in the receiving country and institutions which, in search of interlocutors, turned to these 'leaders' and accorded them prestige, thus enhancing their status (Joly, 1987). Another group of leaders consisted of religious men, predominantly Muslim, Hindu or Christian. With the shifting of politics from remigration to integration, various new types of leaders, often academics and professionals, gained access during the 1980s to political parties in the receiving countries. The majority of these 'ethnic representatives' are men, but women have also been elected at local, national and European levels.

Women on the Move: Towards an Inclusive Politics of Organising

Women have always been active in the European black and ethnic minority communities, but few, if any, studies have addressed the gender of ethnic leadership in Europe. Alongside men, women have worked in organisations to further the aims and to defend the rights of their people, to facilitate integration into the receiving society, and/or to contribute to the preservation of their identity as an ethnic group (Mullard et al., 1990; Rex et al., 1987). Yet the leadership of these organisations is usually male-dominated. The exclusion of women from leadership positions is problematic, considering the fact that male dominance reinforces both the existing patriarchal lines within ethnic communities as well as within the dominant society.

Given the gender exclusiveness of leadership, women chose to form their own groups, either within the existing 'ethnic' organisation, or independently, in order to fight the simultaneous effects of gender and racial discrimination and to deal with problems of subordination, as women, within their own cultural domains. Thereby, women were among the first to cross ethnic boundaries with the purpose of coalition building. There are various reasons for this. First, black, ethnic minority and refugee women could identify with each other on the grounds of their struggle as women within their own communities, and as the 'Other' in relation to the women's movement. Second, it seems that women, because of their exclusion from power positions in 'ethnic' organisations, are suffering less from the effects of government politics of divide and rule. Third, their exclusion from leadership positions liberated women to a certain degree from ethnic nationalisms and competitive feelings towards other ethnic organisations. As a result, an increasing number of black and ethnic minority women in Western Europe participate in cross-ethnic networking: in Britain, in the Netherlands, in Germany, France and other European countries (Bryan et al., 1985; Essed, 1994; Oguntoye et al., 1986; Dooh-Bunya, 1990).

In all fairness to the male-dominated 'ethnic' organisations, it must be said that there too commonality of experiences in the new situation, in matters of education, housing, immigration laws, and the labour market, stimulated the formation of cross-ethnic and cross-national alliances (Ntoane, 1994). It seems, however, that these alliances are more often than not incidental or one-off coalitions rather than lasting associations. Women, on the other hand, have been pioneers in the establishment of sustainable cross-ethnic organisations: nationally as well as on a European level. Today, associations where women of African, Asian, Latin American and other backgrounds work together have emerged all over Western Europe: in England, France, Germany, Norway, the Netherlands, Italy, Spain, Portugal (Kraft and Ashraf-Khan, 1994).

Although the specific histories of these organisations are unique, one can identify a certain progress in the nature of women's organisations which usually reflects the level of consciousness and the orientation towards the future. When major emphasis was placed upon return to the country of origin and the politics there, women often organised on the basis of national background. At a later stage, increasing involvement with the economic and social rights in the receiving country motivated women to join forces with others in similar situations. Thus, associations emerged on the basis of regional or continental affiliation (e.g. Caribbean women; African women; Asian women; Mediterranean women). The next step in broadening our reach meant the establishment of networks between African, Caribbean and Asian migrants, to include the interests of women who migrated from the former colonies, as well as women who migrated in the context of labour migration from Southern European and North African countries (e.g. OWAAD in Britain; Flamboyant in the Netherlands). A number of these cross-ethnic women's organisations have survived over many years (Salimi, 1994; Weldeghiorgis, 1994).

Of a more recent date is the situation where 'established' minority women's groups reach, more and more, to newly arriving people, in particular refugee women. In the absence of sufficient documentation on this issue, I can only judge from my own experience and networking that women have been in the forefront when it came to establishing organisations which bring together black, ethnic minority and refugee interests. These cross-ethnic initiatives are politically important because they form a platform from which to relate more directly the problems experienced within the South which are causing millions of people to flee (underdevelopment, ethnic and religious wars, military coups, environmental disasters etc.) and problems that people from the South are facing in the North (racial violence; xenophobia; institutionalised discrimination on the labour market, in housing and in education).

Because I am familiar with Dutch cross-ethnic initiatives, I will use as an illustrative example the experience in the Netherlands. The late 1980s and 1990s witnessed the emergence of a few all-inclusive women's organisations, which explicitly aim to facilitate local co-operation between black, ethnic minority and refugee women.[2] Apart from local initiatives, there is one national organisation, an umbrella organisation called 'TIYE International', a platform for black, migrant and refugee national women's organisations in the Netherlands.[3] TIYE operates from an integrationist perspective, which can be inferred from the fact that their main aspiration is to be in the same situation as white women. Their policy outline states that it is TIYE's aim to provide black, migrant and refugee women in Europe with the same access to employment, appropriate working conditions and control over economic resources as white women. At the same time, TIYE adheres to a multicultural perspective with the demand that the notion of women's emancipation should be defined inclusively, in order to appeal to all women, irrespective of cultural or ethnic background. TIYE pursues inclusive politics not only through the facilitating of mutual cooperation projects, but also in the fact that black, ethnic minority as well as refugee women are represented in their organisational structure, aims and policies. It is worth mentioning that TIYE politics do not only claim to promote the process of equality for women from the South in the North. They also seek to promote interaction between North and South thus making a connection between the struggle of people from the South who live in the North, and the broader development issues in the South.

The global experience of women's movements has increasingly led feminists to point out that gaining access to decision-making, public office and the administration of laws is crucial for women to be able to influence issues. In order to facilitate access to existing (white) women's lobby groups, ethnic minority and refugee women have joined forces on inter-European levels. The European Black Women's Network[4] is a good example of this. Officially launched in 1993, the European Black Women's Network emerged initially from a conference called in Brussels in 1991 by a member of the EC Green Party, a black woman. The purpose of the conference was to assess the problems with which black and ethnic minority women are confronted and to create a network. Women who attended this conference agreed that their network should be independent, that is, not linked with any particular political party. The idea was to form a network of organisations from which could emerge a pressure group at the European level to present claims, to exchange and evaluate experiences and to reinforce solidarity between all women. The notion of 'black', in the name of the association, is used in a political sense to represent groups who are discriminated against on account of racial or ethnic factors. These include people of colour from the colonies and former colonies, Turkish and other non-colonised people who migrated to the North of Europe in the context of labour migration during the 1960 and 1970s, and refugees of colour. With respect to refugees, this organisation was among the first to bring together claims of so-called established minorities as well as those of recent migrants; in particular, refugees. The political implications are that women, through their own initiative, develop strategies to prevent different kinds of migrants (labour migrants, migrants from the former colonies, economic and political refugees) being played off against one another. Moreover, the network is designed to increase mutual solidarity among women in an increasingly xenophobic and hostile Europe. Depending on legal status (whether you are a national of a member state, whether you only have a temporary residence permit, whether you are a refugee or whether you are illegally in the country) some women are allowed to participate in EU organisations and others are not. Because the network tends to be inclusive, rather than exclusive, relevant information can also reach those who are excluded from participation in EU organisations. Further, through communication, sharing of information and mutual support, those who are being excluded can also exert influence on the European decision-making processes.

Through meetings, conferences and personal contacts, the network facilitates communication and exchange of information between black and migrant women within the European Union. The network is the beginning of a platform to voice the needs of black, migrant and refugee women; to monitor European politics and participate in decision-making processes at all levels of the European policy-making structure; to develop and propose legislative policies, in particular with respect to racism and sexism; and to produce positive images of women of colour and women from the South in economic and social life. The future will tell how viable cross-ethnic and cross-European networking turns out to be.

Notes

1. If put into effect, the 24 hours rule will only apply to green border asylum seekers (those who reach the Dutch borders over land, through Belgium and Germany). This policy anticipates the putting into effect of the Schengen Agreement which states that refugees who have been turned down by one of the member states should not be accepted by any of the others.
2. Examples are, for instance, Zami and TIYE.
3. The information presented here comes from a TIYE flier and the TIYE response to the European 'Green book on social policy', 28 March 1994.
4. Information on the European Black Women's Network largely draws from a speech presented by its current chair, Ms Martha Osamor.

References

Amin, S. (1988) *Eurocentrism* (London: Zed Books).

Anthias, F. and Yuval-Davis, N. (1992) *Racialized Boundaries. Race, Nation, Gender, Colour and Class and the Anti-Racist Struggle* (London: Routledge).

Barker, M. (1981) *The New Racism* (London: Junction Books).

Bryan, B., Dadzie, S. and Scafe, S. (1985) *The Heart of the Race* (London: Virago).

Castles, S. (1993) 'Migrations and Minorities in Europe. Perspectives for the 1990s: Eleven Hypotheses'. In J. Wrench and J. Solomos (eds) *Race and Migration in Western Europe* (Oxford: Berg) pp. 17–34.

Castles, S. and Miller, M. (1993) *The Age of Migration* (London: Macmillan).

Cock, J. (1992) *Women and War in South Africa* (London: Open Letters).

Cooke, M. and Woollacott, A. (1993) (eds) *Gendering War Talk* (Princeton: Princeton University Press).

Desta, A. (1994) 'Female Asylum Seekers in the Netherlands'. In M. Misckke and A. Roerink (eds) *The Future: Women and International Cooperation* (Oegstgeest: Vrouwenberaad Ontwikkelingssamenwerking) pp. 25–7.

Dooh-Bunya, L. (1990) 'Movement for the Defence of Black Women's Rights', PCR Information, Special Issue *Women Under Racism: A Decade of Visible Action* (Geneva: WCC) pp. 25–8.

Elshtain, J. (1987) *Women and War* (Brighton: The Harvester Press).

Enloe, C. (1983/1988) *Does Khaki Become You? The Militarization of Women's Lives* (London: Pandora).

Essed, P. (1990) *Everyday Racism: Reports from Women in Two Cultures* (Claremont, CA: Hunter House) (extended English edition of *Alledaags Racisme*, first published in 1984).

Essed, P. (1991) *Understanding Everyday Racism: An Interdisciplinary Theory* (Newbury Park, CA: Sage).

Essed, P. (1994) *Diversiteit: Vrouwen, Kleur en Kultuur* (Baarn: Ambo). English language edition forthcoming under the title of *Diversity: Gender, Color and Culture* (University of Massachusetts Press – forthcoming).

Feteke, L. and Webber, F. (1994) *Inside Racist Europe* (London: IRR).

Joly, D. (1987) 'Associations Amongst the Pakistani Population in Britain'. In J. Rex, D. Joly and C. Wilpert (eds) *Immigrant Associations in Europe* (Aldershot: Gower) pp. 62–85.

Kraft, M. and Ashraf-Khan, R. (1994) (eds) *Schwarze Frauen der Welt. Europa und Migration* (Berlin: Orlanda Frauenverlag).

Lutz, H. (1991) *Welten Verbinden: Türkische Sozialarbeiterinnen in den Niederlanden und der Bundesrepublik Deutschland* (Frankfurt a.M. Verlag für Interkulturelle Kommunikation).

Mitter, S. (1986/1991) *Common Fate, Common Bond: Women in the Global Economy* (London: Pluto Press).

Moghadam, V. (ed.) (1994) *Identity Politics and Women* (Boulder: Westview Press).

Mullard, C., Nimako, K., and Willemsen, G. (1990) *De Plurale Kubus: Een Vertoog Over Emancipatiemodellen en Minderhedenbeleid* (Den Haag: Warray).

Ntoane, L.C. (1994) 'Black Leadership: An Absolute Necessity'. Paper presented to the *Sheeba Refreshers Meeting*, Driebergen, on the theme of Leadership, 4–5 March 1994.

Oguntoye, K., Opitz, M. and Schultz, D. (eds) (1986) *Farbe Bekennen* (Berlin: Orlanda Frauenverlag).

Osamor, M. (1994) 'Black Leadership in Politics'. Paper presented to the *Sheeba Refreshers Meeting, Driebergen*, on the theme of Leadership, 4–5 March 1994.

Phizacklea, A. (ed.) (1983) *One Way Ticket. Migration and Female Labour* (London: Routledge and Kegan Paul).

Phizacklea, A. (1990) *Unpacking the Fashion Industry* (London: Routledge).

Rex, J., Joly, D. and Wilpert, C. (1987) (eds) *Immigrant Associations in Europe* (Aldershot: Gower).

Salimi, R. (1994) 'Schwarze Menschen in Land der Mitternachtssonne'. In M. Kraft and R. Ashraf-Khan, (eds) *Schwarze Frauen der Welt* (Berlin: Orlanda Frauenverlag) pp. 62–6.

Schrijvers, J. (1993) *The Violence of Development: A Choice for Intellectuals* (Utrecht: International Books and New Delhi: Kali for Women).

Dijk, T.A. van (1993) *Elite Discourse and Racism* (Newbury Park: Sage).

Vickers, J. (1993) *Women and War* (London: Zed Books).

Vrouwenberaad Ontwikkelingssamenwerking (1994) Working document for expert meeting on: 'On the Move: Conflict Situations and Migration: Consequences for Women'. Conference on *The Future: Women and International Cooperation*, Amsterdam, 27 May 1994.

Weldeghiorgis, E. (1994) 'Afrikanische Migrantinnnen in Italien'. In M. Kraft and R. Ashraf-Khan, (eds) *Schwarze Frauen der Welt* (Berlin: Orlanda Frauenverlag) pp. 67–70.

West, C. (1993) 'The New Cultural Politics of Difference'. In B. Thompson and S. Tyagi (eds) *Beyond a Dream Deferred* (Minneapolis: University of Minnesota Press) pp. 18–40.

Wrench, J. and Solomos, J. (eds) (1993) *Racism and Migration in Western Europe* (Oxford: Berg).

Yuval-Davis, N. (1994) 'Identity Politics and Women's Identity'. In V. Moghadam (ed.) *Identity Politics and Women* (Boulder: Westview Press) pp. 408–24.

Yuval-Davis, N. and Anthias, F. (eds) (1989) *Woman–Nation–State* (London: Macmillan).

3   'After the Last Sky, Where do the Birds Fly?' What can European Women Learn from Anti-Racist Struggles in the United States?

Gloria Wekker

The title of this chapter is a line from Mahmoud Darwish's poem 'The Earth is Closing in on Us',[1] which resonated with me in a special way. The title summarises and brings together several threatening factors which cannot be addressed here in detail, but which frame my topic. It is in the context of several serious crises that we came together as European feminists (in the eighth European Forum of Left Feminists conference), as the *fin-de-siècle* is rapidly approaching, to reconfirm our 'sisterhood', 'the ties that bind us' and simultaneously to face the forces which divide us, in order to re-invigorate effective, political, feminist action. By coming together, in Bernice Reagon Johnson's words, 'we are positioned to have the opportunity to have something to do with what makes it into the next century. And the principles of coalition are directly related to that' (Reagon Johnson, 1983: 356).

Let me unpack some of those threatening skies above us as humans. Under those skies, I have continuously changing perspectives: as a world citizen, as a resident of the North, as a European, as an immigrant, as a black woman. The exercise of identifying these threats illuminates the complexity of the 'imagined communities' of which we are all part. In the first place, it is evident that we, especially the people in the North, have collectively made a mess of it environmentally. It should be equally clear that there is no sky after the one above us. As ecofeminist Maria Mies notes:

> Most people in the affluent societies live in a kind of schizophrenic or 'double-think' state. They are aware of the disasters of Bhopal and Chernobyl, of the 'greenhouse' effect, the destruction of the ozone layer, the gradual poisoning of ground-water, rivers and seas by fertilizers, pesticides, herbicides, as well as industrial waste,

and that they themselves increasingly suffer the effects of air pollution, allergies, stress and noise, and the health risks due to industrially produced food. They also know that responsibility for these negative impacts on their quality of life lies in their own lifestyles and an economic system based on constant growth. And yet (except for very few) they fail to act on this knowledge by modifying their lifestyles. (Mies and Shiva, 1993: 57)

There are discernible patterns to the choices the North makes as to where to invest its considerable resources, money, intellect and energy. For example, the Netherlands, instead of creating favourable conditions for large numbers of young immigrants, Turks, Moroccans, Surinamese and Antillians, to find their way in Dutch society, chooses to expand our alienated universe by 'cyberspace-dating' on Internet. Instead of undertaking expensive research to make 'our' (read the rich world's) life-span longer, all of us might be better served by engagement in research, thought and praxis which would make this planet a more equitable and healthier place, for as long as we are here and for those to come after us.

Secondly, living under global political skies, the major political changes of recent times in Eastern and Western Europe, the Soviet Union, the Middle East, South Africa, Central and South America, signal major realignments in the structuring of the world political order (Brah, 1993). An increasing economic and technological globalisation is accompanied by unprecedented migratory movements and by the dark clouds of political fragmentation into nationalist movements, neo-racisms, ethnocentrisms and an inward turning cultural gaze, preoccupied with an essential, monolithic national identity. The lame, laissez-faire attitude of a 'unified' Europe towards the genocide in the former Yugoslavia fits well within this inward looking tendency. Women's positions are articulated in special ways within nationalisms, both by men and by women themselves. On the one hand, religious, ethnic and cultural identities are generally based on patriarchal images of women. 'Our' women need to be controlled, in dress, in appropriate behaviour, in their sexuality. This almost always amounts to more violence and more inequality for women (Mies and Shiva, 1993). Degradation, violation and extermination of 'their' women, as the symbolic markers of the collectivity, can be 'read' as messages passed between men of opposing collectivities about the intrinsic worth of the group. On the other hand, women are not only victims or being acted upon within the discourses and practices of nationalisms: they actively participate in national projects and struggles, as has been the case in the former Yugoslavia, South Africa and Palestine, and they play major roles in the inculcation and reproduction of collective myths, symbols and identifications in the younger members of the collectivity (Anthias and Yuval-Davis, 1992).

Thirdly, threatening clouds mark the Western European skies above those of us, however diverse, who live an existence of (im)migration, exile, as (illegal) aliens, refugees or nomads (Braidotti, 1993), and who have, in the process, been defined as Other. It is also clear that in the Dutch situation, we are confronted almost daily with racist threats from White Power groups and from politicians, who question our entry into, or presence in, the Netherlands. Racist encounters for people of colour on public transport, while shopping, in the educational system and in the media are our daily lived reality (Essed, 1990). The threatening skies of nationalist exclusions take many forms. These include: the constant questioning and undermining of the legitimate presence of people of colour in Western European countries, the lumping together of widely divergent groups as monolithically undesirable and the consistent association of immigrants with criminal, deviant and socially undesirable behaviour, such as drugs trafficking and 'backwardness'. All of these forms contribute to the underpinning of current brands of nationalism with racism. Just as racism in Britain has been shown to be an inherent part of the hegemonic Anglo-Saxon ethnicity (Anthias and Yuval-Davis, 1992; Gilroy, 1987; Sivanandan, 1982), hegemonic versions of Dutch national identity are deeply imbued with notions of being white and of partaking in Christian religion (Willemsen en Nimako, 1993). Yet, as Homi Bhabha notes: 'The Western metropole must confront its postcolonial history, told by its influx of postwar migrants and refugees, as an indigenous or native narrative internal to its national identity' (1993: 26).

The fourth, and final, threatening sky I wish to explore concerns the intersection of racism and gender. For the sky under which I would like to feel most secure, the feminist movement, is also not devoid of threats and danger. Much as I would like vigorously to be able to underwrite Virginia Woolf's famous dictum 'As a woman I have no country. As a woman I want no country. As a woman, my country is the whole world' (Woolf, 1938), I cannot. Woolf's statement is attractive in implying a disloyalty to patriarchal civilisation, a disregard of narrow nationalist definitions and a sisterhood across national/ethnic boundaries. However, it is impossible for me to embrace this aphorism. It is not only that as women of Third World origin in Western Europe we are often assigned to a country or culture (Bhavnani, 1993), whether or not we want to be, it is also and more poignantly that being able to be aloof and detached from any country is the privilege of high caste and whiteness and can only be asserted when there is no challenge to belonging (Walker, 1984). We need to look closely and incisively at our supposed 'sisterhood'. The practices of individual feminists notwithstanding, mainstream feminism as a whole has not begun to accept responsibility for its role in the perpetuation of global and local oppressions (DasGupta, 1994). I am especially concerned here with forms of racism and nationalism which are thriving within the feminist movement, but not acknowledged and not dealt with.

In this chapter I seek to share some of the lessons that can be learnt from the experience of United States' women in combating racism. I am interested both in situations where North American women have operated successfully and in issues where we should learn from their experiences but not take their lead. I will have to narrow and situate this topic in educational spheres, in particular the academy, since this is the situation with which I am most familiar. My central question is thus: what is it that European women can learn from United States' women in anti-racist struggles in the academy?

First, I will situate myself and the locations from which I speak. Subsequently, given the tortuous debates in the Netherlands about which phenomena qualify to be called 'racisms' and 'nationalisms', I will address definitional issues and describe some characteristic features of racisms and nationalisms, with special reference to the situation in the Netherlands. Next, in the light of this, I will address four issues which illustrate some commonalities and differences in the situation of women of colour in the academy in the United States (and in Canada in one instance) and in the Netherlands. These issues are: firstly, the importance of an oppositional consciousness for professors and students of colour in a situation where struggle is inevitable; secondly, the avoidance of traps such as the 'only minority' or the 'model minority' theses, which serve to construct structural inequities as cultural and to undermine the development of a broader solidarity movement between various groups; thirdly, the importance of transnational and transethnic identifications; and fourthly, the insistence on the intersection of the category of gender with other social constructions such as social class, ethnicity and sexuality. The final section of the paper will draw some general conclusions which suggest ways in which it is possible to build coalitions between women of colour and others.

I will be arguing that there are different historical factors and different current blends of exclusionary and inclusionary forces operative in each of the issues I discuss, which have consequences for educational settings and the 'naturalness' of whiteness in each setting. I want to add that this chapter is not based on research, but rather on the analysis of lived experiences and of observations both in the United States and in the Netherlands. Quite consciously, it will be fragmentary, not exhaustive; more poetics than percentages; more subjective than abstract; less concerned with painfully reaching for definitions than reaching for your hearts and minds, which is also painful, but in a different sense. Coalition building, I am convinced, does not proceed from naming or elucidating the correct theory, but from our commonly felt need for survival, which is what is at stake. I am not engaged in the hegemonic 'race for theory', which, as Barbara Christian aptly notes, is so often accompanied by a language which mystifies rather than clarifies our condition (Christian, 1989).

Since all knowledge emanates from specific historical, socio-political locations, I want to situate myself as a black Dutch woman, who was born in Surinam and grew up in the Netherlands. As an adult, having completed my Master's degree in Anthropology at the University of Amsterdam and having worked as a public servant for a number of years, I went to the United States to do my Ph.D in Anthropology at the University of California at Los Angeles. I did research in Surinam, went on to teach Women's Studies at Oberlin College in Ohio and I am now associated with the Women's Studies Department in the Humanities faculty at the University of Utrecht in the Netherlands. It was as an adult that I came to know the experience of being a migrant (to the United States) intimately, since I was too young to realise the parameters of this existence when I first came to the Netherlands. Two reasons, which are also pertinent to my topic, stand out in explanation of why I went to the United States in 1987. In the first place, I was aware that I needed more background in African-American Studies and the Dutch academy could offer none at that time, and secondly, I needed a brand of Women's Studies that wasn't lilywhite and that would show me an intricacy, a breadth and depth that would allow me to understand the constructions of self and sexualities of Afro-Surinamese working-class women, on whom I eventually wrote my dissertation (Wekker, 1992, 1994). In order fully to appreciate this state of Dutch academic affairs, it is necessary to delve deeper into local constructions of who does and who does not belong to the national collectivity, and whose world is reflected in the educational system, even in a feminist universe.

Some Definitional and Conceptual Issues

Key among the many factors that differentiate between local, contextualised brands of racism and nationalism in the United States and the Netherlands are the main locations where empire was constructed (internal versus external dominion), the relative size, stature and period of the two nations as imperialistic 'giants' and different blends of inclusionary and exclusionary tendencies towards residents.

I will address the latter two variables in the course of this chapter, but regarding the first it is important to clarify my position now. I agree with Brah (1993) that a distinction between a 'racism of the interior' and a 'racism of the exterior' 'could perpetuate the erroneous view that European racisms directed against people outside Europe were not an internal dynamic of the historical constitution of "Europe"' (Brah, 1993: 21). So, for example, when Mr 'Whisky' Sisodia in Salman Rushdie's *The Satanic Verses* drunkenly stammers: 'The trouble with the Eng-english is that their hiss-hiss-history happened overseas, so they do-do-don't know what it means' (Rushdie, 1988: 343), one is bound to question the convenience of that escape. The same problem applies to the Dutch.

From the point of view of the oppressed, however, it may have made quite a difference whether the hegemonic power was present all the time or, as in Surinam during long periods of its history as a Dutch colony, was largely in absentia. The survival strategies, including a vivid collective consciousness of racism, which blacks in the United States had to forge, were probably of a different order from the ones blacks in Surinam developed. Thus, when in the 1970s almost half of the Surinamese population came to settle in the former metropole, they were less prepared to deal with racism than their North American counterparts.

For the purposes of this chapter, I will start by first unravelling racism from nationalism, although in reality, under certain circumstances, they tend to intersect and influence each other. Ultimately, of course, we need to engage in anti-racist struggle that intersects with anti-nationalist struggle. Anti-racist struggle is struggle which deconstructs and undermines the mechanisms by which ethnic minorities are constructed as deviants from the 'normal' and excluded from power and other important resources (Anthias and Yuval-Davis, 1992: 22). Anti-nationalist struggle is struggle which deconstructs and undermines the mechanisms by which an 'imagined community', the national collectivity, is constructed as an exclusive ethnic category, which is defined by common origins, common destiny and common culture (Anthias and Yuval-Davis, 1992).

In the Dutch context, there are many branches to the tree of the denial of racism (cf. Essed, 1990, 1991). Apart from a general cloak of silence around the topic, there are many convenient misunderstandings such as that racism, if it exists at all, is located in the bottom layers of Dutch society, not among the elite. Another branch of this tree is that the term 'racism' should only be applied to extremist, organised forms. Then there are the more intellectual varieties of dodging the issue, which make the proposed definitions unattainable and hence make it very hard indeed ever to demonstrate racism satisfactorily. For example, Bovenkerk et al. suggest that racism is 'a coherent, conscious set of ideas based on a race theory' (Bovenkerk et al., 1985), while Fennema (1993) defines it as 'those forms of reasoning that contain a quasi-biological element in an otherwise cultural argument'. In general, the situation in the Netherlands is characterised by the dominant ethnic group being the ultimate authority on the criteria by which behaviour or speech is to be called racist. An astounding amount of biblical leniency, forgiveness and tolerance toward members of their own group is collectively demonstrated in this exercise by judges, academics, employers, personnel officers and politicians. The greatest fear of the dominant group apparently is that blacks undermine their own credibility and position by flinging the taboo accusation of racism around too loosely and at the slightest provocation. At the same time, however, there is minimal willingness systematically to investigate the contours of ethnic inequality on the labour market, for instance. This is exemplified by a recent law for the Enhancement of Proportional Labour Participation of Allochtonous People (Wet Bevordering Evenredige Arbeidsdeelname Allochtonen) that requires employers with more than 35 employees to register their personnel by ethnicity. Originally intended as a form of 'contract compliance', the law was thoroughly emaciated by the time it was accepted by

Parliament. Employers are asked to indicate what they intend to do about raising the percentage of their employees who originate outside the Netherlands, but there are no sanctions attached to the law. This should be seen against the backdrop of an overall registered unemployment rate of 5 per cent for 'indigenous' Dutch at the end of the 1990s, while the corresponding numbers for immigrant groups ranged from 21 per cent for Antillians to 31 per cent for Turks (Smeets, 1995).

Racism, as I define it, is 'beliefs, statements and acts which inferiorise certain ethnic groups on the basis of their not belonging to the culture of origin of the dominant ethnic group within the state apparatus'. Essed's innovative concept of 'everyday racism', which she coined by centring on the experience of black women, stresses some key concepts: 'everyday racism is the integration of racism into everyday situations through practices (cognitive and behavioral) that activate underlying power relations' (1991: 50). I understand racism not as a unitary, homogeneous field, but rather as plural. Racisms (anti-Jewish, anti-black, anti-Turk, anti-Muslim, anti-Romany, etc.) are built up and actualised in connection with perceptions of specific groups and their histories. Some authors make a distinction between colonial racism, which targets groups who originate in the (former) colonies but which, supposedly, is on the wane, and more prevalent forms of nationalist racisms, which are directed against recent immigrants with a different culture, notably people with Islamic backgrounds (Fennema, 1993). Thus, it can be assumed that the racism which an Afro-Surinamese woman encounters will differ from that experienced by a Turkish woman of the same class. Racisms are also gendered, which means that notions of masculinity and femininity pertaining to a particular group are constructed in different manners (Brah, 1993). Thus, for instance, Turkish men and women of the same class will encounter different forms of racism.

The concept of 'nationalism', too, is contextually specific and, like racism, one of its aims is to draw boundaries between who belongs and who does not belong to the collectivity. There is a vast amount of controversy and debate about the precise meaning of the concept of nationalism and its interrelationships with ethnicity, gender, citizenship and the workings of the state. Like racism, there is no one nationalism around in any one society at any one time. Differences of class, place of birth, ethnic origin, religion, political beliefs, gender and other factors radically affect the specific kinds of collective ideologies which different segments of a population hold and the ways in which they construct their boundaries (Anthias and Yuval-Davis, 1992: 42). What is specific to the nationalist project and discourse is the claim for a separate political representation for the collectivity (Anthias and Yuval-Davis, 1992: 25). Viewed in this way, it is clear that there are many possible areas where nationalisms and racisms intersect.

Wherever a delineation of boundaries takes place, as is the case with every ethnic and national collectivity, processes of exclusion and inclusion are in operation. These can take place with varying degrees of intensity, and with a variety of cultural, religious and state mechanisms. But exclusions of 'the Other' can become a positive and inherent part of national ethnicities. Nazi Germany and apartheid South Africa were two examples in which such exclusions became a major and even an obsessive preoccupation for the national culture. But, to a lesser degree, many, if not most, other ethnicities of hegemonic national collectivities include elements of racist exclusion within their symbolic orders (Anthias and Yuval-Davis, 1992: 39). Anti-racist struggle coincides with anti-nationalist struggle when the automatic mechanisms that depict migrants as deviants, as excluded from the dominant ethnicity, are undermined.

Consciousness and Struggle in the Academy

A key difference in the situation of women of colour in the academy in the United States and in the Netherlands is that in the latter case the first communities of colour came into the country from the 1950s onwards (Indonesians and Moluccans), while the most numerous ethnic groups (Surinamese, Antillians, Turks and Moroccans) mostly did not arrive until the 1970s. Since women of colour have been in the United States for centuries, there is thus a meaningful difference in the actual length of time 'minorities' in each of the settings have had to develop strategies of entry into and survival within academia.

Minority groups in the United States have traditionally valued education as one of the main avenues for social advancement. As college undergraduates, minority women enrol in numbers pro-portionate to their distribution in the general population, but in graduate and professional schools, representation falls far below this level. Minority women are earning 6 per cent of all bachelor's degrees, 6.3 per cent of all Master's degrees, 3.1 per cent of doctorates and 2.6 per cent of first professional degrees, such as law and medicine (Hunter College Women's Studies Collective, 1983: 422). Across the country, less than 2 per cent of college faculties are black and black women are a very small percentage of that number. Of a total of 3200 institutions of higher education, only 15 are headed by black women (Wilkerson, 1986: 90). Overall, the educational gains that were made by blacks during the 1970s have rapidly eroded during the 1980s. The higher costs of education, the difficult position of historically black colleges and increasing dropout rates at all levels of the educational process all contribute to this (Wilkerson, 1986).

The much smaller scale of Dutch society and the shorter period in which ethnic minority groups have sought educational advancement should not blind us to the seriousness of the situation in the Netherlands. To my knowledge, at this moment there are less than a handful of women of colour working in tenured positions in Dutch universities. This means that in terms of black female role-models who speak out, who encourage students, who legitimise particular academic interests, we are faced with a serious problem. We (my generation) are our own role-models, inventing ourselves as we live. We do not have our own Audre Lorde (1984), Gloria Anzaldua (1990), June Jordan (1985), Trinh T. Minh-Ha (1989), bell hooks (1991), Chandra Mohanty (1990, 1991) or Gayatri Chakravorty Spivak (1988). This should tell us something urgent about how harsh is the Dutch academic climate in general (including the feminist climate) to women of colour and the academic interests we seek to pursue.

The majority of students of colour in the Netherlands are not enrolled in the 'highest' academic stream of tertiary education, but matriculate in schools for lower, middle and higher professional training (LBO, MBO and HBO). The situation in the non-academic segments of the educational market is slightly more favourable in terms of numbers of students and professors of colour, yet curricular content and the structures of the schools remain as monolithically white as if there never had been any shift in the composition of the population. As far as educational success of students in the HBO segments is concerned (not taking the students in the 'welfare' sectors into account) 90 per cent do not make it through the exam at the end of their first year (propedeuse).[2] In her excellent study of everyday racism, the first to focus centrally on the experiences of black women with racism in the Netherlands, Philomena Essed has outlined the treatment that black students receive in the educational system: being consistently underrated, trivialised, not understood and unfairly evaluated (Essed, 1990).

Thus while the actual treatment of black students may not differ very much between the United States and the Netherlands, an important difference is that – due to, among other factors, black people's consciousness, their history of struggle and resulting Affirmative Action policies – students and professors of colour in the United States will find, in most cases, that they belong to a community. They will not be the lone, isolated figures we so commonly find in academic education in the Netherlands. Communities of colour in the United States, together with their allies, have opted for open confrontation of the hegemonic educational system, with ensuing legal battles to demand ethnic studies programmes and equitable numbers of faculty and students of colour. So far, the response of ethnic minority communities in the Netherlands has, by and large, been one of accommodation, silent discontent, dropping out. Dutch society, traditionally founded on religious pillars, is built on consensus and compromise. The buzz–concept 'multiculturalism' can easily absorb new cultures, as long as they do not fundamentally question prevailing power arrangements (Willemsen en Nimako, 1993; Essed, 1991); that is, as long as the fundamental whiteness of the educational system and process is not interrogated. One of the many challenges ahead of us here will be to work at building a liberated consciousness and community among people of colour and among our allies.

(Women) professors of colour can be seen as the bishops in a game of chess, who, often at great cost, have made it into hostile territory. One of the consequences of the ratio of white students versus students of colour is that a black professor will often have to teach a predominantly or exclusively white class. This is the case in many disciplines, in the United States, Canada and in the Netherlands. Himani Bannerji, a South Asian Professor of Women's Studies and Sociology at York University in Canada, painfully sums up some dimensions of that experience:

> The social relations of teaching and learning are relations of violence for us, those who are not white, who teach courses on Gender, Race and Class to a white body of students in a white University. I want to hide from this gaze. I am a real person who is angry at having to prove to real people grown accustomed to racism, that it has a history, political economy, culture, a daily exis-

tential dimension. Skeptical, brutal, shame-faced questions dart
out at me; a white woman defends the killing of a young black
man, herself a part-time member of the police force, her husband
implicated in the killing. I hear her, I see the stony faces of the
black students in the class, the uncomfortable body motions of
some white students. I hear a few hisses. My body feels tense and
hot, I want to shout at her, just plain scream – 'you fucking racist
idiot', 'you killer', but I cannot. The theatre of teaching, its script
does not permit me to do that. If I have to say it, I have to say it
pedagogically; exact a teaching moment out of it ... The point
is coming across, the meaning of racism is becoming evident and
wider; but in the meanwhile there is me, there is she ... Of
course I dissociate. (Bannerji, 1991: 7)

Bannerji and so many others like her go on teaching, almost wilfully
inflicting this violence on themselves daily, because they/we choose
to decolonise, to teach anti-racism, not only for ourselves, but for
others as well. This is the stuff, our life's blood, of which coalition
building and survival are made.

There is also another side to this experience. As Linda Carty reminds
us:

As a Black woman now teaching university in a society where
this is extremely rare, I am aware, like the few other 'non-white'
women in a similar position, of the unique opportunity I have to
redress some of the historical inaccuracies perpetrated by Euro-
centric scholars, including feminists, who refuse to recognize the
changing nature of the social world ... The opportunity presents
an exciting challenge for 'non-white' women bringing our feminist
praxis inside the university. We have a regular audience which
we could not otherwise encounter on a daily or even weekly basis.
(Carty, 1991a: 41)

Clearly, we will not, individually, be able to change the power
relations and existing knowledge. We will need to ally ourselves with
white scholars who are prepared to risk the power accorded them
by virtue of their race and class and possibly gender. Similarly, we
will need to build bridges to other minority scholars, both nationally
and internationally (see the discussion below).

The Traps of the 'Model Minority' and 'The Only Minority' Models

In our quest for a more equitable educational situation, we should avoid two pitfalls that characterise the North American situation: the 'model minority' thesis (Asian Americans) and the 'only minority' concept (African Americans). Both propose a culturalist explanation for material inequities and serve to undermine the sense of solidarity between 'non-white' groups that is necessary fundamentally to change relations of power. Advanced by hegemonic scholarship, but, to a significant extent, subscribed to by the respective groups themselves, these concepts effectively serve as instruments of divide and rule, not only in the educational field but also on wider social terrains, such as the economy. In the Dutch situation also, there are grounds to fear that there will be comparable developments.

In order to evaluate this, it is necessary to consider the different configurations of 'ethnicity' in the United States and in the Netherlands. In the United States, since the 1960s, in the aftermath of the Civil Rights Movement and the emergence of the new ethnicity (the search for cultural roots [Willemsen en Nimako, 1993]), 'everybody is ethnic'. White groups, who apparently belong to the dominant ethnicity in society, call themselves Polish-, Irish-, Italian-, Greek-, etc. Americans. At first sight, there is thus a remarkable and, from a Dutch perspective, wholesome quality of egalitarianism to this system, where next to diverse white ethnic groups we also find various ethnic groups of colour. It seems as if the American concept of citizenship is broad and varied enough to accommodate cultural and colour differences, that it is, in effect, 'colour-blind'. This benevolent broadness should not blind us, however, to the different structural barriers that white and non-white groups face in having their claims to equality accepted. There are very real power differences between ethnic groups that correspond with the ethnic hierarchy, in which white Anglo-Saxons are firmly at the top.

The insight that 'everybody belongs to an ethnic group' carries potential benefits in educational situations. Although it is often no more than mere rhetoric and there is a distinct tendency to individualise, make into folklore and psychologise ethnic differences in the United States, without analysing the historical and material bases of racist structures (Mohanty, 1990), it offers possibilities which are still sorely missing in a Dutch context.

I am thus arguing that notions of citizenship in the United States do not *a priori* hinge on ethnicity, but that one's life chances, at the same time, are very much related to being white or non-white. In the Netherlands, on the other hand, there is simultaneously a (receding) welfare state, which allegedly takes care of its residents, regardless of citizenship, and a stubborn insistence on a citizen, 'someone who belongs', being white and Christian. There are thus different blends of inclusivity and exclusivity operative in both situations. Ethnicity in a Dutch context only pertains to those who have come from elsewhere ('newcomers', 'foreigners', 'allochtonous people'), not to the dominant ethnicity (Willemsen en Nimako, 1993). The use of the concept of 'race' pertaining to people has dwindled in the postwar years, and is now only used in connection with plants and animals. Yet, the concept of ethnicity carries both 'ethnic' and 'racial' connotations (Willemsen en Nimako, 1993). On a recent television talkshow, for example, the Blue Diamonds, a popular singing duo who have lived in the Netherlands for at least 40 years but who are originally from Indonesia, appeared as guests. The members of the panel asked them questions like: 'What do you people eat?' and how certain things were done 'at home', meaning Indonesia. The message was clearly brought home to the viewers that no matter how long they had lived in the Netherlands, they would for ever remain 'foreign', in both senses of the term.

The national self-concept, narrow as it is and homogenising of both those who are included within it and those outside its boundaries, precludes widespread acceptance of the notion that one can be both Dutch and Surinamese, Turkish and Dutch. One way to problematise existing boundaries would be for people of colour to start calling themselves by these hyphenated terms. Although it would by no means remove the structural barriers to equal treatment, it would serve to undermine largely unspoken and unconscious assumptions about white homogeneity and Christianity as necessary ingredients of who belongs to the Dutch nation. Since this is the case, people of colour in the Dutch academy face a predicament. Where whiteness is not interrogated as a particularly powerful ethnic category, it becomes naturalised and frozen. I will return to this issue later.

The United States still harbours an exclusively white-on-black concept of racism (Martinez, 1994). Even though there are other large segments of the population, Native Americans, Asian/Pacific Americans and Latinos, who also do not belong to the upper ethnic stratum in American society and who also suffer from various forms of racism, the crucial historical axis in race relations has been and continues to be the white–black paradigm. Martinez explains why the bi-polar model became dominant:

> Many reasons exist for the persistence of the white/Black paradigm of racism; they include numbers, history and the psychology of whiteness. As slave labour became economically critical, 'blackness' became ideologically critical; it provided the very source of 'whiteness' and the heart of racism ... The exclusively white/Black concept of race and racism in the U.S. rests on a western, Protestant form of dualism woven into both race and gender relations from earliest times. In the dualist universe there is only black and white. A disdain, indeed fear of mixture haunts the Yankee soul; there is no room for any kind of multi-faceted identity, any hybridism. (Martinez, 1994: 58, 59)

There is thus a prevalent construction that only African Americans can suffer from racism and that the experiences of other people of colour come under the heading of exploitation and repression for reasons of culture and nationality. To the extent that not only large segments of African American communities but also other groupings have come to accept this thesis, a competitive game, the 'Olympics of oppression', is set up, in which those groups who stand to gain most by joining forces, lose the most.

A variation on this theme is the 'model minority' thesis, pertaining to Asian Americans. It tends to stress the success of this group, which is attributed almost always to a cultural emphasis on education, hard work and thrift (Woo, 1989). In reality, the thesis clearly does not hold for the vast majority of Asian Americans, who have immigrated to the United States since 1970 and who are suffering from discrimination in a variety of fields, such as housing and lack of access to capital. Only a small percentage of Japanese Americans and an element of the Chinese American population, who have lived in the United States for more than three generations, are doing well. Yet, more importantly, the 'model minority' thesis serves to justify the status quo in that it helps to explain away any problems that other groups might have as simply being due to different cultural values or failure of individual effort. It induces people to ignore structural barriers and inequities (Woo, 1989).

This is a situation where the Dutch can learn from what has happened in the United States in order not to follow in the same trajectory. In the Netherlands there is a tendency (as there is in the United States) to hold up certain minority groups, for example, Indo's[3] and Hindustani Surinamese, as model minorities. Equally divisive and pernicious is a tendency among segments of the Surinamese population in the Netherlands to consider themselves historically and culturally closer and thus more acceptable to hegemonic Dutch culture than Islamic or African peoples. The development of a minimal common political identity, a migrant identity (Lutz, 1993), is severely hampered by these tendencies. It is thus important to take stock of these tendencies in the Dutch situation.

Transnational Identifications

What is striking about United States nationalism is, on the one hand, an intellectual denial of the notion of the United States as an imperialist power, while on the other hand there is a very powerful ideological system, central to the education of every American, that the United States has a mission to the world (Barsamian, 1993). This mission consists of both developing and policing the world and, interestingly, goes hand in hand with a vast ignorance, geographical and otherwise, about the rest of the world. Nationalism takes, in Elizabeth Martinez's words, the following forms:

> U.S. political culture is not only Anglo-dominated but also embraces an exceptionally stubborn national self-centeredness, with no global vision other than relations of domination. The U.S. refuses to see itself as one nation sitting on a continent with 20 others all speaking languages other than English and having the right not to be dominated. (Martinez, 1994: 56)

With a number of notable exceptions, United States intellectuals too are caught in this web of national self-centredness. Few, such as Lorde (1984) and Jordan (1985), have a truly internationalist outlook.

The Netherlands has a troubled colonial past, with former colonies in the East Indies and Surinam and current connections with the Dutch Antilles and Aruba in the framework of the Kingdom of the Netherlands. Sectors of the hegemonic population have not yet come to terms with 'the loss' of Indonesia and New Guinea, or with no longer being able to justify or openly express feelings of superiority towards people of colour and those who symbolically join them. These notions find expression from time to time in decisions on immigration and entry into the Netherlands. This is demonstrated, for example, in the Poncke Princen and Attorney General Gonsalves affairs in 1993/94.[4] Within the Netherlands itself, whiteness, as power, is consistently silently reproduced. This occurs both through curricular content and through the relative absence of professors of colour. As a young girl going to school in the Netherlands, I was continually alienated by having my culture of origin represented as backward, primitive, still in transit to the more elevated stage Dutch society had reached.

In the Dutch feminist tradition, there is an internationalist outlook, an openness to ideas from abroad. The same quality characterises black women's attitudes, with the added factor that the works of our North American and Canadian sisters have often assisted our emotional and intellectual survival. As Philomena Essed mentions in her contribution to this volume, the positive side of our situation here is that we have developed an internationalist outlook, leading to transnational and transethnic identifications. The downside is that our attitude, again, may have been too accommodating so far: making do with whatever we can lay our hands on from abroad and not developing our own frameworks of awareness, knowledge, analysis and power. There is much work to be done here both within black and within white circles.

Women's Studies: The Importance of Gendered Intersections

The great contribution of feminists of colour in the United States has been to point out the inadequacy of the ways in which gender, the central organising concept of Women's Studies, has been theorised. Gender, conceptualised as hierarchy and inequality between men and women, has been shown in the 1980s to be an empty category if it is not understood in its intersections with race, class and sexuality. Lesbian and heterosexual women of colour, postcolonial, Third World and poor women were instrumental in challenging this hegemonic conception of gender, which provided understandings only of the lives of white, middle-class women.

In the Netherlands these insights have not yet gained much ground. With a few exceptions, white Dutch feminists persist in

thinking and writing as if the dynamics which fuel gender inequality
are only discernible when other power relations are least visible, if
not invisible (Carty, 1991b). One only needs to look at the content
of the Dutch Women's Studies journals, and the ethnic composition of their editorial boards, to ascertain that whiteness and its
accompanying privileges have been thoroughly 'naturalised'. The
point is not to add some women of colour and their texts to a
department or a journal, although that too needs to happen. What
is at stake is, in the words of Sandra Harding:

> As long as inclusive tendencies in Women's Studies stay at the
> level of studying Others, Women's Studies remains part of their
> problem. Here is where the determination to take responsibility
> for who we are becomes crucial. What would it mean, for instance,
> for white feminists to develop their scientific and political programs
> to take responsibility for who we are as whites, beyond merely
> being the friend or ally of women of colour by supporting the
> advancement of their persons and texts? For one thing, it would
> require providing less partial and distorting descriptions and expla-
> nations of the racial conditions of white women's lives and how
> these conditions affect the lives of women of colour here and around
> the world. (Harding, 1990: 17)

Conclusions and Strategies

In this chapter I have considered what European women can learn
from the anti-racist struggle in the United States academy. Although
there are many differences between Europe and the United States,
there are also similarities. Most important, in my estimation, is the
lack of historical and contemporary awareness of racism displayed
by blacks and whites in the Netherlands. The building of community
among blacks, and working from potentially fruitful transnational
and transethnic identifications, must be priorities if this situation is
to be rectified. Our white, potential allies must also educate themselves
about racism. Interrogation of whiteness and its attendant, unspoken
privileges is not just optional, but a prerequisite for coalition building.
Women's Studies that do not acknowledge the intersections of their
central category, gender, with other axes of differentiation, stay
irrelevant to the majority of the world's women.

We should avoid the national self-centredness that is so characteristic of United States nationalism. It harbours a vast ignorance about
the rest of the world and tends to think of relationships with that
world only in dominant–subordinate terms. Equally we should not
fall into conceptual traps, such as the 'only minority' or the 'model
minority' theses, that tend to attribute structural inequities to cultural
differences and hence to sow divisiveness.

Some of the points I have been trying to make on anti-racist and
anti-nationalist struggle are best illustrated by an insurgent speech
by Bernice Reagon Johnson, one of the powerful singers in the black
(a cappella) group, Sweet Honey in the Rock:

> It must become necessary for all of us to feel that this is our world.
> And that we are here to stay and that anything that is here is ours
> to take and to use in our image. And watch that 'our' – make it
> as big as you can ... The 'our' must include everybody you have
> to include in order for you to survive. You must be sure you
> understand that you ain't gonna be able to have an 'our' that don't
> include Bernice Reagon Johnson, cause I don't plan to go
> nowhere! That's why we have to have coalitions. Cause I ain't
> gonna let you live unless you let me live. Now there's danger in
> that, but there's also the possibility that we can both live – if you
> can stand it ... (Reagon Johnson, 1983: 368)

Epilogue

I will end on a note which also speaks to me with extraordinary
resonance, because it embodies some of the worlds I inhabit. It is a
poem by my friend Abena Busia, a Ghanaian poet and professor of
comparative literature at Rutgers University, living in New York
City, from her exquisite and wistful collection of poetry *Testimonies
of Exile* (1990). The title of the poem is 'All my friends are exiles':

All my friends are exiles,

born in one place, we live in another
and with true sophistication,
rendezvous
in most surprising places –
where you would never expect to find us.

Between us we people the world.

With aplomb and a command of languages
we stride across continents
with the self-assurance of those who know
with absolute certainty
where they come from.

With the globe at our command,
we have everywhere to go,
but home!

Notes

1. Quoted in Busia's (1990) poem 'Migrations'.
2. This percentage comes from an unpublished report on the educational situation of minorities at the HBO level. It was personally communicated to me by researcher Gharietje Choenni.
3. Indo's are people of mixed heritage, mostly Indonesian and Dutch, who had to flee to the Netherlands during Indonesia's war of Independence. See also note 4.
4. Poncke Princen was a Dutch soldier in the army that was sent to Indonesia during what has euphemistically become known as the 'policional actions' (politionele acties), the war waged by the Dutch against Indonesia's independence (1946–49). Princen walked over to 'enemy ranks', joining the Indonesian nationalists, stayed in Indonesia and eventually obtained Indonesian nationality. Forty-five years after this occurred, his entry into the Netherlands to visit his children and grandchildren was obstructed by powerful factions of veterans and politicians in Dutch society, who argued that allowing entry to this traitor would rip open wounds that have not yet had time to heal!

   The Gonsalves' affair blew up and over during the summer of 1994, after media publications revealed that Gonsalves, now Attorney General in the Netherlands, had during his duty as a colonial public servant in Dutch New Guinea, in the late 1940s, shot and physically abused several Papuans. There was no reason, according to the member of the cabinet responsible for such decisions (Minister of Justice Kosto), to reconsider his current position in the light of these historical facts.

References

Anthias, F. and Yuval-Davis, N. (1992) *Racialized Boundaries. Race, Nation, Gender, Colour and Class and the Anti-Racist Struggle* (London/New York: Routledge).

Anzaldua, G. (ed.) (1990) *Making Face, Making Soul. Haciendo Caras. Creative and Critical Perspectives by Women of Color* (San Francisco: an Aunt Lute Foundation).

Bannerji, H. (1991) 'Re: Turning the Gaze', *Resources For Feminist Research/Documentation sur la Recherche Feministe*, vol. 20, nos 3–4.

Barsamian, D. (1993) 'Edward W. Said. The Pen and the Sword: Culture and Imperialism', *Z-Magazine*, July/August.

Bhabha, H. (1993) 'Beyond the Pale: Art in the Age of Multicultural Translation'. In R. Lavrijsen (ed.) *Cultural Diversity in the Arts. Art, Art Policies and the Facelift of Europe* (Amsterdam: Royal Tropical Institute).

Bhavnani, K-K.(1993) 'Towards A Multicultural Europe?: "Race", Nation and Identity in 1992 and Beyond'. *Feminist Review*, vol. 45, pp. 30–45.

Bovenkerk, F. et al. (1985) *Vreemd Volk, Gemengde Gevoelens* (Meppel: Boom).

Brah, A. (1993) 'Re-Framing Europe: En-gendered Racisms, Ethnicities and Nationalisms in Contemporary Western Europe', *Feminist Review*, vol. 45, pp. 9–28

Braidotti, R. (1993) 'Nomads in a Transformed Europe: Figurations for an Alternative Consciousness'. In R. Lavrijsen (ed.) *Cultural Diversity in the Arts. Art, Art Policies and the Facelift of Europe* (Amsterdam: Royal Tropical Institute).

Busia, A. (1990) 'All my friends are exiles'. In *Testimonies of Exile* (Trenton, NJ: Africa World Press).

Carty, L. (1991a) 'Black Women in Academia: A Statement from the Periphery'. In H. Bannerji et al., *Unsettling Relations. The University as a Site of Feminist Struggle* (Boston: South End Press).

Carty, L. (1991b) 'Women's Studies in Canada: A Discourse and Praxis of Exclusion', *RFR/DRF, Transforming Knowledge and Politics*, vol. 20, nos 3–4.

Christian, B. (1989) 'The Race for Theory', *Cultural Critique*, vol. 6.

DasGupta, S. (1994) 'Reinventing the Feminist Wheel', *Z-Magazine*, September.

Essed, P. (1990) *Everyday Racism: Reports from Women of Two Cultures* (Alameda, CA: Hunter House).

Essed, P. (1991) *Understanding Everyday Racism: An Interdisciplinary Theory* (Newbury Park, CA: Sage).

Fennema, M. (1993) 'Twee Soorten Racisme. Oude Superioriteitsgevoelens en Nieuwe Vijandbeelden'. In G. Pas (ed.) *Achter de Coulissen: Gedachten over de Multi-Etnische Samenleving* (Amsterdam: Wetenschappelijk Bureau GroenLinks).

Gilroy, P. (1987) *There Ain't No Black in the Union Jack* (London: Hutchinson).

Harding, S. (1990) 'The Permanent Revolution', *The Women's Review of Books*, vol. 7, no. 5, p. 17.

hooks, b. (1991) *Yearning. Race, Gender and Cultural Politics* (Boston: South End Press).

Hunter College Women's Studies Collective (1983) *Women's Realities, Women's Choices. An Introduction to Women's Studies* (New York/Oxford: Oxford University Press).

Jordan, J. (1985) *On Call. Political Essays* (Boston: South End Press).

Lorde, A. (1984) *Sister Outsider. Essays and Speeches* (Trumansburg, NY: The Crossing Press).

Lutz, H. (1993) 'Migrantenidentiteit. Migratie als Erfenis'. In G. Pas (ed.) *Achter de Coulissen: Gedachten over de Multi-Etnische Samenleving* (Amsterdam: Wetenschappelijk Bureau GroenLinks).

Martinez, E. (1994) 'Seeing More Than Black and White. Latinos, Racism and the Cultural Divides', *Z-Magazine*, May.

Mies, M. and Shiva, V. (1993) *Ecofeminism* (Halifax/London: Fernwood Publications and Zed Books).

Minh-Ha, T.T. (1989) *Woman, Native, Other. Writing Postcoloniality and Feminism* (Bloomington/Indianapolis: Indiana University Press).

Mohanty, C. (1990) 'On Race and Voice: Challenges for Liberal Education in the 1990s', *Cultural Critique*, winter, pp. 179–208.

Mohanty, C. et al. (1991) *Third World Women and the Politics of Feminism* (Bloomington/Indianapolis: Indiana University Press).

Reagon Johnson, B. (1983) 'Coalition Politics: Turning the Century'. In B. Smith (ed.) *Home Girls: A Black Feminist Anthology* (New York: Kitchen Table Press).

Rushdie, S. (1988) *The Satanic Verses* (London: Viking Press).

Sivanandan, A. (1982) *A Different Hunger* (London: Pluto Press).

Smeets, H. (ed.) (1995) *Jaarboek Minderheden 1995* (Houten/ Zaventem/Lelystad: Bohn Stafleu Van Loghum Koninklijke Vermande bv).

Spivak, G. (1988) *In Other Worlds* (London: Routledge).

Walker, A. (1984) *In Search of our Mother's Gardens* (London: Women's Press).

Wekker, G. (1992) 'I Am Gold Money, (I Pass Through all Hands, But I Do Not Lose My Value): The Construction of Selves, Gender and Sexualities in a Female, Working-Class, Afro-Surinamese Setting', Dissertation, UCLA.

Wekker, G. (1994) *Ik Ben een Gouden Munt. De Constructie van Subjectiviteit en Sexualiteit van Creoolse Volksklasse Vrouwen* (Amsterdam: Feministische Uitgeverij Vita).

Wilkerson, M. (1986) 'A Report on the Educational Status of Black Women During the UN Decade of Women, 1976–85'. In M. Simms and J. Malveaux (eds) *Slipping Through the Cracks. The Status of Black Women* (New Brunswick/Oxford: Transaction Books).

Willemsen, G. en K. Nimako (1993) 'Multiculturalisme, Verzuilde Samenleving en Verzorgingsstaat. Naar een pluralistische Democratie'. In G. Pas (ed.) *Achter de Coulissen: Gedachten over de Multi-Etnische Samenleving* (Amsterdam: Wetenschappelijk Bureau Groenlinks).

Woo, D. (1989) 'The Gap between Striving and Achieving: The Case of Asian American Women'. In Asian Women United of California (eds) *Making Waves: An Anthology of Writings by and about Asian American Women* (Boston: Beacon Press).

Woolf, V. (1938) *Three Guineas* (London: Penguin).

4 The Boundaries of Community: Gender Relations and Racial Violence

Theresa Wobbe

In the late 1980s, hatred of foreigners and racism became the order of the day in German politics. In 1992, 23 people were killed in racist attacks and thousands were the victims of violence. From 1991 to 1992, the number of attacks reached 2584, an increase of 74 per cent. Some 70 per cent of these attacks were carried out by young people in radical right-wing organisations (Willems, 1993), most of whom are men (Birsl, 1994). This does not mean that women are not involved in racist activities.

In this chapter I would like to emphasise one particular aspect of racist violence and to argue that more attention should be given to the act of violence itself. I will link the issue of 'race' and rape to the construction of rape in the western hemisphere, focusing mainly on Germany, but using some examples from other countries. I will firstly give an example to clarify the context of community and gender in which such rapes occur and the common interlinking of 'race' and rape. Secondly I will focus on the intersection of violence and the rhetorical structures used in rape narratives. The final section of the chapter will argue that the social construction of 'belonging' functions through gender difference. Against this background the concept of 'openness to vulnerability and the power to violate' can clarify how a powerful instrument of social closure becomes evident. I will suggest that the interrelation of gender relations, the construction of community (*Gemeinschaft*) and racist violence all need to be considered in order to understand why it is that racism forms such a stable part of everyday German life.

Communities and Gender

In her outstanding article 'Split Affinities: The Case of Interracial Rape', Valerie Smith argued in favour of the development of methods of analysis for interpreting the ways in which race and gender are inscribed in cultural productions (Smith, 1992). She deconstructed the rhetoric surrounding an incident which came to be known as the 'Central Park rape' in the United States. The following description of this incident illustrates the interrelation of constructions of community, gender relations and boundaries of belonging.

On an evening in April 1989, a young white woman jogger was raped repeatedly in Central Park, Manhattan, by a group of black and Puerto Rican adolescent males. The rape victim, an investment banker, emerged from her coma after two weeks but appears to have sustained some brain damage. This incident evoked a great deal of racist rhetoric in the media, in which neither the rape victim nor the other women who had been raped during that week in New York City were at the centre of debate. Valerie Smith concludes: 'Rape here is clearly not represented as a violation of a woman's body alone. Rather, in the terms of interlocking issues of race, class and gender, these crimes suggest that certain women's bodies are more valuable than others' (Smith, 1992: 278).[1]

In addition, the media debate about the 'Central Park rape' initiated a discussion about to whom the Manhattan Central Park 'belonged'. The sexual violence one woman had suffered became the symbolic representation or signifier of the violation of a specific community. The white Anglo-American business people of Manhattan considered themselves violated in that 'their' place, the Central Park, had been 'attacked'. The social problem of rape was thus transformed into a racial problem. The incident of the raped woman served as a powerful symbolic representation in the construction of a racial discourse about the boundaries of belonging.

Violence and Rhetoric

Many women are familiar with the experience of being attacked and violated in private and public spaces because of their vulnerability as women. Social spaces like streets, parks, stations and stadia are generally frequented and occupied by women in a radically different way than by men.

There is a link between the violence of racism and everyday violence against women. In Germany the stereotype of 'the Turkish man who rapes the German woman' signals this linkage. This stereotype represents one construction of foreigners as rapists of

Germans. This in turn implies that 'foreigners' are exclusively men, who threaten Germans, who are exclusively women. This stereotype is extremely powerful, and its social construction is so evident precisely because of the existence of sexual violence as a social and cultural phenomenon. Rape narratives can function as a ground rule, or basic pattern, because of the fact that women and men occupy different positions in public spaces and in the private sphere. The lack of protection experienced by women who, in addition to the very fact of their being women, belong to different cultural, ethnic, national and religious communities and to different classes and generations, is an indication of their specific location, role and function in their communities. It corresponds to their social vulnerability, which is constructed through gender as well as race and class.

Rape narratives such as those mentioned above (see Markus, 1992) establish a differentiation within each gender as well as between women and men. The narrative of 'the Turkish man who rapes the German woman' implies that German/white women are the only victims of rape and that German/white men do not rape. Non-German/black men are constructed as 'rapists', whereas non-German/black women are constructed as not being raped.[2] This narrative trope has many implications, particularly political ones. As lawyer Kimberlé Crenshaw argued in her considerations about the Anita Hill/Clarence Thomas hearing, black women are excluded from alternative feminist narratives of sexual abuse. According to her interpretation 'the central disadvantage that Anita Hill faced was the lack of available and widely comprehended narratives to communicate the reality of her experience as a black woman to the world' (Crenshaw, 1992: 404). The traditional feminist discourse about rape as well as the traditional anti-racist discourse about lynching did not coincide to draw attention to 'Hill's intersectional identity' (1992: 406). Crenshaw focuses on issues of social power which ensured that Anita Hill was not heard outside dominant discourses. Thus the Anita Hill/Clarence Thomas hearing constituted 'a classic show-down between antiracism and feminism' (1992: 405) which established a multiple marginality for Hill.

Historian Ruth Harris demonstrates, in her research on rape, race and nationalism in France during the First World War, the central relevance of gender relations and rape narratives which were used in war propaganda. She shows how 'the idea of France as a raped woman became part of the repertoire of propagandists' (Harris, 1993: 172). According to Harris, patterns of identification surrounding the imagery of rape had little to do with women's experiences but were linked with shifting visions of national boundaries. The traumatic experiences of the women actually raped were not represented in the collective national memory and were 'finally even denied as part of a manufactured "atrocity hysteria" in the aftermath of the war' (1993: 204).

The Social Construction of Belonging

In the context of debates on woman, nation and state, Floya Anthias and Nira Yuval-Davis (1992) have argued that women participate in ethnic and national processes. Women have been located, not only as 'biological reproducers', but also as 'reproducers of the boundaries of ethnic/national groups', as 'transmitters of its culture' as well as 'signifiers of ethnic/national differences – as a focus and symbol in ideological discourses used in the constitution, reproduction and transformation of ethnic/national categories' (Yuval-Davis and Anthias, 1989: 7).

Yuval-Davis and Anthias (1989) offer a framework within which the intersection of race and gender can be examined. According to them, 'an axis can be found within constructs of collectivity and belongingness (that is, ethnic phenomena) postulated through notions of common origin or destiny, not in terms of cultures of difference but in terms of the specific positing of boundaries' (Anthias and Yuval-Davis, 1992: 2). They emphasise that ideological boundaries involve material practices (1992: 4). In the context of gender difference and racist violence I would like to add the dimension of everyday interaction together with the dimension of the body to Yuval-Davis and Anthias's conceptions. Women are often the signifiers of communities not only ideologically and discursively but also with their bodies. More generally, as a powerful instrument of social closure (Weber, 1978) gender relations occupy one of the central dimensions in the construction of community/*Gemeinschaft*. All forms of closure presuppose ways of defining belonging and 'otherness'. Women are a specific focus of, and marker in, this process of social closure because they represent the community in as far as they maintain the cultural past, present and future of the group and as the signifiers of the 'social body'. They thus represent the boundary between 'us' and and the 'Other'. Bryan S. Turner's theory of 'bodily order' (Turner, 1984) reflects that dimension of the 'social body'. He argues that all social systems have solved the problem of the past, present and future in four dimensions: the reproduction of population through time; the restraint of desire as an interior body problem; the regulation of population space; the representation of bodies in social space as a task facing the surface or 'exterior' of bodies (Turner, 1984; Shilling, 1993).

Georg Simmel offered a sociological framework for this mode of closure in everyday life. He suggested that the stranger is nearby in the sense of social space but far away in terms of social time. The stranger represents an incongruous 'synthesis of nearness and remoteness' (Simmel, 1971: 45). From the perspective of 'ethnic collectiveness', the presence of the stranger is a challenge 'to the reliabilities of orthodox orientation points and the universal tools of order making' (Bauman, 1990: 149). In the context of gender relations this challenge connoted by the presence of the stranger generates a specific social meaning. The synthesis of nearness and remoteness becomes a physical-affective dimension between the sexes in everyday interaction. As will be argued, this physical-affective dimension is central to the understanding of the violence of racism and everyday violence against women in a sociological framework.[3]

Openness to Vulnerability and the Power to Violate

The power difference inherent in the vulnerability and violation of women is not simply a matter of biology. The possibility of violating others or of protecting oneself against physical attacks are not merely 'natural', but linked to the socially constructed imbalance of power between men and women. We also find this kind of power difference between black and white people, between minorities and majorities, between the socially weak and the socially strong. The potential vulnerability of a black man is connected to the social connotations of his body and the criminal associations attached to his skin colour. According to this stereotype, his skin colour is inferior to that of his white counterpart. This interpretation is based on the construction of skin colour as a social signifier, in which gender, race and class interconnect. The dual possibilities of violation of others or protection of self are connected to these constructions of social signifiers.

The concept of vulnerability and the power to violate (*Verletzungsoffenheit* and *Verletzungsmächtigkeit*; Popitz, 1986; Wobbe, 1993a) provides the opportunity to deconstruct the patterns which establish racialised rape narratives.[4] This concept reflects the physical dimension of the personal capacity to violate or to protect, but clarifies the fact that these capacities (for men and women) are not grounded in biological or physiological facts, but in social constructions. Generally speaking, the construction of community/*Gemeinschaft* intersects with the construction of vulnerability and the power to violate/*Verletzungsoffenheit* and *Verletzungsmächtigkeit*. The mode in which society is structured is bound up with the construction of the boundaries of gender and race.

This concept sheds light on what happens when acts of violence take place. These acts which are an expression of the power to inflict bodily harm and impose violence on others, differ from expressions of other forms of power. The attacker violates the whole person, not merely her/his physical body. The physical is inseparable from the integrity of the person.

Us and Them

The stereotype of foreign men attacking women suggests that sexual violence against women is of key significance. It does not, however, imply that women are the ultimate victims. The degree of access to power and the very decision to implement that power to violate are determining factors. In connection with the social construction of vulnerability, the interrelation of gender and race can be described more precisely by linking them to the concept of minorities and majorities. This concept allows the consideration of some important but largely neglected factors. In this section we will consider everyday racism and its relation to women's position in society.

The research group of the Deutsches Jugendinstitut at Leipzig conducted interviews with young people in East Germany at the time of the transformation of the political and social system of the former GDR. They were especially interested in the question of how nationalist, authoritarian and racist stereotypes worked. According to the researchers the violence of gender relations has significant relevance for the creation of racial patterns. This can be seen in the following quote by a girl interviewed as part of this research: 'I think foreigners belong in their own country. As a German girl, it's really awful to be harassed by that kind of people. It's no wonder people are against them. When they're here they've just got to live by our morals' (Friedrich et al., 1991: 87). In this context 'our morals', as

the girl puts it, are equated with the absence of sexual violence.
According to her, the power to violate comes from the 'Other', from
foreign men. In this construction 'foreigners' always signifies men,
whereas women are equated with 'Germans', i.e. the women who
'belong to German men'.

This stereotype, together with other constructions that 'violence
comes from outside', have become part of everyday thinking. This
is illustrated by the following quote from a West Berlin girl: 'I'm
not against them. I'm afraid of them. When a Turkish man or an
Arab comes towards me, I get scared; when a German man walks
up to me I'm not afraid, because I just don't expect any trouble from
him' (Farin and Seidel-Pielen, 1991: 129). Her statement suggests
that it is obvious who is alien and, therefore, dangerous and who is
native and, therefore, sexually harmless. Generalising from this, we
can see that what this girl anticipates from a foreigner, as opposed
to what she anticipates from a fellow countryman, constitutes the
dividing line between 'us' and 'them'. The boundary between 'us'
and 'them' also indicates the limits and intersections of social obligations and social norms.

To take this further, the absence of social responsibilities towards
particular groups implies the freedom to violate and attack. In
present-day Germany, white wives of African men suffer discrimination, such as being called 'nigger-whores', and threats from
right-wing radicals shouting 'Kill the nigger-whores!' At an East
German camping-ground black mothers were confronted with a
horrendous social metaphor, a well-known one in the former GDR:
their children were called 'lumps of charcoal'. The mothers were
attacked and ordered to give their children over to the attackers with
the words: 'Hand over the charcoal!' The fatal dimension of drawing
dividing lines between 'us' and 'them' cannot be overlooked.

These incidents and slogans indicate the way in which racism makes
itself felt in daily life. It shows how racist violence alters the coor-
dinates of social norms and reduces the value of those who are subject
to physical attack. It illustrates the ways in which ordinary people
can become victims in public spaces, and it demonstrates the vulnerability of those who do not fit the stereotype of 'Germans'.

Right-Wing Rock Music

From a cultural studies perspective, youth bands, particularly in
rock music, are useful in highlighting popular constructions of

typical Germans and indicating shifts in those conceptions. During the 1980s, German rock music underwent a change in that aggressive sexist songs as well as national socialist symbols and right-wing lyrics became increasingly common. Hans W. Giessen has argued that rock music functions as an indicator of social processes, but that political and academic institutions have not recognised this (Giessen, 1993). For our purposes, rock music presents one example of how 'Others' are stereotyped in the popular imagination.

The success of the group *Böhse Onkelz* with their 'highly racist track record' (Hennesey, 1992)[5] particularly alarmed the public when the group got itself into the hit parade in September 1992 . However, the lyrics of songs by two other groups also illustrate the ways in which rock music constructs 'outsiders'. The well-known group *Stöhrkraft* sings the song, 'In some years' with the following lyrics:

We fight for the German fatherland.
Everywhere you look,
you can see how the country floods.
Foreign folks [Völker] nest
and they claim to be German.

Another song by *Stöhrkaft* is called 'Fighting Dog' (*Kampfhund*). This song advocates the chasing of 'dark danger' during the night in order to annihilate them without 'any mercy or moral'.[6]

German right-wing rock music also promotes violence against Turkish people, who make up Germany's largest minority.[7] In the song '*Deutschland wach auf!*' ('Wake up, Germany!') by the group *Volkszorn*, which roughly translates as 'Public Incitement', an order is given to kill and to rape Turkish people:

Kill their children!
Rape their women!
Wipe out their race!
So you can terrorize them to death.

The above example indicates two social dimensions of the vulnerability of the female sex that are bound up with inherent problems in the construction of society. Firstly, every society can be threatened from outside and is in danger of being 'overrun'. One specific construction of a mode of retaliation is of overpowering the enemy through rape. The mass rape of Jewish and non-Jewish Polish and Russian girls and women by German soldiers can be taken as an historical example of this, as can the mass rape of German girls and women by Allied soldiers during the liberation from National Socialism. Secondly, every society is faced with the problem of sustaining and handing down its social and cultural practices from generation to generation. This brings the problem of ensuring that continuity is not endangered by 'too many foreigners coming into the country'.

Belonging to a community is most frequently determined by birth or marriage (Anthias and Yuval-Davis, 1992: 5). This mode of belonging is exclusive in that it implies that others cannot or may not belong to the collective. Thus, one means of dealing with this can be through control over the segregation and merging of communities in a manner familiar to us through ethnological or cultural anthropological examples. Another way is through marriage regulations. Women are of particular significance for society's continuity, since this continuity is linked to the determinants of human existence, namely with 'birth' and 'mortality' (Arendt, 1958). There is a connection between the openness to vulnerability of a community and the female sex through the fact that women are, in a very specific way, particularly relevant to the past, present and future of their communities. Women ensure the reproduction of society through the corporeality of their reproductive achievement and also make possible the passing on of sociocultural traditions.

The Historical Dimension

We are familiar with the kind of violent discourse from National Socialist persecution and genocide, which constitutes incitement to wipe out another race by killing those who are crucial to its past, present and future. Joan Ringelheim, who, in the 1980s, initiated the feminist debate on 'Women and the Holocaust', put the following question on to the agenda:

> ... were more Jewish women than men actually killed during the Holocaust? This question is important because it is death which defines the Holocaust. The Nazi genocide ... was a killing operation which not only selected Jews, among others, to be killed, but also distinguished among Jews. Jews were not a mass of undif-

ferentiated persons to the administrators of this process. At the very least, they were Jewish men, Jewish women and children. Deportation lists distinguished by sex. (Ringelheim, 1992a: 391)[8]

According to Ringelheim, an analysis of gender differences between men and women is incomplete unless we also consider the different ways in which they were defined with respect to National Socialist genocide; namely the dimension of annihilation. Seeking answers to the question of the chances of survival for Jewish women and men, Ringelheim examined data from the concentration camps. She demonstrates that National Socialist selection and deportation policies were different for women than for men. The deadly National Socialist 'racial struggle' was specifically targeted at women, as the potential bearers of the next Jewish generation.

Women were often the largest population available for the killing operations after men had emigrated, been evacuated or been taken into forced labour. Ringelheim emphasises the fact that Jewish women were 'connected to the race struggle of National Socialism because they carried the next generation of Jews' (1992a: 393). In this, Ringelheim refers to Himmler's statements:

We came to the question: what about the women and children? I have decided to find a clear solution here too. In fact I did not regard myself as justified in exterminating the men – let us say killing them or having them killed – while letting avengers in the shape of the children ... grow up. The difficult decision had to be taken to make this people disappear from the face of the earth. (from Smith and Peterson, 1974: xxx)[9]

As Joan Ringelheim shows, Jewish women with or without children were killed primarily because of their relevance to the future of their community (Ringelheim, 1990, 1992a, 1992b).

Minorities and Majorities

The social dimension of threat can be illustrated through an example connected with recent racist violence in Germany. In Thale,[10] in the Quedlingburg district, on the night of 17–18 of October 1992, ten young people, male and female between the ages of 13 and 21, attacked a mixed hostel of former contract workers. Initially shooting at the building with flares, they then forced their way inside, smashing up the furniture, beating up the women and men who lived there and shooting at them with blanks. Eventually the males tried to rape three Vietnamese women; the police only just managed to stop them. In many cases, people reacted with more horror to this crime because of the fact that white girls were watching and less because of the terror it meant for the Vietnamese women.

A reconstruction of the event makes it possible to describe the rape – the unique aspect of the crime – as, in part, a re-establishment of 'belonging'. The hostel inhabitants had initially invited young people from Thale over for a meal. These young people had in turn invited them over in order to get to know each other better. This development 'bothered some people'. The hostel was attacked on the following night. Because the boundary dividing those who belong from those who do not had been shifted slightly, those young people who opposed this shift implemented their power to violate with the aim of re-establishing the old boundaries of the communities.

The attempted rape goes far beyond this. The violence inflicted on women, namely on their persons and on their bodies, is a violation that is experienced by them with their own physical selves. 'We cannot withdraw out of our own bodies in the relationship to another person' (Popitz, 1986: 70). This perspective can be related to the construction of gender difference. Set in the physical-affective construction of the female sex it is vulnerable to the opposite sex. As it is impossible to separate oneself from one's body, the power imbalance between the sexes is experienced by women as an existential subjugation. Rape, the direct act of violating the physical and therefore the personal integrity of women, reveals the naked truth: that they exist at the mercy of their violators. The subjugation of women is then linked to the subjugation of the entire group. In the example of the young people's attack, the Vietnamese men were also vulnerable. They were not able to protect themselves and/or the entire group. All the same, they did not experience the vulnerability on their own bodies that the Vietnamese women did.

The context of this incident shows that women's roles are not merely imposed upon them: 'women actively participate in the process of reproducing and modifying their roles as well as being actively involved in controlling other women' (Yuval-Davis and Anthias, 1989: 11). In that situation the white German young females in the group of young people had access to violation of other women because they defined themselves as belonging to the group which had the power to violate. This does not, however, exclude the possibility that in another constellation, as women, they themselves could be vulnerable.

Contrary to the assumption that racism is ungendered, it becomes evident that gender distinction is relevant to the violent drawing of boundaries between majorities and minorities.[11] The construction of gender difference goes hand in hand with the construction of the power to violate and its reciprocal vulnerability. The female sex denotes a group upon whose person, body and life the construction of belonging – an existential subjugation – is implemented and engendered.

The existential significance of women's vulnerability is something that we have witnessed through mass-murder in the former Yugoslavia. The mass rape of Muslim girls and women, the mass subjugation of their bodies and their person, is used by male perpetrators as a modern 'strategy of expulsion', as 'ethnic cleansing' (Stiglmayer, 1994).[12] This strategy is carried out on the bodies of girls and women in an unmercifully cruel way, for these women – whose own social and personal existence is irreparably damaged – are forced to create the future of the other community by extinguishing their own community.

Conclusion

Since German unification, politicians have encouraged a strong national identity. In doing so, they have not only ignored the very problem of racism, but inadvertently sanctioned it. They have thus excluded many nationals who, whilst being part of society, do not fit stereotypes of typical Germans and have, as a result, become the target of violence. When 'experts' seek to condemn right-wing radicalism and racism in Germany they are often ignoring the power of the normalisation process through which attacks are encouraged. They fail to consider the perspectives of those groups who have the power to violate and of those who are vulnerable. I have argued that it is important to focus simultaneously on groups which are especially vulnerable to violence, and on those groups which have the power and the freedom to violate others. Contrary to what is generally assumed, gender differences are relevant to racial definitions of belonging. As a powerful instrument of social closure, gender relations are a central dimension in the construction of communities (Yuval-Davis and Anthias, 1989; Anthias and Yuval-Davis, 1992). The synthesis of closeness and distance becomes a physical-affective dimension between the sexes in everyday interaction. This physical-affective dimension is central to the sociological under-standing of the everyday violence of racism and sexism. It shows the extent to which the boundaries of community intersect with the social body that women represent.

In this chapter I have emphasised the dimensions of everyday life and interaction. Other modes of closure emerge in institutions and in large-scale structures. The different scales of closure have to be included in considerations of gender relations and racism. The inter-section, for instance, between face-to-face relations, imagery represented in the mass media, and the political discourse about the 'us' and 'them' can be related to the meaning of the social body as well as to the vulnerability of the female sex.

Sexism and racism are worlds of violence. In order to understand the mechanisms which sustain them, we desperately need to take into account the link between gender relations and racist violence. If we do not, then violence becomes the order of the day, and the victims of that violence become more vulnerable. If violence becomes more powerful and increases, we will lose, to an ever greater degree, the chance to act collectively in a shared world (Arendt, 1958).

Notes

1. For a discussion of race and rape in general see Davis (1981), Brittan and Maynard (1984), bell hooks (1990), Andersen and Collins (1992); for race and gender in science see Stepan (1990).
2. For a discussion of race, gender and feminist politics see hooks (1990), Davis (1981), particularly Chapter 11, 'Rape, Racism and the Myth of the Black Rapist'. Regarding public space see Ardener (1993).
3. Gesa Lindemann (1993) offered the concept of the physical-affective construction of the body and of gender difference Following the German phenomenological anthropologist Helmuth Plessner and ethnomethodological sociology, she argues that the physical-affective reality of gender difference has to be considered as a construction in the social field. This concept is based on a distinction in phenomenology between the difference in the German language between the body as

'Körper' and the body as 'Leib', that is between the objective
instrumental body and the subjective-affective body; for this theoretical context see Honneth and Joas (1988). I have discussed
this concept elsewhere in the context of race and gender; see
Wobbe (1994a and 1994b). For the reception of that German
phenomenological tradition in British sociology of the body see
Turner (1992).
4. The categories of H. Popitz refer to the difference between the
body as 'Körper', which is able to violate others, and the body
as Leib, which can be hurt since it is a physical-affective body.
See note 2.
5. Giessen (1993) refers to Hennesey (1992).
6. See Giessen (1992) and Binder (1993).
7. See Lutz (1991).
8. See also Ringelheim (1990 and 1992b), Katz and Ringelheim
(1983), Milton (1984), Wobbe (1993c).
9. See also Bock, 1991.
10. I would like to thank Mr Wolfgang Janotta, from Thale Catholic
Priest's Office, for the information contained in his letter of 17
November 1992, which I reproduce here.
11. This also implies, although this cannot be gone into here, that
women from the majority can have an interest in racist behaviour
and can be actively prepared to consolidate their status within
their community through the exclusion of other women and
men, cf. Wobbe (1993a and 1993b).
12. See also the massacres of female children in Rwanda: Claire
Brisset, 'Le massacre programmé des enfants rwandais', *Le Monde*
2 August 1994 (Les petites filles 'elles ont été tuées plus systé-
matiquement par les massacreurs. Tel est l'enjeu du génocide:
faire disparaitre les futures femmes').

References

Andersen, M.C. and Collins, P.H. (eds) (1992) *Race, Class, and Gender*
(Bemont, CA: Wadsworth).
Anderson, B. (1983) *Imagined Communities* (London: Verso).
Anthias, F. and Yuval-Davis, N. (1992) *Racialized Boundaries. Race,
Nation, Gender, Colour and Class and the Anti-Racist Struggle* (in asso-
ciation with Harriet Cain) (London/New York: Routledge).
Ardener, S. (ed.) (1993) *Women and Space. Ground Rules and Social
Maps* revised edn, (Oxford: Oxford University Press).

Arendt, H. (1958) *The Human Condition* (Chicago: Chicago University Press).

Bauman, Z. (1990) 'Modernity and Ambivalence', *Theory, Culture and Society* Special Issue: *Global Culture*, vol. 7, pp. 143–69.

Binder, A. (1993) 'Constructing Racial Rhetoric: Media Depictions of Harm in Heavy Metal and Rap Music', *American Sociological Review* vol. 58, pp. 753–67.

Birsl, U. (1994) *Rechtsextremismus: weiblich-männlich? Eine Fallstudie* (Opladen: Leske & Budrich).

Bock, G. (1991) 'Equality, Difference and Inferiority: Motherhood, Antinatalism and Gender Relations in National Socialist Racism'. In G. Bock and P. Thane (eds) *Maternity and Gender Policies, Women and the Rise of the Welfare States* (New York/London: Routledge).

Brittan, A. and Maynard, M. (1984) *Sexism, Racism, and Oppression* (Oxford: Blackwell).

Crenshaw, K. (1992) 'Whose Story is it, Anyway? Feminist and Antiracist Appropriations of Anita Hill'. In T. Morrison (ed.) *Race-ing Justice, En-Gendering Power. Essays on Anita Hill, Clarence Thomas, and the Construction of Social Reality* (New York: Pantheon Books) pp. 402–40.

Davis, A. (1981) *Women, Race and Class* (New York: Random House) (particularly Chapter 11, 'Rape, Racism and the Myth of the Black Rapist').

Farin, K. and Seidel-Pielen, E. (1991) *Krieg in den Städten* (Berlin: Rotbuch).

Friedrich, W., Netzer, W. and Schubarth, W. (1991) Ostdeutsche Jugend. Ihr Verhältnis zu Ausländern und zu einigen aktuellen politischen Problemen (Leipzig: Deutsches Jugendinstitut).

Giessen, H.W. (1992) Zeitgeist populär. *Seine Darstellung in deutschsprachigen postmodernen Songtexten* (St Ingbert).

Giessen, H.W. (1993) 'Ich sing ein deutsches Lied. Chauvinistische Poptexte und der neue Rechtsradikalismus', *Soziale Welt*, vol. 44, pp. 556–69.

Harris, R. (1993) 'The Child of the Barbarian. Rape, Race and Nationalism in France During the First World War', *Past and Present*, vol. 141, pp. 170–206.

Hennesey, M. (1992) 'An Ominous Note: German Act Fans Neo-Nazi Flames', *Billboard*, 24 October 1992.

Honneth, A. and Joas, H. (1988) *Social Action and Human Nature* (Cambridge: Cambridge University Press).

hooks, b. (1990) *Yearning, Race, Gender, and Cultural Politics* (Boston: South End Press).

Katz, E. and Ringelheim, J. (1983) Proceedings of the Conference Women Surviving the Holocaust, Occasional Paper (New York: Institute for Research in History).

Lindemann, G. (1992) 'Die leiblich-affektive Konstruktion des Geschlechts. Für eine Mikrosoziologie des Geschlechts unter der Haut', *Zeitschrift für Soziologie*, vol. 21 pp. 330–46.

Lindemann, G. (1993) *Das paradoxe Geschlecht* (Frankfurt aM: Suhrkamp).

Lutz, H. (1991) *Welten Verbinden – Türkische Sozialarbeiterinnen in den Niederlanden und in der Bundesrepublik Deutschland* (Frankfurt aM: Türkei-Studien).

Markus, S. (1992) 'Fighting Bodies, Fighting Words: A Theory and Politics of Rape Prevention'. In J. Butler and J. Scott (eds) *Feminists Theorize the Political* (New York/London: Routledge) pp. 385–403.

Milton, S. (1984) 'Women and the Holocaust: The Case of German-Jewish Women'. In R. Bridenthal, A. Grossman and M. Kaplan (eds) *When Biology Became Destiny: Women in Weimar and Nazi Germany* (New York: Monthly Review Press).

Popitz, H. (1986) *Phänomene der Macht. Autorität-Herrschaft-Technik* (Tübingen: Mohr Siebeck).

Ringelheim, J. (1990) 'Thoughts about Women and the Holocaust'. In R.S. Gottlieb (ed.) *Thinking the Unthinkable: Meanings of the Holocaust* (New York: Paulist Press).

Ringelheim, J. (1992a) 'Postscript: Women and the Holocaust: A Reconsideration of Research'. In C. Rittner and J.K. Roth (eds) *Different Voices. Women and the Holocaust* (first published 1985).

Ringelheim, J. (1992b) 'Verschleppung, Tod und Überleben. Nationalsozialistische Ghetto-Politik gegen jüdische Frauen und Männer im besetzten Polen'. In T. Wobbe (ed.). *Nach Osten. Verdeckte Spuren Nationalsozialistischer Verbrechen* (Frankfurt aM: Neue Kritik) pp. 135–60.

Shilling, C. (1993) *The Body and Social Theory* (London: Sage Publications).

Simmel, G. (1971) *'The Stranger'. On Individuality and Social Form* (Chicago: Chicago University Press).

Smith B.F. and Peterson A.E. (eds) (1974) *Heinrich Himmlers: Geheimreden 1933–1945* (Frankfurt aM: Propyläen).

Smith, Valerie (1992) 'Split Affinities: The Case of Interracial Rape'. In M. Hirsch and E. Fox Keller (eds) *Conflicts in Feminism* (London: Rouledge) pp. 271–87.

Stepan, N.L. (1990) 'Race and Gender: The Role of Analogy in Science'. In D.T. Goldberg (ed.) *Anatomy of Racism* (Minneapolis/London: University of Minnesota Press) pp. 38–57.

Stiglmayer, A. (ed.) (1994) *Mass Rape. The War against Women in Bosnia-Herzogovina*, translated by Marion Faber, Foreword by Roy Gutman, Afterword by Cynthia Enloe (Lincoln: University of Nebraska).

Turner, B.S. (1984) *The Body and Society, Explorations in Social Theory* (Oxford: Blackwell).

Turner, B.S. (1991) 'Recent Developments in the Theory of the body'. In M. Featherstone et al. *The Body, Social Process and Cultural Theory* (London: Sage) pp. 1–35.

Turner, B.S. (1992) *Regulating Bodies. Essays in Medical Sociology* (London/ New York: Routlege).

Weber, M. (1978) *Economy and Society* (Berkeley/Los Angeles and London: California University Press).

Willems, H. (1993) *Fremdenfeindliche Gewalt. Einstellungen, Täter, Konflikteskalation* (Opladen: Leske & Budrich).

Wobbe, T. (1993a) 'Die Grenzen des Geschlechts. Konstruktionen von Gemeinschaft und Geschlecht'. *Mitteilungen, Institut für Sozialforschung an der Johann Wolfgang Goethe-Universität* Frankfurt aM, no. 2, pp. 98–108.

Wobbe, T. (1993b) 'Die Schwelle des Körpers, Geschlecht und Rasse', *Feministische Studien*, vol. 11, pp. 110–16.

Wobbe, T. (1994a) 'Violentia: Überlegungen zur Verschränkung von Rassismus und Sexismus'. In J. Huber and A.M. Müller (eds) *'Kultur' und 'Gemeinsinn'* Interventionen von Jessica Benjamin et al. (Basel: Stroemfeld) pp. 19–34.

Wobbe, T. (1994b) 'Die Grenzen der Gemeinschaft und die Grenzen des Geschlechts'. In T. Wobbe and G. Lindemann (eds) *Denkachsen. Zur theoretischen und institutionellen Rede vom Geschlecht* (Frankfurt aM: Suhrkamp), pp. 177–207.

Wobbe, T. (1993c) 'Different Ways of Remembering: Rethinking Women's History under National Socialism'. Paper presented on the panel 'Dilemmas of Remembrance: Women and the Holocaust Reconsidered', 9th Berkshire Conference on the History of Women, Vassar College, 11–13 June 1993.

Yuval-Davis, N. and Anthias, F. (eds) (1989) *Woman–Nation–State* (London: Macmillan).

5 Gender, Orientalism and the History of Ethnic Hatred in the Former Yugoslavia

Dubravka Žarkov

The common representation of the war in the former Yugoslavia in the national media of the former Yugoslav republics, as well as in the international media, is that it is a product of 'centuries of ethnic hatred' in 'the Balkans'. Different interpretations are given, with cultural (traditional versus modern), religious (Orthodox versus Catholic; Christian versus Muslim) or ideological (totalitarian, i.e. communist, versus democratic) differences all being argued to have contributed to the war. However, the 'ethnic hatred' explanation and the 'ethnic character' of the war are hardly questioned. The central discourse presented is one in which the history of the former Yugoslavia is represented exclusively as a 'history of ethnic hatred'. This representation is often merged with an Orientalist discourse of 'the Balkans' (Bakic-Hayden and Hayden, 1992), in which the former Yugoslavia is represented as divided into two irreconcilable and incompatible parts: West and East. According to this argument, the western, Catholic, modern part of the country strives for democracy and civil society, while the eastern, Orthodox Muslim, traditional, even tribal, part is still satisfied with a communist totalitarian system. Bakic-Hayden and Hayden (1992) focus on authors from Slovenia and Croatia as the main proponents of the Orientalist discourse. They give numerous examples from speeches delivered by Croatian and Slovenian politicians, from texts of well-known Croatian and Slovenian scholars published in professional social science journals and from newspaper texts of some national and international journalists. In this 'Orientalisation' of the Balkans, the Orthodox church, 'Byzantine' culture or the 'Muslim Balkans' do not belong to the 'symbolic continent of Europe' (1992: 9). What should not be forgotten, however, is that Orientalist discourse is used by the 'Orientalised' as well. In Serbia, which is itself the main target of Slovenian and Croatian 'Orientalisation', the same discourse has been used in representation of the Albanian population of Kosovo, particularly since the beginning of the 1980s, and is still used with regard to the war.

It appears, thus, that both the discourses of the 'history of ethnic hatred' and the 'Orientalisation' of the Balkans have been adopted and shared, albeit for different reasons, by many, seemingly opposing, political groups in the former Yugoslav republics and outside the designated geo-political territory of the former Yugoslavia. In this chapter, I focus on these two discourses within the territory of the former Yugoslavia. International aspects of their use will only be touched upon where necessary for comparison or clarification.

The Use of Discourses

During the socialist period (approximately 1944–89)[1] of the former Yugoslavia the 'history of ethnic hatred' was declared to belong to the past and destined to be duly forgotten. In the former Yugoslavia, the Second World War had been represented as a war of ethnic hatred, in which more victims died of a so-called 'brother's hand' than from German bullets. At the same time, however, the Second World War was considered to have been a socialist revolution in which partisans had brought about what was thought impossible – ethnic harmony. Socialist history, thus, in its official representation, both grew out of and departed from the 'history of ethnic hatred'. It itself started off with a 'history of brotherhood and unity'.

Various measures were introduced to make 'brotherhood and unity' work. Among them, in 1961, was the introduction into the census of a new category: 'Yugoslavs'. It was a separate, non-ethnic category, created to strengthen identification with the Yugoslav socialist system, and, hence, to be a category of unity. The Yugoslav census also offered other possibilities, such as to opt out of an ethnic iden-tification altogether, i.e. not to define oneself ethnically, or to define oneself regionally.[2] Hence, to be a Bosnian – which was clearly a territorial, not an ethnic reference – was officially a part of a 'nation-ality column' in the census, and a right guaranteed by the constitution. Thus today's use of the term 'Bosnians', particularly in international political discourse, in a way that limits the group only to Muslims is unjust to the members of other ethnic groups who live or lived in Bosnia (and Herzegovina) and who also consider themselves Bosnians (and Herzegovinians). This is particularly clear when talking to refugees. Whatever their ethnic or religious identity, many still say that they consider themselves to be Bosnians.

In 1971 Muslims were given the chance to declare themselves an 'ethnic group'. A population that previously defined themselves ethnically as Albanian, Serb, Croat, etc. and shared Islam as their religion, thus had the opportunity to change their ethnic affiliation to 'Muslim'. This brought significant changes to the ethnic stratification of the former Yugoslavia. First, it particularly affected the category 'Yugoslavs', by reducing dramatically the number of people who declared themselves as such. The largest number of persons declaring themselves as 'Yugoslavs' between the 1960s and 1970s were from Muslim religious backgrounds. Secondly, it constructed a specific link between 'ethnic' and 'religious' identity. The defining of one religious group as a separate ethnic group paved the way to defining ethnicity as synonymous with religion, and thus reducing the possibility of defining ethnic groups as religiously diverse. Thus, if no Muslim could be a Serb or a Croat, then no Serb could possibly be anything but Orthodox, and no Croat could be anything but Catholic. What was the political climate in which these various options for self-identification were created? How did they change, and what were their effects? These issues have only recently become the object of study, and then only for some aspects of the issues central to the understanding of the category 'Yugoslavs' (Lendvai, 1991; Petrovic, 1990).[3]

Against the background of these, in many ways, ambiguous policies and political practices with regard to the 'nationality question' (Ramet, 1990, 1992), the defeated, pre-socialist 'history of ethnic hatred' was always present. The self-glorification of socialism needed the narrative of a perpetual bloodshed in the past in order, by way of contrast, to glorify its victorious present. It needed the 'pre-socialist history of ethnic hatred' in order to create and sustain the 'socialist history of brotherhood and unity'.

In the late 1960s and early 1970s, with rising nationalism, there was an easy acceptance of the idea that the history of the former Yugoslavia was the 'history of ethnic hatred'. According to some Yugoslav authors this period had far-reaching political consequences. Proponents of many different political projects for the future were, during these few years, engaged in a political struggle which proved crucial for the development of the country in the 1980s and 1990s, the period which included the disintegration of Yugoslavia and the war (Rus, 1971; Stojanovic, 1972; Sekelj, 1990, 1991).

The reasons for the adherence of nationalists to the 'history of ethnic hatred' lay not, as in the case of socialist discourse, in pinpointing the starting point of the 'new history' of the 'new society'. Although this 'starting point' is important for nationalist history, it often has to be blurred, pushed back into the primeval past, too far back to be remembered. Nationalists have to prove that their particular nation has always been there, in history or territory.[4] For nationalists from the former Yugoslavia, socialism was just an unfortunate digression, imposed on them by totalitarian communist rule; a means by which they were forced to forget these primeval times. The idea of perpetual bloodshed thus did not provide nationalists with a contrasting discourse designed to make their ideology attractive (in the way it was used in socialism). Instead, it was used to signal continuity with pre-socialist times, the return to the most valuable roots. It was the very essence of their nationhood: narratives of victims and heroes, of 'century-long aspirations' and 'eternal longings' of their nation (which survived despite being surrounded by ethnic hatred). It is that hatred and violence against their ethnic group and their heroic resistance to it that constitutes the nationalist representation of history. Thus, for this nationalist discourse, the history of ethnic hatred and violence is the only possible history. Since it always accuses only the 'Others', and presents its own nation exclusively as a victim of ethnic hatred of these various 'Others', this interpretation of the past simultaneously provides justifications of present and future nationalist projects.

In the context of post-socialist developments, the discourse on the 'history of ethnic hatred' in the former Yugoslav republics has yet another role to play. Merged with the 'Orientalisation' of the Balkans it provides a counter-reference to the newly achieved, fought for, European identity. For nationalists in Croatia and Slovenia, in particular, the socialist past of the former Yugoslavia, its 'history of ethnic hatred' and the bloody war in the Balkans are all merged. At the same time they belong to a past that is over and finished with. By adopting a new, European identity, they have distinguished themselves from that past politically and culturally. As in other East European, former socialist states, the official discourse of newly created former Yugoslav states is of democracy, not nationalism.[5] Nationalism is represented primarily as a cultural project or a liberal political project of nation-state-building (Koch, 1991). Alternatively, it is represented only as a transitional phase, albeit an unfortunate one (Hobsbawn, 1992). In other words, European identity as a means to achieve a Western European democratic society. By becoming new 'post-socialist' states, Croatia and Slovenia have not only distinguished themselves from the 'totalitarian communist history' of socialist former Yugoslavia. They have distinguished themselves, historically and territorially, even more from the 'bloody Balkan history', arguing that, really, geographically, they do not belong to the Balkans, but are part of Central Europe. Not even the romanticised narrative of a different kind of Balkans – the Balkans of patriotism, heroism and martyrdom, so dear to nationalist ears in Serbia – are accepted as part of their history. They are, simply, from another continent, European, not Oriental.

That the connections between politics, history and territory have to be carefully (re)defined and (re)negotiated was apparent throughout the socialist period of the former Yugoslavia. Both within its own borders and in its relationships with neighbouring states, many disputes about territory were linked to different interpretations of history: the Kosovo and Macedonia 'questions' still loom over many political heads. It is not surprising, then, that after the first shock which struck the 'symbolic continent' of Europe when it was faced with a war on its geopolitical territory, some (self-deceiving, defence-) mechanisms of differentiation were quickly set off. First, it is not just *any* war, but an ethnic war; second, it is not really in Europe, but in the Balkans. So, '… back to Europe, where we have always belonged', the Slovenian Prime Minister said in one of his first speeches. In Zagreb, the cinema 'Balkan' was, after 1989, renamed cinema 'Europe' (Drakulic, 1993).

Socialism, nationalism and post-socialism (discussed above) cannot be understood as discrete and consecutive historical periods in the development and disintegration of the former Yugoslavia. Nationalism, in particular, is much more than a transitional phase from 'socialism' to 'post-socialism'. I have tried to show that nationalism – as a discourse and a political practice – has been a significant force throughout the socialist period. In addition, the so-called 'post-socialism' still has much more to do with both the socialism and nationalism of the former Yugoslavia than is usually admitted. Thus, nationalism, socialism and post-socialism are interrelated processes, for which the construction and representation of history as the 'history of ethnic hatred' and Orientalist discourse are significant constitutive elements, as the discussion above indicates. In the sections which follow, I will address some of the consequences of those processes.

Is the Future Ethnic?

If the only history is the history of ethnic hatred, then, the only way of being is of being ethnic. 'Ethnic purity' becomes both the ultimate criteria of membership in the community and the ultimate aim. The 'imagined community' (Anderson, 1991) becomes a 'natural group' whose 'purity' is defined through naturalised notions such as 'the blood' and 'the soil'. Thus, it becomes natural that a person is only, and necessarily, a Serb, a Croat, a Muslim, and even more so, that one is born and will remain as such.

Naturalised definitions of an 'ethnic group' construct a need, enthusiasm even, for maintaining constant guard over the 'purity' of the group. It also provides a justification of the war as the way in which to protect the 'ethnic group' and its 'purity'. For, if the only history is the history of ethnic hatred, then ethnic violence and ethnic war come as its natural consequences. The notion that the war is essential for the protection and preservation of an ethnic group is reflected in the now common Serbian expression: 'Serbs were always losing in peace and winning in war', meaning that only war brings survival, while peace is equivalent to death.

Furthermore, the perpetuation of such a history is unavoidable, since there is a recursive relationship between ethnic war and ethnic hatred. Ethnic war feeds ethnic hatred, ethnic hatred produces ethnic war and so on, until the end of time, or until the ethnic boundaries are so fixed that it becomes impossible to transgress them, that is, until 'the blood' and 'the soil' no longer 'mix'. These 'mixtures' are assumed to have objective, even physical reality, throughout Yugoslav socialism. The so-called 'ethnically mixed' marriages, or the 'ethnically mixed' territories, have become ever more physical. As easily as one can touch, and smell, and feel the texture of blood and soil, one can 'mix' them or 'set them apart' in marriages and territories. The assumed physical nature of 'the blood' and 'the soil' has not changed, nor have the ways in which they are constructed. What has changed are the values ascribed to these 'mixtures'. In socialism they were praised as victorious artefacts of 'brotherhood and unity', while nationalism condemned them as treason to the 'purity' of specific nations. In both cases, however, it is 'purity' that is normalised and constructed as natural.

Against the background of the Orientalised Balkans, the Yugoslavian naturalised war between 'naturalised' ethnic groups makes any hope of resolution unnatural and impossible, even among the groups and individuals who oppose the war. I was, for example, sitting in Amsterdam, at a meeting of a group of young people who left the former Yugoslavia because of the war.[6] They were from various parts of the country, discussing what their contribution could be to the situation back home. There were strong disagreements, which led some to despair. A young man behind me suddenly said: 'Look at us! Just look at us! We can't agree about anything even here. What a shit we are! Balkanians! We are real Balkanians.' This internalisation of the Orientalist definition of the people from the Balkans may transcend a single, exclusionist, ethnic definition, but only in order to re-establish its own exclusionist natural norms. Dialogue, peaceful solutions, negotiations: these means are not constructed as belonging to the bloodthirsty, primitive Balkanians, only hatred, bloodshed, and victimising. Thus, it is not only the Balkans' past and present which belong to the discourse of 'ethnic hatred'. It is the Balkans' future, too.

Perhaps the most devastating possible consequence of the 'history of ethnic hatred' in the 'Orientalised Balkans' is the fact that the future begins to be imagined in ethnic terms. For, by precluding alternative projects, this exclusive 'ethnic future' naturalises, in history, the ethnic way of being. It also constructs the ethnic war not only as a historical way of being, but as natural. The continuity between the 'ethnic past' and the 'ethnic future' is, thus, established and the reminders of other possibilities are hidden, erased or reinterpreted. Changes in city and street names, the 'purification' of language, the destruction of monuments built during socialist times, and of cultural and religious monuments significant to other ethnic groups living on the same territory, are examples of things that were happening across the former Yugoslav territory long before the war started, as if all these events were preparing people to forget, quickly and, apparently, painlessly, that anything other than ethnic hatred and ethnic wars had ever been possible, or will ever be possible.

Ethnicity and Gender

Feminists have always approached and analysed female sexuality as a crucial site of other social and cultural relations. The control, construction and representation of the female body and its sexual capacities, identities and images have been perceived as significant elements of social life. In anthropology, especially in Mediterranean studies and studies of the Balkans, sexuality – both male and female – has been perceived as an organising principle of social life.[7] However, feminists have argued that it is through gender hierarchy that male and female sexuality find their place in social relations.

In Orientalist discourse, the 'Other' is defined as having a very specific kind of sexuality: the uncontrolled and uncontrollable, instinctive and primitive (Said, 1978; Jansen, 1989; Lutz, 1991). Further, male and female sexuality are constructed as differentiated within Orientalist discourse, but also as different from European sexuality. Female 'oriental' sexuality is constructed as more dangerous to 'occidental' men than to 'oriental' men, while male 'oriental' sexuality is constructed as particularly dangerous to 'occidental' women. This gendered 'Orientalisation' of sexuality which distinguishes 'civilised' from 'primitive' peoples, enables 'Europe' to maintain its difference from 'the Balkans' as much as it once enabled the distinction between the 'Western World' and the 'East'. At the same time, however, it lends itself to the discourse of the 'history of ethnic hatred'. Naturalised definitions of 'ethnic purity' which allow for membership of the group to be defined only through 'pure blood', i.e. through birth into the community, are inevitably concerned with both 'the Other' and with the sexuality-as-danger that comes from 'the Other' (who is, of course, gendered). Thus, the perceived danger is gender-specific, making practices aimed at women and men also gender-specific.

As Orientalist discourse converges with the discourse of ethnic hatred, gender specific practices are focused on the control of male and female sexuality, and of male and female sexual bodies. This control is concerned with members from one's own ethnic community as much as with those who are perceived to belong to the 'Other', even though the practices and policies of control and subjugation of the former often differ from those used against the latter. The sexual mutilation of men reported in the war in the former Yugoslavia is certainly a gruesome example of a gender-specific practice towards men who are constructed as 'the Other'. Calling men 'women' is another example, as is the labelling of men who oppose war 'homosexuals', or rejecting them as not being 'real' Serbs, Croats, Muslims. All these examples illustrate the fact that male sexuality is constructed as an element in the controlling and defining of the boundaries of an 'ethnic group'.

Construction of 'ethnic purity' as natural and the ultimate criterion for membership in an 'ethnic community' creates a specific place for female sexuality in the maintenance of the boundaries of the group. If 'pure blood' can only be transmitted through a 'pure birth', then the control of women's bodies and sexual behaviour is essential for the 'purity' of the 'ethnic group'. Even more so, the very existence and physical survival of the 'pure-ethnic-group' – for, in national-ist discourse, the group only 'exists' as 'pure' – is perceived as dependent on the control of female procreative sexuality.

While Orientalist discourse and the discourse of ethnic hatred both create 'ethnic purity' as their 'natural norm', gender hierarchy creates the subjugation of women as its 'natural norm'. The existing gender hierarchy constructs the control of female sexuality and the female body as a measure of male sexual and social power, including the power to define the 'Other'. It is this subjugation of the feminine as opposed to the masculine 'Other' that underpins the labelling (discussed above) of men as homosexuals or as women.

Inasmuch as 'ethnic purity' depends on the definition of the 'ethnic Other', gender hierarchy depends on the definition of the female/feminine 'Other'. Thus, if the boundaries of the ethnic community are defined by the 'Other', they are defined by both the ethnic and the female 'Other'. This subjugation of the female/ethnic 'Other' constructs and appropriates the female body as a natural weapon of the 'ethnic war'. It is appropriated in discursive terms, in symbolic, universalising categories such as 'the Mother' or 'the Victim'. For the symbols, identities and values of the 'ethnic group' are appropriated and represented through engendered, feminine metaphors. The most common of these are: the birth of the group; the sacred soil that must not be polluted; the pure origin that stands no mixture; the motherland that needs to be defended; the motherland mourning the death of the sons killed by the enemy; and the motherland which sends her sons to the war.

Where the only history is the 'history of ethnic hatred', the appro-priation of the female body is not only discursive. In the political practice of the 'ethnic war', the female body is physically present and, consequently, dealt with in bodily, if not mortal, terms. Thus, rape is a 'natural' element of an 'ethnic war'. It is a 'natural' element of male power to define the boundaries of its own 'ethnic group' by defining women of the 'Other' through rape, and thus defining the female body as the *ethnic female body*.

Rape is a 'natural' element of every war, so much so that, until recently, it was not even recognised as a war crime. In the Orientalisation of sexuality, men rape women because (among other things) men's sexual capacities are seen as unbridled, as uncontrollable. In the war in the former Yugoslavia almost all international observers – UN, Amnesty International, Helsinki Watch – point to the rape of women as a means of intimidation of the whole group, i.e. with implicit or explicit political motivation. Their information points to the *systematic* use of rape by Serbian forces, but emphasises that rape is used by all sides. Still, it is impossible to prosecute the perpetrators. The international War-Tribunal in The Hague, for instance, needs proof of an explicit order to commit rape from a commander to his forces.[8] Otherwise, rape is considered an arbitrary act and the sole responsibility of a single soldier. A man rapes a woman.

A man who rapes a woman is still such a 'natural' element of our societies that hardly any rape can make a difference. Only if and when rape is declared a crime against the state, a nation, a community is the difference established. Ironically, rape becomes a political concern only when it ceases to be a crime against the woman and becomes exclusively a crime against the group to which a woman is assumed to belong. From ancient Greece, to Panama, to the Gulf War, and now to the former Yugoslavia, rape has been used by the armed forces of these same states, nations, communities, as a means of both conducting and justifying the politics of wars and invasions (cf. Brownmiller, 1975; Aron et al., 1991; Lazaro, 1990; Farmanfarmaian, 1992). At the same time, it was used as a means of demonising the 'Other'. It is always the 'Other' – the primitive, the uncivilised, the Orientalised, the male 'Other' – who rapes 'our' mothers, sisters, daughters.

The same dynamics are happening in the war in the Balkans. Justifying and demonising practices become a vicious political circle. While the warring sides were loudly accusing the 'enemy' for the rapes, they often turned deaf ears to demands that their own forces be investigated. Raped women often became flags waved by the warring parties and the stories about rape became more important than the rapes.

The national and international media have reproduced the rape-stories of conquest and of suffering, reinforcing the Orientalist narrative of the 'Other'. In the Serbian media, it is the Serb woman who is the symbol of suffering, while Croat and Muslim men are constructed as the demonic symbol of the rapist. In the international media, however, the Serb man is turned into the symbol of all rapists, and the Muslim woman into the symbol of all victims. In both cases, nevertheless, the same process of ethnicisation of the perpetrator and the victim is in play, obscuring the many significant elements involved in these rapes.

Turning rape exclusively into a crime against an ethnic community obscures the fact that women are raped both because they are the 'female Other' and the 'ethnic Other'. It denies both the gender-specific character of rape as sexual violence against women and the hierarchical gender relations in which women are subject to sexual violations by men, be it in war or peace. On the other hand, perceiving rape exclusively as a crime of men against women denies the complexity of social processes in which the war-rape occurs. Gender relations are always part of other social and political relations, and gender identities are constitutive elements of other identities. The construction of rape exclusively as a crime against women denies the fact that, precisely because of their symbolic and social functions – including the function of maintaining 'ethnic boundaries' – women are targets of rape in an 'ethnic war'. Rape is, thus, a specific, gendered and political strategy.

Conclusion

In this chapter, I have tried to show that the relationship between practices of the war in the former Yugoslavia and their representation is complex. Feminist analysis thus has to be concerned with both specific practices towards women and the representation of those practices, as well as with the relation between the two. There are certain discourses through which *practices are both constructed and represented*. These include the discourses of the 'history of ethnic hatred' and 'the Orientalised' Balkans. By constructing a reality in which an 'ethnic group' and an 'ethnic war' are the only and *'natural'* ways of being, these two discourses have consequences for women and men living on this territory, as well as for gender relations and sexual politics. By defining an 'ethnic group' through 'natural' norms of purity, the sexual bodies of men and women are constructed as 'ethnic boundaries'. The existence of a gender hierarchy makes the female body the primary focus of practices through which these boundaries are defined and dealt with. Consequently, rape is the strategy of an 'ethnic war', as much as abortion legislation might be a strategy of an 'ethnic peace' and a 'mourning mother' is as necessary to the discourse of the 'history of ethnic hatred' as a 'mother-courage'.

Feminists from the former Yugoslavia are painfully aware of these consequences especially because relations between feminist groups from different territories of the former Yugoslavia have been influenced by ethnic divisions. Nevertheless, despite the differences, cooperation and solidarity still persist among many women and women's groups which defy the discourses of ethnic hatred. You will not, however, read about cooperation and solidarity in either the international or the national newspapers, since cooperation does not fit into the picture of primitivism, hatred and war. Nevertheless, as long as solidarity exists between women's or other groups, it will be a reminder of other possibilities, even if these are obscured, erased or reinterpreted in nationalist discourses.

Notes

I am grateful to Michael Chai, Lena Inowlocki, Professor Willy Jansen and Helma Lutz for their insightful suggestions on the text, and to Ann Phoenix for careful and patient editing.
1. The years are, in many ways, arbitrary. For the beginning of the socialist period may also be placed in 1941, i.e. the beginning of the Second World War on the territory of, then, the Kingdom of Yugoslavia. In Yugoslav history books, the beginning of that war was always referred to as being the beginning of a socialist revolution. Also, in 1943, during the war, deputies gathered in Jajce to declare the foundation of the new socialist state and, in the 1945 referendum, the return of the King was finally rejected and the Republic adopted as a state form.

    1989 was also more than the end-point of a 'socialist period'. In that year, the first post-Second World War multi-party elections were organised and held in all the Republics of SFR Yugoslavia. In the years that followed, the socialist state of Yugoslavia, which was created after the Second World War, disintegrated. However, whether or not it was the end of the 'socialist period' is still a matter of debate among scholars who analyse the process (see in particular Sekelj, 1991).
2. In 1981, for example, the options were grouped and ordered as follows:

- First on the list are six nations ('*narodi*'): Crnogorci, Hrvati, Makedonci, Muslimani, Slovenci, Srbi;
- Then there are fourteen minorities ('*narodnosti*'): Albanci, Bugari, Cesi, Italijani, Madjari, Nemci, Romi, Rumuni, Rusi, Rusini, Slovaci, Turci, Ukrajinci, Vlasi;
- The next option is 'the others' ('*ostali*');
- Then, those who did not opt for any of the possibilities offered, a right granted according to paragraph 170 of the Constitution ('*nisu se izjasnili prema clanu 170 Ystava SFRJ*'); in other words, those who refused to answer the question;
- Then, the category 'Yugoslavs' ('*izjasnili se kao Jugosloveni*');
- Then, those who opted for the regional definition ('*izjasnili se u smislu regionalne pripadnosti*');
- Finally, 'unknown' ('*nepoznato*').

3. Lendvai discusses how political changes in the 1980s in the former Yugoslavia have affected the ways in which people define themselves in the census. Petrovic presents some statistical data on how these changes have affected the so-called 'ethnically mixed' marriages since the 1960s.

4. Furthermore, the 'starting point' approach to history (as adopted by socialism) is too dangerous for nationalism, if it is the sole reference. That was particularly clear in the debate about political/territorial claims on Kosovo, the South Serbian Province. Historians, ethnographers, archaeologists all competed to present proof as to who was first, where, and when. Albanian scholars from Kosovo argued that ancient Albanian tribes populated the Kosovo area in the times long before Slavic tribes even came to that territory. Defeated in the 'starting point' argument, the Serbian side presented an argument about 'whose presence left the more important trace', i.e. they argued that there was a highly developed and sophisticated Orthodox culture cradled in Kosovo during the medieval period. None of the sides reflected upon the discourses they drew upon in order to construct their arguments.

5. There is, nevertheless, an uneasy relationship between democracy and nationalism in the former Yugoslav Republics (see Hayden, 1992 and Katunaric, 1991). For the 'discomfort' about democracy in Slovenia see Gaber (1993). For the role of democracy and nationalism in the representation of the warring sides see Gerrits (1992).

6. At the beginning of the war young men who wished to avoid mobilisation were among the first to leave the country, often for the Netherlands (particularly Amsterdam). Their reasons and motivations varied, but what they have in common is that they were not willing either to kill or to be killed. Many wives and friends joined them later. Some estimates are that about 200,000 people left for these reasons. In all the former Yugoslav republics, authorities still refuse to grant them pardons, and if they go back they will face martial law and be put on trial for deserting the army. Many pleas to allow them amnesty and safe return, from parents and national and international political and humanitarian organisations, have been addressed to the presidents and other authorities. All have been rejected.

7. See for instance: Davis (1977), Delaine (1991), Denich (1974), Dwyer (1978), Gilmore (1985, 1986), Goddard (1987), Jansen (1987, 1993), Simic (1969), Souriau (1980), Wolf (1969).

8. This is a press-statement made by Mr Kalshoven, the Chairperson of the United Nations Committee on War Crimes, following the public hearing on the Rape of Women in Former Yugoslavia (Parlement Europeen, Direction de la Presse, 23 February 1993, pp. 6–7). The European Parliament Resolution on Rapes in Yugoslavia, released on 10 March 1993 (in paragraph C3) demands that the 'systematic abuse of women be considered a war crime', indicating, thus, that it is not the case at present. On the legal aspects of rape as a war crime see 'Helsinki Watch War Crimes in Bosnia-Hercegovina', vol. II, pp. 394–7 (1993).

References

Anderson, B. (1991) *Imagined Societies – Reflections on the Origin and Spread of Nationalism* (London: Verso).

Aron, A. et al. (1991): 'The Gender Specific Terror of El Salvador and Guatemala', *Women's Studies International Forum* nos. 1–2, pp. 37–47

Bakic-Hayden, M. and Hayden R. (1992) 'Orientalist Variations on the Theme "Balkans": Symbolic Geography in Recent Yugoslav Cultural Politics', *Slavic Review* vol. 1, pp. 1–16.

Brownmiller, S. (1975) *Against Our Will; Men Women and Rape* (New York: Simon and Schuster).

Davis, J. (1977) *People of the Mediterranean* (London: Routledge and Kegan Paul).

Delaine, C. (1991): *The Seed and the Soil – Gender and Cosmology in Turkish Village Society* (Berkeley: University of California Press).

Denich, B. (1974) 'Sex and Power in the Balkans'. In M.Z. Rosaldo and L. Lamphere (eds) *Women, Culture and Society* (Stanford: Stanford University Press) pp. 243–63.

Drakulic, S. (1993) *Balkan Express – Fragments from the Other Side of War* (London: Hutchinson).

Dwyer, D.H. (1978) *Images and Self-Images – Male and Female in Morocco* (New York: Columbia University Press).

European Parliament Resolution on Rapes in Yugoslavia (10 March 1993) Geneve: UN.

Farmanfarmaian, A. (1992) 'Sexuality and the Gulf war; Did You Measure Up?', *Genders* vol. 13, pp. 1–30.

Gaber, S. (1993) 'The Limits of Democracy: The Case of Slovenia', *Journal of Area Studies*, Special Issue: Antagonism and Democracy in Former Yugoslavia, no. 3, pp. 57–64.

Gerrits, A.W.M. (1992) 'Some Comments on the Civil War in Yugoslavia', *Helsinki Monitor*, vol. 3 no. 1, pp. 54–6.

Gilmore, D.D. (ed.) (1986) *Honour and Shame and the Unity of the Mediterranean* (Washington DC: American Anthropological Association).

Gilmore, D.D. et al. (eds) (1985) *Sex and Gender in South Europe – Problems and Prospects* (Washington: American Anthropological Association).

Goddard, V. (1987) 'Honour and Shame – the Control of Women's Sexuality and Group Identity in Naples'. In P. Caplan (ed.) *Cultural Construction of Sexuality*, (London: Tavistock) pp. 166–92.

Hayden, R.M. (1992) 'Constitutional Nationalism in the Former Yugoslav Republics' Paper presented at the conference on 'Nation, National Identity, Nationalism', University of California, Berkeley, 10–12 September 1992.

Hobsbawm, E.J. (1992) 'Ethnicity and Nationalism in Europe Today', *Anthropology Today*, vol. 8, no. 2, pp. 3–8.

Jansen, W. (1989) 'Ethnocentrism in the study of Algerian Women'. In A. Angerman et al. (eds) *Current Issues in Women's History* (London and New York: Routledge) pp. 289–311.

Jansen, W. (1987) *Women Without Men – Gender and Marginality in an Algerian Town* (Leiden: E.J. Brill).

Jansen, W. (1993) 'Creating Identities – the Interplay of Gender and Religion in Jordan'. In M. Brugmann et al. (eds) *Who's Afraid of*

Sexuality? Questions of Identity (Amsterdam and Atlanta GA: Rodopi) pp.157–69.

Katunaric, V. (1991) 'Uoci novih etnopolotickih raskola – Hrvatska i Bosnia i Hercegovina', *Sociologija*, vol. 33, no. 3, pp. 373–85.

Koch, K. (1991) 'Back to Sarajevo or Beyond Trianon', *The Netherlands Journal of Social Sciences*, vol. 27, no. 1, pp. 29–42.

Lazaro, J. (1990) 'Women and Political Violence in Contemporary Peru', *Dialectical Anthropology*, vol. 15, pp. 233–47.

Lendvai, P. (1991) 'Yugoslavia without Yugoslavs: the Roots of the Crisis', *International Affairs*, vol. 67, no. 2, pp. 251–63.

Lutz, H. (1991) 'The Myth of the "Other": Western Representation and Images of Migrant Women of So Called "Islamic Background"'. In S. Allen, F. Anthias and N. Yuval-Davis. (eds) Gender, Race and Class, Monographic Section of the *International Review of Sociology*, vol. 2, pp. 121–39.

Parlement Europeen, Direction de la Presse, 23 February 1993, Bruxelles.

Petrovic, R. (1990) 'Actual Ethnogenetic Processes in Yugoslavia', *Sociology* (Supplement), vol. XXXI, no. I, pp. 233–51.

Ramet, S. (1990) *The Evolution of Yugoslav Nationalities Policy: Some Methodological Considerations*, Bradford Studies on Yugoslavia no. 15 (Bradford).

Ramet, S. (1992) *Nationalism and Federalism in Yugoslavia 1962–1991*, 2nd edn (Bloomington/Indianapolis: Indiana University Press).

Rus, V. (1971) 'Sadasnji medjunacionalni odnosi u Jugoslaviji', *Gledista*, nos 5–6, pp. 761–9.

Said, E. (1978) *Orientalism* (London: Routledge and Kegan Paul).

Sekelj, L. (1990) 'Yugoslavia 1945–1986', *Sociologija*, Supplement for the XIV World Congress of Sociology, vol. 32, pp. 65–84.

Sekelj, L. (1991) '"Realno samoupravljanje", "realni nacionalizam" i dezintegracija Jugoslavije', *Sociologija*, vol. XXXIII, no. 4, pp. 587–99.

Simic, A. (1969) 'Management of the Male Image in Yugoslavia', *Anthropological Quarterly*, vol. 42, pp. 89–101.

Souriau, C. (1980) *Femmes et Politique Author de la Mediterranee* (Paris: Harmattan).

Stojanovic, S. (1972) 'Od postrevolucionarne diktature do socijalisticke demokratije – Jugoslavenski socijalizam na raskrscu', *Praxis*, vol 9, nos 3–4, pp. 375–98.

Wolf, E. (1969) 'Algeria'. In E. Wolf, *Peasant Wars of the Twentieth Century* (New York: Harper & Row) pp. 211–50.

6 From National Economies to Nationalist Hysteria – Consequences for Women

Tatjana Djuric

Translated by Dubravka Zarkov

During the last few years the former Yugoslavia has experienced political and economic fragmentation and civil war as destructive effects of nationalism and ethnic mobilisation. In these dramatic political processes, women have been increasingly marginalised as political subjects, and at the same time have become ever more numerous 'consumers' of the devastating effects of these processes. My intention in this chapter is to discuss nationalism in former and contemporary Yugoslavia from the perspective of the relationship between socialist state ideology of the so-called 'national economies' and present nationalist hysteria. In current debates on the war in Yugoslavia and the disintegration of Yugoslavia, these economic aspects of nationalism and their profound consequences for women are often neglected.[1] They are, however, central to the chapter.

My discussion of the disintegration of Yugoslavia is largely based on the analysis of internal processes of Yugoslav socialism, and their consequences. It is important to note, however, that in the light of changes throughout Eastern Europe and the fall of communist regimes, it is also necessary to consider other elements. Comparisons with other countries are necessary to the understanding of some aspects of these processes of transition and transformation, not least because the Yugoslavian example seems to be the only one within Eastern Europe where internal violence has been a key feature. These questions are, however, beyond the scope of this chapter.

This chapter argues that the economic and political processes of the disintegration of the former Yugoslavia are, by and large, the products of the internal contradictions of the system. These internal contradictions were created by illegitimate socialist rule, the acute identity crisis of Yugoslav society, the lack of democratic traditions, the prevalence of illiteracy and the authoritarian attitudes of the majority of the population.[2] The political use of nationalism by the ruling oligarchies of former Yugoslav republics has induced the process of economic and political disintegration of the country (Kresic, 1993). A significant consequence of those politics is the deterioration of the social position of women in the former Yugoslavia. The socialist system did proclaim women's rights to employment, political participation, abortion and so on, but at the same time it reproduced the patriarchal system. In socialism, patriarchal and sexist ideology was a foundation on which nationalist hysteria built chauvinism and militancy. Women became symbols of nationalist politics and at the same time ever more numerous victims of war and every other violence.

In the first part of the chapter, I deal with the concept of 'national economies'. I argue that the concept was created as an answer to the problems of social modernisation, in the late 1960s, in socialist Yugoslavia. I relate this to the effects of the economic and political use of nationalism and the disintegration of Yugoslavia. The second part of the chapter considers the gap between the officially declared equality between the sexes and the 'on-the-ground' situation of women in socialist Yugoslavia.

The final part of the chapter identifies the contradictions between the almost total marginalisation of women's political activities in the newly formed socialist Yugoslavia on the one hand and discusses the importance of women, in their traditional roles, in nationalist parlance. On the other hand, I also give some attention to the general economic and political situation in the present-day socialist Yugoslavia, where ethnic mobilisation and the civil war add to the overall deterioration in women's circumstances.

National Economies or Socialist State-Promoted Nationalism?

The economy was always considered one of the important elements that differentiated Yugoslavia from other socialist East European countries.[3] This was especially true in the 1950s and 1960s, with the introduction of self-management and the Great Economic Reform of 1965.[4] The Reform was supposed to be an answer to the ever more obvious modernisation crisis of the socioeconomic development of the country. The term 'modernisation crisis' indicates that the crisis was a result of the development strategy characteristic of modernisation processes. The basic orientation of this strategy was achieving a speedy, high and extensive rate of industrial development based mainly on the increased use of labour power. This kind of strategy resulted in the structural disproportion of the economy: industry got primacy over agriculture, and heavy industry over light industry.

Two economic principles formed the basis of the Yugoslav economic reform philosophy of the 1960s. The first was a tolerance of the market economy (the so-called 'socialist market economy'). The second was a loosening of state control and the decentralisation of economic decision-making processes (through the 'self-managing units'). These were supposed to rid the economy of structural imbalance and make it more effective. There was, however, no adequate change in the political system to accompany the economic reform and this created a risky discrepancy between the economic and political systems which, until then, were both strictly controlled by the state and Communist Party.

It took only a couple of years for the economic effects of the Reform – such as price liberalisation and a high rate of redundancy – to increase social unrest. Too many social groups were hard-hit by these particular effects, and were not provided with any compensatory alternatives. The Reform, furthermore, had a significant, although unintended, political effect. Namely, that self-management was perceived as possibly taking away economic power from the ruling elite, and thus weakening their political power. The political instability of the regime, and the fear of losing political monopoly, made the ruling elite give up the Reform, using the difficult social situation and the threat of major social unrest as an excuse.[5]

For these reasons, the idea of the free market and an efficient economy were swiftly abandoned. The idea of decentralisation, however, was preserved. At the end of the 1960s and the beginning of the 1970s the new process of redefinition of the economic system began. Anti-market orientation was strengthened and at the same time federal, economic and financial institutions such as the National Bank of Yugoslavia were decentralised.

Significantly, the same period was marked by the rise of political opposition to the communist one-party rule. Democratisation, decentralisation and political pluralism were political ideals of the opposition forces. As in Western Europe, these ideals were put forward by the so-called new Left – young intellectuals and students.

They demonstrated on the streets of Belgrade, Zagreb and Ljubljana, just as they did on the streets of Paris.

Of all these ideals, the one appropriated and reinterpreted by the political elite of the former Yugoslavia was that of decentralisation, turning it into pluralisation of the power centres. This, however, had very specific features. It was not characterised by differentiation of society, nor by creating autonomous social and political structures. Instead, it followed territorial and national prerogatives (Sekelj, 1991).

The process of transferring the economic functions of the federal state to the constitutive republics began after 1968. With the Constitution of 1974, republics were declared responsible for their own economic development and for the economic development of the federal state. In practice, this meant that the federal state was stripped of not only responsibility but also any opportunity to influence the economic development of its constitutive republics. It also meant that no republic had a say in any other's economic affairs (Goati, 1987). The ruling bureaucracies and elites of each republic held all the economic power over their territories. This exclusive economic power of the republics on their own territory was further backed by the processes of transferring the political functions of the Federation onto the republics. By the same Constitution of 1974, the republics were granted nation state status within the federal Yugoslav state.

The concept of an 'agreement economy' was constructed, to operate at all levels of the economy. Its sole purpose soon became to create the space for negotiations among the republics, and between the republics and still-existing federal institutions. In other words, its purpose was to regulate the distribution of political and economic power. Even this 'distributive' function of the federal state, however, was hardly realised. The republics had veto power, which was effectively used to undermine the execution of the economic decisions seen as 'unfavourable' for the particular republic. The prerogatives of the federal state, though minimal, were thus often paralysed (Goati, 1987).

At the level of a single enterprise, the concept of the 'economy without force' was created. The concept was built on the assumption that the enterprises would conduct their business by mutual agreement and negotiations about price, quality and quantity of products etc., without the 'force' of the market or the federal state. In practice, business and development policy of the enterprises were taken over, controlled and directed by the republic on whose territory those enterprises happened to be.

The giving of unlimited economic power over their own territories to the republics played a large part in the creation of closed national economies. In 1976 only about 3 per cent of all enterprises extended beyond the borders of a single republic, and in 1985 only about 2 per cent were still there. Inter-republic trade throughout the 1970s was not more than between 20-25 per cent (OECD Report, 1986: 116), and 99 per cent of all investments came from within the republics (SZS, 1986: 43). At the same time, a multiplication of industrial capacity began in each republic. Decrease in inter-republic economic cooperation and dependence was substituted for, and followed by, an external dependence on foreign indebtedness (Ocic, 1983). The most dynamic economic process throughout the 1970s and 1980s was thus the process of closing up.

The failures of national economies, however, were for a long time obscured by the high input of foreign financial aid and loans.[6] The price which political elites, both federal and republic, decided to pay in order to maintain their power was the foreign debt of US $20 billion, when the economy was in ruins and unable to repay it.

At the beginning of the 1980s the most significant economic problems were thus high and rapidly increasing rates of inflation, increases in unemployment, especially among the young, educated female workforce, the rapid increase in numbers living in poverty, followed by increasing socioeconomic stratification and a widening 'rich–poor' gap.[7] In the mid-1980s it became obvious that the consequences were not only economic.[8] Economic and political processes of decentralisation in the former Yugoslavia went hand in hand and turned into a process of disintegration. The socialist regime was unable to resolve the modernisation crisis of the 1960s and this led to the structural crisis of the 1970s, and finally to the political state crises of the 1980s and 1990s (Sekelj, 1991).[9] The transfer of economic and political power from the federal institutions to the republic created a sovereignty on the nation-based territory of the republics and the increasingly populist regimes which supported them (Popov, 1993).

Different projects for the future of the former Yugoslavia were discussed and suggested by both the political elite and their opposition throughout the mid and late 1980s: unitarian versus asymmetric federalism, federalism versus confederalism, a multi-party system versus reform of the Communist Party etc. In order to further the process, the weak union of the national communist parties (i.e. the Federal League of Communists) was broken apart. The conflicts within the Leagues of Communists of Serbia and Slovenia, and conflict between

the two, in the late 1980s, marked the end of the Federal League
of Communists of SFR Yugoslavia. The Leagues of Communists
of the Republics did not survive much longer. Defeated in the
elections in Croatia and Slovenia, and forced to change the hated
name of communist in other republics, in the late 1980s they faced
the emergence of other political parties. The socialist legacy, however,
largely determined the nature of the rising political opposition.
Insufficient articulation of anti-totalitarian democratic alternatives
in the context of closed nation-state republics facilitated the success
of nationalist ideologies. Thus, the idea of the political pluralism of
'post-Yugoslav, post-socialism' turned into the reality of ethno-
pluralism, not so different in its authoritarian nature from the
Yugoslav socialism it claimed to replace (Golubovic, 1991; Kresic,
1993; Sekelj, 1990, 1991). It is too simplistic to reduce these processes
of disintegration to a conflict between the developed, liberal North
and the despotic, communist South. The repressive social system of
the former Yugoslavia manipulated, for its own purposes, the
democratic social forces throughout the country with much success.
The same is now true for the nationalist elites in power in all former
Yugoslav republics. This does not mean that there are no non-nation-
alist forces, only that their power seems to be too weak to resist
manipulation and/or marginalisation.

The only remaining federal institution at the beginning of the 1990s
– the self-proclaimed guardian of the federal state and of the ideal
of 'Yugoslav-ness' (Jugosloventsva) – was thus, tragically and
ironically, the army, still called the Yugoslav National Army. The
war, then, should not have been a surprise, but, despite the fact that
the political and economic processes described above portended the
danger of disintegration, it was a surprise for the vast majority of the
population in the former Yugoslavia. Many political moves made
by national leaders – Milosevic and Tudjman in particular – and by
the political oligarchies of the former Yugoslav republics were
leading the direction of war. Until their responsibility is socially
evaluated (particularly the responsibility of the regime in Serbia) peace
will be impossible. The trade war between Serbia and Slovenia, the
war of propaganda on national TV programmes and other media,
the build-up of arms in the Federal Army and national and ethnic
militia in Croatia, Slovenia and Bosnia are all part of this responsibility. The politics of republican leaders were based on threats and
blackmail, on nationalist indoctrination and provocation. Yet, despite
all that was happening, nobody believed that war would start. It was

perhaps because of this that the war actually started: not believing that war was possible simply hindered any action to prevent it.

Changing Images and Persistent Realities: Socialist Women Between Emancipation and Tradition

Gender relations are mostly neglected in debates on nationalist processes in general, and in analyses of nationalism in the former Yugoslavia in particular. The same goes for analyses of the relationships between socialism, nationalism and gender, although the complexities of the relationship between socialism and women have been minutely studied.[10] In the case of Yugoslavia, there are a few feminist authors who have written on these issues (Drakulic, 1987; Meznaric and Zlatkovic, 1991; Milic, 1993; Papic, 1993). The argument in this section of the chapter is firstly that the actual position of women in socialist Yugoslavia was much worse than publicly represented, especially with regard to their economic position and participation. Secondly, the increase of nationalism brought about an even worse situation. On the one hand, deterioration occurred because of the overall worsening social and economic situation in the country. On the other hand, assumptions about the 'proper' role of women (which were part and parcel of nationalist ideologies) contributed to the faster deterioration of women's position and to the exclusion of women from the public sphere, particularly after 1989.

The concept of women's emancipation was part of official socialist theory. It referred to the realisation of equal rights and opportunities for women in a socialist society (i.e. equality between the sexes), and to the entry of women into the sphere of social production. The purpose of the women's emancipation project was not, however, the liberation of women. The concept of liberation would mean the destruction of the very patriarchal nature of society, and transformation at all levels, including sexuality, the family, household and personal as well as the freeing of women from all forms of oppression. The socialist women's emancipation project never went beyond the 'women's question' into the transformation of gender relations. Consequently, both images of women and women's position at various levels of society were highly ambiguous (Zarkov, 1991).

Women shared equal legal rights with men in the spheres of education, employment and political participation, and they had the right to divorce and abortion. But the socialist state granted women legal equality while maintaining traditional gender relations, and their related structures both in family and in society. The *de jure* equality, moreover, could not lead to *de facto* equality, because the gendered social structures were either precluding women from assuming the rights they had been granted, or were marginalising and ghettoising them when they did.[11]

In the 1981 census, women comprised 51 per cent of the total population of the former Yugoslavia (from 48 per cent in Kosovo to 52 per cent in Croatia (SGJ, 1991: 441–2)). If the position of those defined as dependants are examined, however, women have continued to be over-represented since the Second World War. In 1948, 67 per cent of women were classified as dependants. This decreased at a snail's pace to 63 per cent in 1980 (SGJ, 1991: 131). The proportion of women classified as dependent varied considerably in different republics: 90 per cent of women were classified as dependants in Kosovo; 69 per cent in Bosnia-Herzegovina; 69 per cent in Montenegro; 63 per cent in Macedonia; 58 per cent in Serbia (with Provances); 58 per cent in Vojvodina; 52 per cent in Croatia, and 50 per cent in Slovenia (SGJ, 1991: 442, 448). The high rates of female dependency indicate that women's position in these patriarchal societies is primarily as mothers, wives and unpaid workers in the home. Interestingly, the 1991 census of SFRJ (the former Yugoslavia) notes that data on female dependency were not compiled, not even as projections (SGJ, 1993: 53).

The data presented above indicate the unequal partnership between women and men in participation in the social life of the former Yugoslavia. The same picture emerges from analyses of data on education, employment/unemployment, and political participation, which were all regarded as pillars of women's emancipation in socialism.

Rates of illiteracy, for instance, which from 1948 were steadily falling, show an interesting dynamic. Rates of female illiteracy in 1948 were two and a half times higher than those of male illiteracy: 15 per cent of the male and 38 per cent of the female population. In 1981, however, it was almost four times higher: 5 per cent of males and 17 per cent of females were still illiterate. Although illiteracy rates decreased with increases in economic development in particular republics, illiterate women outnumbered men in all the former Yugoslav republics. In the educational structure of the SFRJ population, 68 per cent never completed their school education, only completing primary education (equal percentages of men and women at 69 per cent). Differences open up from the secondary level onwards. Some 26 per cent of the population completed secondary education: 33 per cent of all men and only 19 per cent of women. Only 6 per cent have higher educational qualifications (BA and higher): 7 per cent of men and 4 per cent of women. However, the participation of women has improved from 37 per cent of the student body in 1945/46 to 52 per cent in 1990/91. In 1945 there was not a single woman with a Ph.D, while in 1990 women comprised 28 per cent of all those with a Ph.D (SGJ, 1991: 375–8). Nevertheless, in comparison with men, discrimination against women increased, even as their level of education increased. This is particularly true at the university level, where the number of female students is highest at the BA level and lowest at doctoral level (SZS, 1986: 115). There is a similar situation in the teaching profession. In 1990/91 women comprised 64 per cent of teachers in primary schools, 51 per cent in secondary schools and 30 per cent at higher levels (high schools and universities) (SGJ, 1991: 339–43).

The structure of unemployment has not changed since the 1950s, with women comprising just over half of those unemployed: 53 per cent in 1952 for SFRJ, 53 per cent in 1991 for the same territory, and 54 per cent in 1992 for SRJ. The unemployment rates for women without qualifications decreased from 68 per cent in 1952 to 53 per cent in 1990, indicating that, on the one hand, women without qualifications were more easily employed, and on the other hand, that women's level of education had improved. In the same period, women's overall rates of employment increased from 29 per cent to 40 per cent (SGJ, 1991: 100). Nevertheless, the real picture of female employment requires the analysis of their representation within various sectors of the economy. Viewed this way, there has been a steady segregation of women into 'female' jobs, which are, more often than not, labour intensive and low paid. Thus, improvement in women's education did not help women to get better paid or more interesting jobs (Kavcic, 1990). The new job areas that slowly opened to women soon became stereotyped as 'female' and low status, affecting women's pay and employment benefits. Although there was less of a gap between 'female' and 'male' jobs in the more developed republics of the former Yugoslavia (Kavcic, 1990), the problems that women faced did show basic similarities across republics. Marina Blagojevic (1991) showed in her research that in all republics of the former Yugoslavia it was gender, far more than ethnicity, that determined women's disadvantaged position in the labour market and their low wages.

Data on women's political participation in national and regional parliaments and in the local political bodies confirms this. In 1990, women held 5 per cent of all seats in the Federal Assembly of SFR Yugoslavia (SGJ, 1991: 438). In the Parliaments of the republics of the former Yugoslavia the figure varies from 2 per cent in Serbia to 11 per cent in Slovenia and only in the municipal structures are women more visible. Thus, although socialism proclaimed equality, there has been no change in the gender power structure, either in the family or in society. The patriarchal system, where maternity is the prevailing cultural pattern of female existence, still prevails. Women as mothers still do most of the household work, unpaid and unrecognised, and often with their only job satisfaction being the success of their children.[12]

Those women who are socially successful often adopt male models of behaviour and 'put on men's shoes'. They are seldom successful in using the position they have attained for creating new opportunities for other women. Women who have escaped some of these patriarchal pressures were, and still are, a minority, despite their enormous efforts to work for change. Among these women are the few feminist groups which were first to criticise and dismiss socialist concepts of emancipation as false and utilitarian. However, they did not have much success among the majority of women in the former Yugoslavia. 'Feminist' is still a pejorative word, and it is a personally and politically degrading term in Yugoslav political and public life.

Nationalist Hysteria is Here, But Where are the Women?

The discussion in the previous two sections of this chapter points to some processes that led to war in the former Yugoslavia in terms of the convergence of economic and nationalist developments. It also indicates the position that women had in these economic and political developments. In this section I will focus on the Federal Republic (SR) of Yugoslavia, its economic and political situation and women's role in it. Most of the data on women used in this section is from research done by women which, perhaps, indicates that only women are interested in researching women.

As the biggest marginal group in society, women take part in these processes in specific ways. Their general social situation deteriorated rapidly during the dramatic changes that have been happening in the former Yugoslavia. Neither the new state-status nor the recently created political systems gave women what they promised to the population as a whole. As many feminists have argued, it is not only because of the generally poor economic situation, but also because of the patriarchal cultural patterns common to both the former Yugoslav socialist elite and the current nationalist politics and policies of the new states. Furthermore, in the newly created states, women are among those who produce and defend patriarchal values in the family and in society, as much as they were in the socialist state. They have become symbols of nationalist policies and, willingly or unwillingly, are the 'mothers of the nations'. They are also among the most numerous victims of the devastating consequences of nationalist hysteria.

This condition, of nationalist hysteria, is the basic condition of SR Yugoslavia today (Bibo, 1991). The social integration of citizens is based on consensus about two main assumptions: firstly, that Serbs as a nation are threatened by extinction, and secondly, that there is an international conspiracy against Serbs. All the hardship and misery that the citizens of Serbia are enduring due to international sanctions are interpreted within these two basic assumptions, and no space is left for different interpretations. Nation is accorded the highest value, and national, primordial, voluntaristic political criteria are the only criteria of belonging to society (Kuzmanovic, 1992). In this situation, the expression of a plurality of values and interests, either through political institutions and parties, or actions resulting from public opinion, is almost impossible. Currently, many opposition parties are as nationalist as the ruling parties in all former Yugoslav territories. This was indicated by research done during and after the first multi-party elections (Sekelj, 1991). The individuals and groups whose opinions differ from those presently ruling are treated as traitors and enemies.

The problems that the present states of SR Yugoslavia (Serbia and Montenegro) face, through being unrecognised and boycotted by the international community, are falsely presented with unreasonable and unrealistic solutions being suggested. Questions such as the involvement of Serbia in the current war, and Serbia's responsibility for it, are seldom posed, even by the political opposition. Economic problems are put forward and discussed, but no effort is made to relate them to political causes, or to the war. They are, instead, used to justify mutual accusations of different political parties and party leaders, or related to the United Nations' sanctions, reinforcing the discourse of 'international conspiracy against the Serbs'. The truth is that the economic devastation is total: inflation rises 1 per cent per hour, unemployment is over 30 per cent and there is a lack of basic foods and medicines. Faced with this reality, economic indicators seem completely unsatisfactory to describe the situation. The large majority of the population is faced with the problem of mere survival. For the nationalist state with a populist regime and either weak or even more nationalistic opposition, these conditions of collective deprivation make it easy for apathy, fatalism and pathological fear to flourish. The Programme of Monetary Reconstruction that was introduced on 24 January 1994 has, officially, stopped inflation. However, inflation is still a latent danger because, in SR Yugoslavia, it is not only an indicator of monetary and structural problems in the economy, it is also the price paid for the political choices and decisions made by the political oligarchy. The picture of economic recovery offered by the Programme is unrealistic, for it encourages the illusion that recovery is possible within the closed system, i.e. within the economic blockade.

Within these economic and political conditions, women find themselves more and more excluded even from the spheres which they previously occupied in the socialist state. Their overall social position has worsened, and they are losing many previously unquestioned rights, the right to abortion being one of the most significant. Ironically, it was not lost thanks to Serbian President Milosevic. In May 1994, the Serbian Parliament adopted new legislation on abortion which largely limited the abortion rights of women. Feminists addressed the Serbian President, demanding that he should refuse to sign the legislation, in which case it could not be applied. He agreed, and returned the legislation to the Parliament for further debate, noting that it encroached on the basic rights of women. Thus, ironically, one of the basic rights for women was temporarily preserved by the same force against which many feminists struggle. There are other incredible examples. For example, the Police Academy in Belgrade refused the opportunity to enrol women.[13]

In a situation of total economic and political deprivation, women constitute the majority in different social strata and groups that are faced with important limitations: increasing unemployment, impoverished retired people, and high percentages of workers in 'female' jobs (health and education). Negative trends in education, employment and political participation that were already established in the socialist state continue to be part of the new Yugoslavia. For instance, in the 1992 election in SR Yugoslavia, women won less then 3 per cent of the seats (SGJ, 1993: 36). Their position within university hierarchies has worsened. According to the latest research, women comprise 1 per cent of members of the Academy of Science of SR Yugoslavia and women have never held the post of Rector at the University of Belgrade (Milivojevic, 1994). In employment, gender inequalities prevail. Research done by Slobodanka Markov and Fuada Stankovic (1991) shows that women are seldom at the top of management hierarchies. Only 2 per cent are directors, and then mainly in small enterprises. Feminists from the newly recognised states of Slovenia and Croatia warn that the employment situation for women has considerably worsened since the independence gained in 1990. This paradox of 'democracy' – women losing the few rights they previously had just when the general population of the respective state is supposed to gain more rights – is not exclusive to former Yugoslav republics. The Eastern European situation in general, since the 'velvet' and other 'revolutions', shows the same characteristics in almost all areas of public life (SIGNS Forum, 1991; *Feminist Review*, 1991; Helsinki Watch, 1992; Funk and Mueller, 1993; Kuzmanovic and Zarkov, 1993).

The continuity of patriarchal patterns of gender inequalities in children's socialisation is maintained in the current system of education. A group of feminist authors has done an analysis of the latest primary school textbooks in SR Yugoslavia (Plut, Rosandic et al., 1994). They conclude that sex discrimination prevails from the very first textbook for the youngest pupils. The sex roles presented for family and professional relationships give men and women specific, segregated places in both. Individual characters are mainly male and the family represented is the nuclear, heterosexual, modal family of mother, father and son.

In nationalist parlance, on the other hand, women are given a special place. They are 'mothers of the nation' and 'protectors of offspring'. There are, however, dreadful consequences of these constructions, since women have been specifically targeted victims of the current war, both in its propaganda and its effects on the ground. Patriarchal and sexist ideology intersect with the increased militarism of everyday life to portray men as the defenders and women as the ones to be defended. So, when women adopt nationalist politics, they often do it in a manner which is consonant with their place within a system of patriarchal domination – as mothers of the heroes and victims. However, Papic (1993) found that significant numbers of women adopt nationalism as an expression of equality with men. Nevertheless, few women are actually involved in the creation of nationalist policies or practices. Women are seldom politicians, part of the military, journalists, or in other professions closely associated with the current war.

It does seem that although women share economic and political deprivation with men, they are less likely to share men's extremism. Women, for example, were slow to adopt the nationalist politics of the former republics' oligarchies. In 1990, women were significant supporters of the Reform Group of ex-Prime Minister Ante Markovic and his liberal, pro-Yugoslav, democratic orientation. Compared with men, women voted for green parties more often, and their support of nationalist parties was half that of men (Puzigaca, 1990). Since 1990, women are the majority of the activists in anti-war and anti-nationalist campaigns. Feminist and autonomous women's groups who are actively opposed to nationalism, sexism and war are numerous, including: the Women's Party, Women's Lobby, Women's Parliament, Woman and Society, Women in Black, SOS line for Women and Children Victims of Violence, Group for Women Raped in War, Centre for Rape Victims, Women's Studies, etc. Their activity, however, is often limited to the big urban centres, Belgrade being the most significant, and their influence, if not on women then on society in general and nationalist politics in particular, is limited.

Thus, despite the activism of many, it seems that women remain loyal prisoners of families and their patriarchal 'fate'. Today, they fight an increasingly difficult fight to feed their families. Like their grandmothers used to, they now bake bread and, as a novelty, 'embargo cookies', as well as trading 'sanction recipes' designed to make something out of nothing.

Conclusion

Citizens of SR Yugoslavia, and Serbian people in particular, carry a heavy responsibility for the current situation in the former Yugoslavia. To resolve it, they will have to redefine their national project as a cultural project for civil society. They will have to address the question of the type of state in which they wish to live, democratic or authoritarian. Today, sadly, the majority is concerned with the question of size: they ask how big the state is, or should be (Popovic,

1993). Only when questions of the type of state are posed can any new answers be given. The answer has to be in the direction of peace, and reacceptance of SR Yugoslavia into the world community.

Relations between economic development and the political systems also have to be redefined in order to enable more democratic development for both economic and political processes. However, the problem of nationalism cannot be solved by locking it into the context of social and economic development and the democratic state. For such development does not exclude nationalism, even in the so-called democratic societies of the West. However, an undeveloped and undemocratic society can contribute to the rapid rise of nationalism, as the example of the former Yugoslavia shows.

The experiences of SFR and SR Yugoslavia show how economic and political processes can serve the purpose of obscuring each other, when tightly intertwined with nationalist processes. Their relationship is different in the 1990s from what it was from the 1960s to the end of the unified Yugoslav state. Nevertheless, economic and political processes have constantly reinforced each other, creating a vicious circle with devastating consequences for the people who lived, and still live, in that territory.

Some of these consequences affect women differently from men, but a significant difficulty is that women's problems are often invisible, even to women themselves. While they continue to be reproducers of patriarchal values in society, women reproduce their own deprivation as economically and politically marginalised and rendered socially passive. In order to resolve their situation, they have first to make it visible – to men, but also to women. Women's solidarity and networking is crucial to the project of women getting an effective hold on politics and society. The effort to make women's situation visible has to contribute to the visibility of gender relations within society, and the power hierarchy in which women are deprived. It also has to take into account other social processes, such as nationalism. If attempts to improve gender equality do not do this, they are, in effect, contributing to the strengthening of the very social system they aim to subvert.

Notes

Special thanks are due to Dubravka Zarkov for her support and useful comments on this chapter, and for her efforts in helping women from

SR Yugoslavia to go to the EFLF Conference, for which the paper
which formed the basis of this chapter was written.

I also wish to thank the organisers of the conference for providing
me with this rare opportunity to participate in debate on crucial
questions of nationalism and gender, and Ann Phoenix for her
laborious editing of this text. All comments on, and suggestions about,
the issues discussed in this chapter would be warmly welcomed.

1. There are some exceptions, nevertheless, in debates on economy
   and nationalism in the former Yugoslavia. See, for instance,
   Schierup (1991). Among Yugoslav authors, see Horvat (1989),
   Korosic (1988), Kuzmanovic (1992), Madzar (1990).
2. Ivic and Perazic (1994) note that 1991 data show that one-third
   of all the population of SR Yugoslavia (Serbia and Montenegro)
   and 40 per cent of women have not completed primary education,
   and 60 per cent of the total population has no professional
   qualifications. For discussion of identity crisis and other factors
   associated with disintegration, see Golubovic (1988, 1992).
3. Lendvai (1991), for instance, talks of the specificity of the
   Yugoslav economic project as a point of differentiation, and for
   that reason, as a point of interest for foreign scholars who
   researched the so-called 'original Yugoslav path to socialism'.
4. The 'Great' because the Yugoslav state started the reform with
   a frontal opening towards the market, wide liberalisation of
   prices and mass redundancy of employed workers), and with the
   withdrawal of some macroeconomic instruments (export
   subsidies, taxes on income etc.).
5. Throughout the last few decades the socialist regime of the
   former Yugoslavia had cyclic attitude shifts with regard to
   market economy: due to the pressure of economic difficulties
   the market option would be adopted, only to be abandoned (and
   replaced with a state-planned economy) with the threat of losing
   political monopoly (cf. Kovac, 1986).
6. Foreign accumulation in Yugoslav GNP increased from 6 per
   cent in the 1965-70 period to 8 per cent in the 1971–81 period.
   Foreign investment increased from 19 per cent to 25 per cent
   respectively (Madzar, 1990: 188).
7. The number of unemployed doubled between 1965 and 1975
   (starting from 230,000 in 1965). In 1980 it tripled, and in 1985
   it was already four times higher. The number of unemployed
   women increased from 53 per cent in 1965 to 56 per cent in

1985, while the number of educated/highly educated unemployed persons leapt from 16 per cent to 56 per cent respectively (SZS, 1986: 61).

After 1982, inflation ran out of control. The increase in prices in that year was 30 per cent, while in 1985 it reached 76 per cent (SZS, 1986: 239).

The poverty rate changed from 17 per cent to 25 per cent in the 1978–87 period, thus one-quarter of the Yugoslav population was below the 'poverty line'. During the same period, poverty spread from rural areas into the cities, reaching 'white collar' workers (Milanovic, 1991: 187–200).

8. In 1979 the International Monetary Fund stopped granting financial aid to the former Yugoslavia, when it became obvious that it would not be repaid. The Yugoslav political elite admitted for the first time that the country was faced with 'difficulties'. The words 'economic crisis' were first used only in the mid-1980s, while the words 'political crisis' were publicly introduced and used by politicians only in the late 1980s.

9. The crises were obscured at first by the charismatic personality of the leader, and, after the death of Josip Broz Tito, by the bureaucratisation of his charisma. After Tito's death, the leading political slogan put forward by his successors was: 'After Tito – Tito', the idea being that there would be no change in the political course of the country. This slogan was quickly countered by popular sceptical wisdom, and turned into a mocking slogan: 'After Tito – Titanic'. The germ of tragic truth carried in it was soon to be learned.

10. From a large body of literature I will mention only a few well-known authors, and their work on Eastern Europe and Yugoslavia: Molyneux (1981, 1985), Jancar (1978, 1981), Morokvasic (1984), Denich (1974, 1977), Meznaric (1985), Rosenblum-Cale (1979), Sklevicky (1987, 1989), Wolchick and Meyer (1985) More recent works, and particularly those on changes in Eastern Europe and Yugoslavia, are mentioned elsewhere in the text.

11. The social position of women in East European socialist states has already been well documented, theoretically and empirically (see note 10). Thus, my intention to provide some statistical data on women's situation in the former Yugoslavia is not motivated by the wish to substantiate the truth. My intention is to follow the argument that the already bad situation of women has

worsened with the increase of nationalist politics and adherent ideas about women and their 'proper' place and role in society. Therefore, in this and the following section, I will provide statistical data only as an illustration of that argument.

I will mainly use data from the *Statistical Yearbook of Yugoslavia* (SGJ), from 1991 and 1993. Some are cited in their original form, some I have had to create, for many of the necessary indicators are not used due to the gender assumptions made in current statistical methodology. Furthermore, some of the data are not available, although they do exist. For instance, the 1991 Census was conducted over the whole territory of the former Yugoslavia, but was never processed, due to the disintegration of the country. It is therefore difficult to make direct comparisons between the indicators from 1981 and 1991 in order to give a more substantial statistical analysis.

Some of the data are for the whole former Yugoslav territory (SFRJ), others are for the country created after the breakdown, i.e. the Federal Republic of Yugoslavia, comprising Serbia and Montenegro (SRJ).

12. For example, mothers are custodians of 84 per cent of children in divorce cases.
13. Information from personal contact. Newspapers in which the conditions of enrolment are published are not available.

References

Bibo, I. (1991) *Die Deutsche Hystorie* (Frankfurt: Verlag).

Blagojevic, M. (1991) *Zene izvan Kruga – profesja i porodica* (Belgrade: Institut za socioloska istrazivanja Filozofskog Fakulteta).

Denich, B. (1974) 'Sex and power in the Balkans'. In M.Z. Rosaldo and L. Lamphere (eds) *Women, Culture and Society* (Stanford, CA: Stanford University Press) pp. 243–63.

Denich, B. (1977) 'Women, Work and Power in Modern Yugoslavia'. In Schlegel (ed.) *Sexual Stratification, a Cross Cultural View* (New York: Columbia University Press).

Drakulic, S. (1987) 'Smrtni grijesi feminizma/Decki se zatrcavaju'. In L. Sklevicky (ed.) *Zena i Drustvo: Kultiviranje Dijaloga* (Zagreb: Sociolosko Drustvo Hrvatske).

Feminist Review (1991) Special Issue: *Feminisms and Europe*, no. 39.

Funk, N. and Muller, M. (eds) (1993) *Gender Politics and Post-Communism* (New York: Routledge).

Goati, V. (1987) 'Politicke nejednakosti u nas i ekonomisk razvoj'. *Pogledi*, no. 2, pp. 31–2.

Golubovic, Z. (1988) *Kriza Identiteta Jugoslovenskog Drustva* (Belgrade: Filip Visnic).

Golubovic, Z. (1991) 'Cari lakog politickog cara'. *Borba*, 5–6 October.

Golubovic, Z. (1992) 'The Conditions Leading to the Breakdown of the Yugoslav State. What has Generated the Civil War in Yugoslavia?', *Praxis International*, vol. 12, no. 2, pp. 129–42.

Griffin (1989) *Alternative Strategies for Economic Development* (London and Paris: Macmillan and OECD Development Centre).

Helsinki Watch (1992) *Hidden Victims – Women in Post-Communist Poland*, vol. IV, issue 5.

Horvat, B. (1989) *ABC Jugoslovenskog Socijalizma* (Zagreb: Globus).

Ivic, I. and Perazic, O. (1994) 'Obrazovni nivo stanovnistva i razvoj', *Republika*, vol. 41, pp. 5–6.

Jancar, B. (1978) *Women under Communism* (Baltimore: Johns Hopkins University Press).

Jancar, B. (1981) 'Women in Communist Countries, Comparative Public Policy'. In N. Black and A.B. Cottrell (eds) *Women and World Change, Equity Issues in Development* (London: Sage).

Kavcic, B. (1990) 'Women and Power Structure: The Yugoslav Case', *Sociology*, vol. XXXII, Supplement.

Korosic, M. (1988) *Yugoslovenska Kriza* (Zagreb: Naprijed).

Kovac, M. (1986) 'Neoriginalnost robne privrede'. In *Dugurocni Program Ekonomske Stabilizacije – Tri godine posle* (Belgrade: NIGRO Privredni Pregled).

Kresic, A. (1993) *Politika nacionalizma i udruzivanje baroda*. Paper presented at the Theoretical Basis for Research of Yugoslav Disintegration Conference, June 1993, Belgrade.

Kuzmanovic, T. (1992) 'Promisljane razvoga i slucaj Jugoslavije (Development Thinking and the Case of Yugoslavia)', *Sociologija*, vol. XXXIV, no. 2.

Kuzmanovic, T. and Zarkov, D. (1993) 'Economy and gender in the changing "Second World"'. Paper presented at the Out of the Margin – Feminist Perspectives on Economic Theory Conference, June 1993, Amsterdam.

Lendvai, I. (1991) 'Yugoslavia without Yugoslavs – The Roots of the Crisis', *International Affairs*, vol. 2, pp. 251–63.

Madzar, L.J. (1990) *Suton socijalisticke privrede* (Belgrade: Economika and Institut Economskih Nauka).

Markov, S. and Stankovic, F. (1991) 'Zene u preduzetnistbu i menadzmentu'. In S. Bolcic, B. Milosevic and F. Stankovic (eds) *Preduzetnistvo i sociolgija* (Novi Sad: Matica Srpska) pp. 100–16

Meznaric, S. (1985) 'Theory and Practice. The Status of Employed Women in Yugoslavia'. In S. Wolchik and A. Meyer (eds) *Women, State and Party in Eastern Europe* (Durham: Duke University Press).

Meznaric, S. and Zlatkovic, J. (1991) 'Gender and Ethnic Violence: The Case of Kosovo'. In S. Allen et al. (eds) *Gender, Race and Class*, International Review of Sociology, Monographic Section (Rome: Borla).

Milanovic, B. (1991) 'Poverty in Eastern Europe in the Years of Crisis, 1978–87: Poland, Hungary and Yugoslavia', *The World Bank Economic Review*, vol. 5, no. 2.

Milic, A. (1993) 'Women and nationalism in Yugoslavia'. In N. Funk and M. Muller (eds) *Gender Politics and Post-Communism* (New York: Routledge).

Milivojevic, I. (1994) 'Women and University'. Paper presented at the Workshop on Women's Studies, March 1994, Novi Sad, Yugoslavia.

Molyneux, M. (1981) 'Women in Socialist Societies: Problems of Theory and Practice'. In K. Young et al. (eds) *Of Marriage and the Market* (London: CSE Books) pp. 167–203.

Molyneux, M. (1985) 'Family Reform in Socialist States: The Hidden Agenda', *Feminist Review*, vol. 21, pp. 47–64.

Morokvasic, M. (1984) 'Being a Woman in Yugoslavia: Past, Present and Institutional Equality'. In M. Gadant and A.M. Barrett (eds) *Women of the Mediterranean* (London and New Jersey: Zed Books).

Ocic, C. (1983) *Integracioni i dezintegracioni procesi u privredi Jugoslavije* (Belgrade: MC CKSK Srbije).

OECD (1986) *Economic Survey: Yugoslavia* (Paris: OECD).

Papic, Z. (1993) 'Nacionalizam, patrijarhat i rat', *Republika*, vol. 65, pp. 26–8.

Plut, D., Rosandic, R. et al. (1994) *Ratnistvo, Ptriotizam, Ptriarhalnost* (Belgrade: Centar za antiratny akciju).

Popov, N. (1993) 'Srpski populizam od marginalne do dominantne pojave', *Vreme, Posebni Dodatak*, 135, 24 May.

Popovic, O. (1993) 'Kakvka ili kolika drzava', *Republika*, nos 73–4, p. 13.

Puzigaca, M. (1990) *Istrazivanje javnog mnjenja Vojvodine* (Novi Sad: Agencija SCAN).

Rosenblum-Cale, K. (1979) 'After the Revolutions: Women in Yugoslavia'. In I. Volgyes (ed.) *The Peasantry of Eastern Europe*, vol. II (New York: Pergamon Press).

Savezni Zavod za Statistiku (1986) *Yugoslavia 1945–1985* (Belgrade).

Schierup, C.U. (1991) 'The Post-Communism Enigma – Ethnic Mobilisation in Yugoslavia', *New Community*, vol. 18, no. 1.

Sekelj, L. (1990) 'Yugoslavia 1945–1986', *Sociologija*, Supplement for the XIV World Congress of Sociology, vol. 32, pp. 65–84.

Sekelj, L. (1991) '"Realno samoupravljanje", "realni nacionalizam" i dezintegracija Jugoslavije', *Sociologija*, vol. 33, no. 4, pp. 587–99.

SGJ (1991) *Statistical Yearbook of Yugoslavia* (Belgrade: Savenzi Zavod za Statistiku).

SGJ (1993) *Statistical Yearbook of Yugoslavia* (Belgrade: Savenzi Zavod za Statistiku).

SIGNS (1991) *Forum on Women in Eastern Europe*, vol. 17, no. 1.

Sklevicky, L. (1987) *Zena i Drustvo, Kultiviranje Dijaloga* (Zagreb: Sociolosko Drustvo Hrvatske).

Sklevicky, L. (1989) 'Emancipated Integration or Integrated Emancipated: The Case of Post-revolutionary Yugoslavia'. In A. Angerman et al. (eds) *Current Issues in Women's History* (London: Routledge).

SZS (1986) *Yugoslavia 1945–1985* (Belgrade: Savenzi Zavod za Statistiku).

Tasic, P. (1993) *Kako sam branio Antu Markovica* (Skopje: NIP).

Wolchick, S. and Meyer, A. (eds) (1985) *Women, State and Poverty in Eastern Europe* (Durham: Duke University Press).

Zarkov, D. (1991) 'The Silence which is not One: Sexuality, Subjectivity and Social Change in a Feminist Rethinking of Research on Peasant Women', MA thesis, Institute of Social Studies, Den Haag.

7 Women and Ethnicity in Present-Day Russia: Thoughts on a Given Theme

Natalya Kosmarskaya

Participation in the eighth European Forum of Left Feminists Conference on Gender and Nationalism in Europe turned out to be a very exciting episode in my life. Apart from the warmth of the conference atmosphere which easily made me feel a part of the European feminist and academic community, it was inspiring to be in the thick of challenging, theoretical discussions on nationalism, racism and gender. I was also impressed by the sheer number of women scholars and feminists present – there were more than 80 of them – all deeply concerned about how women of different ethnic and religious affiliations would, in future, live in the unified Europe. All this was very different from the state of affairs in my own country: Russia and the former Soviet Union in general.

First, in the former Soviet Union, researchers have different realities to address. Even when women migrants and refugees are the main focus of research, and even when the everyday hardships in women's lives seem more or less similar, there are marked geopolitical, ethno-social and cultural differences between European countries and the former Soviet Union.

Second, by comparison with Europe, where the gender approach to ethnic phenomena has already gained public and academic recognition, the intersection of gender and ethnicity in Russia seems to be a *terra incognita*, even given the generally poor state of research on gender relations. To illustrate the point, much was said at the Amsterdam conference about possible ways in which to withstand every facet of racism and nationalism against women, as well as the ways in which to exert pressure on the political powers about these issues. In Russia, however, we need extensive and systematic research to be done in different geographical zones and in various spheres of ethnic relations before the relevant data can be presented to the government. Similarly, the problems associated with attempting to

142

build up the anti-racist and anti-nationalist alliances on the European scale were widely discussed at the conference. In Russia, we need alliances to make women's problems, including those concerned with ethnicity, visible to policy-makers and the public.

To finish my comparative argument, the fact that the conference participants were well informed about problems of gender and ethnicity in different countries was in contrast with their lack of familiarity with the situation in Russia and the former Soviet Union in general.

Allowing for all this, I was enthusiastic about the editors' proposal that I should contribute to this book. This seemed to be an important step towards the realisation of my aim of bringing issues of gender into public and academic discussion on the ethnic aspects of Russia's development.

The first part of this chapter presents an overview of the dimensions of women's ethnicity in present-day Russia. The second part discusses some data from my fieldwork on women, ethnicity and nationalism. Many important aspects of the intersection of gender and ethnicity have not been given as much space as they deserve in what follows. This is mainly because of the lack of available empirical research data and statistics. However, the inter-ethnic situation in post-Soviet Russia, official policy responses and the state of research on gender and ethnicity are examined as a necessary background to the chapter.

Ethnic Realities and ...

Since 'perestroika' and the later collapse of a unitary communist state, the countries of the former USSR have been going through a dramatic period of change in the sphere of inter-ethnic relations. The 'inviolable friendship of all the Soviet peoples', 'the free republics' unbreakable union' and the like have shared the destiny of the other communist myths. There is nothing surprising about this.

In a country with 128 nations and ethnic groups living, in many cases, inter-mixed all around the territory, many of the internal frontiers were installed by Stalin quite arbitrarily following his own preferences and whims. Moreover, whole nations became subjects of repressions and deportation, with their lands being occupied by other ethnic groups. Ethnic values and the sense of belonging to a national collectivity were deliberately repressed, quite successfully in some cases, and replaced by a 'proletarian internationalism'. After the collapse of the imperial centre with its military, economic and ideological pressures, nationalisms, separatism and territorial claims could not be bottled up any longer.

With regard to the inter-ethnic situation in present-day Russia, two main problems deserve to be mentioned as influencing the country's development in the longer term. I will call these the 'Russian question' and the 'Caucasian question'. The first one, that is of the Russian-speaking diaspora in the former national republics, has already proved to be very politically sensitive and fraught with serious socioeconomic destabilisation. According to the last All-Union Population Census (1989), there were about 25 million ethnic Russians living in the so-called 'near abroad', together with another 11 million of those who considered Russian to be their native language. This ethnic composition is a result of Russian colonisation of the territories which have been annexed to the Empire for the last 150 years. The process was substantially intensified under the Soviet regime when thousands of Russian-speaking people moved to the peripheries of the USSR to transmit culture and new ideologies and to build up socialist economies. This spreading of the Russians about the territory of the then USSR was most marked between 1939 and 1979 when the proportion of Russians living outside Russia was growing steadily from 9.3 per cent (10 million people) to 17.4 per cent (23.9 million) (Ostapenko and Subbotina, 1992). In the early 1990s, the political independence of the former republics severely undermined the 'superiority complex' and high social status the Russians had enjoyed in the republics for decades. Having been turned into an ethnic minority, they found themselves one day in an environment which was no longer comfortable and friendly. This was for three main reasons: the growing national aspirations of the 'titular' ethnic groups, the achievement of official status by native languages (and hence the ousting of Russian as the main language), and uncertainty and infringements of Russian-speakers' citizenship and property rights in the new states.

The majority of those from the Russian diaspora are following a wait-and-see policy, trying to adapt to these new challenging realities. Others are cherishing plans to migrate or have already returned to Russia. The stream of these migrants is gathering momentum. According to estimates from the Federal Migration Service (FMS), about 2.5 million people, so-called forced migrants together with refugees,[1] crossed Russia's borders in 1993–94. Forecasts for the near future, ranging from 1 to 6 million people likely to become new Russian residents (*Rossiskaya Gazeta*, 1993; *Nezavisimaya Gazeta*, 1993), are rather worrying, not only because this is such an imprecise estimate, but also because of the consequences of such an influx.

Whatever the outcome of academic and public debate on diaspora, whether it is considered to be a tragic heritage of the communist past or as the last great chance for Russia's Renaissance (Vishnevsky, 1994), the realities need to be faced for humanitarian and other reasons. The more newcomers there are competing for jobs, food and housing in a country whose economy is being brought to ruin, which has an already impoverished resident population, the more this will add to the volatile mixture of socially marginalised people in Russia. Similarly, the more victimised and discriminated against their compatriots in the 'near abroad' feel themselves to be (whether or not this is justified), the more oil it pours on the flame of Russian nationalism and chauvinism, and the more trump-cards will be in the hands of the newly formed extreme Right.

As for the second knot of ethnic tensions, the 'Caucasian question', its importance for the future ethno-social scenario of Russia's development has not been fully recognised either by the policy-makers or by the public. The term 'Caucasian' is generally applied to the people coming from the Northern Caucasus and the so-called Transcaucasian republics (Armenia, Georgia, Azerbaijan), large numbers of whom are engaged in 'shuttle' petty trade and other forms of (sometimes semi-criminal) business activities. However, future migrants from Central Asia should also be considered part of the Caucasian question.

The core of the problem lies in the enormous rural overpopulation in the Caucasus, the Transcaucasian area and Central Asia, which is caused by traditionally very high rates of population growth and long-standing land shortages. Taking a very cautious estimate, the level of unemployment in Central Asia amounted, in 1990, to 12.5 per cent of the able-bodied population. (This figure excludes the mothers of large families, i.e. the majority of women in the economically active age group.) Breaking these figures down to specific groups, about 35–40 per cent of the agricultural labour force is excess to demand. Some 30–40 per cent of Armenian and Azerbaijanian school-graduates have practically no chance of finding any job or gaining any educational qualifications within their countries. There is, in addition, little land available for each rural inhabitant (0.22 ha.

in Tajikstan, 0.33 ha. in Georgia, 0.36 ha. in Uzbekistan, about 0.5 ha. in Kirghizia, Azerbaijan and Armenia [Segodnya, 1994]).

With the fall of official restrictions on population mobility which were typical of the Soviet regime, people began to leave their villages in larger and larger numbers. Besides the above-mentioned 'push' factors, the ecological crisis and the erosion of traditional values further stimulated the process. Rural–urban migrations are most common in Central Asia at the moment, but it is likely that there will be a massive exodus of native populations out of the area in the medium and long term, with Russia and Kazakhstan being natural destinations.

As for Armenians, Chechens, Azerbaijanians, Ossets and other 'Caucasians', they have already begun to move to Russia. The social discontent which flares up every now and then in different Russian towns over these so-called 'blacks' (a common insulting nickname for them because of their black hair and dark eyes) might be a portent of serious future tensions or even confrontation. It is worth mentioning here that the political success of the Russian radical nationalists in the elections of December 1993 was largely due to their attacks on the 'Caucasian' ethnic groups in Russia who were constructed as the main cause of the declining economic situation and rise in crime.

It is not only so-called 'ordinary' people who demonstrate ethnic prejudices of this kind. Educated and western-oriented democrats also show such prejudices. The impressions recorded by Joan Urban from the American Catholic University, who comes to Moscow every year for her research on modern political life in Russia, might be relevant here:

> In spite of all the ideological shifts, one thing was unchangeable in the minds of my friend-democrats, that is their open enmity and intolerance against the people coming from the Caucasus – the Chechens, Azerbaijanians, Georgians in particular, even against the Armenians. Sometimes the Muslims of Central Asia were also perceived in this way. But primarily the 'Caucasians' were stubbornly described as being sly, dishonest and ill willed. And more than that: these features, according to my friends, are genetically immanent to the ethnic groups under consideration. (Urban, 1994: 39)

... How Women are Involved

No doubt, all the problems outlined above are seriously affecting women's lives. For all the women of the former Soviet Union, even those living far from zones of open military conflict or serious inter-ethnic confrontation, these problems are just another contribution to the psychological distress caused by general sociopolitical in-stability. For women from the Russian diaspora one of the important stress factors is the atmosphere of uncertainty concerning their future and that of their children. As for women migrants and women refugees, going through a difficult period of resettlement and adaptation to new surroundings, they are obliged to carry additional physical and psychological burdens together with their 'normal' workload, household and maternity obligations.

Statistical data on population mobility is still rather poor and whatever has already been collected by the Federal Migration Service (FMS) and other bodies responsible for dealing with migration is mostly kept out of the public eye. The figures published by the FMS show overall numbers of migrating men and women and their age structure, but do not usually break down gender by educational, professional and family status, ethnicity, and source of income. The relevance of the official data is also restricted by the existing collection technique (until January 1994 no distinctions were made between refugees and forced migrants) and by the fact that only about 30 per cent of migrants apply to the FMS territorial branches and so can be registered. However, the data at my disposal (see Table 7.1) reveal a number of important trends in the gender composition of migrant groups.

There is a moderate excess (3.4 per cent for Russia as a whole) of migrating females over males (this figure includes children). What factors are responsible for these figures? Females are under-repre-sented in the birth to 15-year-old age group, but they appreciably outweigh males in the economically active age group (women outnumber men by 8.7 per cent for Russia, 15 per cent for the Volga-Vyatka region and Eastern Siberia etc.). By retirement age, this difference is even more marked. In most regions there are twice as many women migrants of retirement age than men. This makes these women a special target-group for migration policies.

Micro-level information from a study I conducted in the Oryol region of Central Russia[2] throws new light on the situation of migrant women of working age. Approximately 25 per cent of

Table 7.1: Age and gender composition of forced migrants and refugees registered in Russia between July 1992 and January 1994

Regions of the Russian Federation	Men of all ages %	Women of all ages %	Female/male ratios, specific age groups				
			0–5 years	6–15 years	Working age group	Above working age
Russia as a whole	46.6	53.4	0.98	0.99	1.09	1.85
1. Northern region	44.5	55.5	0.92	1.08	1.18	2.46
2. North-western region	45.6	54.4	1.06	1.01	1.11	1.71
3. Central region	45.1	54.9	1.07	1.03	1.15	1.93
4. Volga-Vyatka region	45.1	54.9	1.08	0.93	1.17	2.20
5. Central-Chernozem region	47.3	52.7	0.96	0.97	1.02	2.12
6. Volga region	46.9	53.1	0.97	1.00	1.05	2.07
7. North Caucasian region	47.8	52.2	0.95	0.95	1.08	1.40
8. Ural region	47.0	53.0	1.00	0.97	1.08	2.21
9. Western Siberia	46.3	53.7	0.99	0.99	1.10	2.33
10. Eastern Siberia	44.3	55.7	1.04	1.13	1.17	2.76
11. Far Eastern region	44.9	55.1	1.02	1.05	1.12	2.45
12. Kaliningrad region	44.9	55.1	1.17	1.17	1.23	1.32

Source: Forced Migrants in Russia. Statistical Bulletin No. 3. Federal Migration Service of the Russian Federation. Moscow, 1994, pp. 32–5.

families being registered as migrant are headed by women. These are not official figures, but just the casual observations of the migration staff. However, although this tendency needs further exploration, it draws our attention to some very important aspects of the impact of migration on women's lives.

First, migration is a threat to families, and the thousands of women living in inter-ethnic marriages (every sixth family was a mixed one in 1989 [Statistical Reference Book, 1992]) are particularly vulnerable in the socio-ethnic setting now typical in the former Soviet Union. According to the macro-level study of mixed families based on the results of the last All-Union Population Census (1989), it was much more common in the former Soviet republics for Russian women to be married to non-Russian men than for Russian men to be married to women of other ethnic groups. The reverse side of the same coin was that the men belonging to the 'titular' nations of the Central Asian and Transcaucasian regions were much more likely to live in mixed marriages than women of the same ethnic groups (Volkov, 1991).

Second, the group of women migrants heading their families might also include women whose matrimonial status is not affected by resettlement. These are single and divorced mothers. Given the high rate of divorce which was usual in the USSR (the latest figures for the former USSR are 950 divorces in 1990 compared with 2666 new marriages) and the large number of children born to unmarried mothers (11.2 per cent of all births in 1990 [Statistical Reference Book, 1992]), quite a large proportion of migrant women are likely to be heads of households.

While it is important to take a humanitarian approach, treating women only as victims of inter-ethnic tensions is an oversimplification. There are, it is true, far too frequently, extreme situations where women have to save their lives by abandoning war zones, areas of conflict and instability. Yet, in the much more routine situation of everyday inter-ethnic contact it is mainly women who find themselves in the very important role of 'contact person' and 'ambassador', irrespective of whether they belong to the ethnic majority or minority.

A very high rate of economic activity has, for a long time, been typical for Soviet women (more than 80 per cent of women were in paid employment in 1989, compared with 87 per cent of men) (Rimashevskaia, 1992). This, however, is only part of the explanation of women's role in inter-ethnic contacts. Due to the gender differentiation which is still prevalent in post-Soviet families, childcare, child rearing, housekeeping and the like are primarily in women's hands. Thus, women are extensively involved in everyday out-of-home contacts, such as standing in queues, visiting shops, schools, hospitals, kindergartens, etc., and are more 'visible', more 'public' than men who spend all day in their workplaces.

This important 'mediating' function makes women, whether they realise it or not, active and influential agents of inter-ethnic relations. At the same time, the demands of such 'contact' obligations add substantially to women's psychological burdens and responsibilities. Women's role in inter-ethnic contexts is thus multiple and, sometimes, unpredictable. A further oversimplification seems to be the 'natural' peace-making skills it is assumed that they have. Indeed, these have become the motifs favoured in political manifestos and at political conferences.

Although women are under-represented in political parties and social movements, there are some women leaders of openly nationalist orientation. One blatant current example is of Fauzia Bayramova, head of the National Independent 'Ittifak' Party, Tatarstan. More importantly, so-called ordinary women, living from hand to mouth, desperately anxious about their children in circumstances of raging crime and instability, facing the loss of jobs, annoyed at high prices and Caucasian 'profiteers' and with a seemingly endless list of other hardships, can easily be manipulated by political extremists. It is for this reason that opposition parties have recognised women as an influential group of voters and aimed special messages at them before the elections in December 1993.

From my personal observation, it is mostly women who comment very emotionally or abusively on the 'blacks' or those who 'have flooded Moscow'. I remember the words of one woman whom I met in one of the now abundant Moscow market-places. Standing near wonderful fruit sold by the notorious 'Caucasians' at exorbitant prices, she exclaimed: 'Look! This is a paradox! They say on TV about economic crisis in Georgia, but the Georgians are so wealthy! Our country is rich but why are all the Russians so poor?' This ethnic stereotyping seems to be common ('all the Georgians are rich ...'). It tends to be coupled with typical Soviet enmity against other people's material wealth ('... and that is why they are bad'), scapegoating 'others' for Russia's troubles and shutting their eyes to the fact that a lot of Russians also make enormous profits from selling fruit in the market-places.

The situation described above is one of many in the sphere of inter-ethnic relations which demand to be thoroughly explored and monitored. It remains to be seen whether social scientists and policy-makers are able to meet the challenge of the burning new realities. The evidence currently available suggests that there are many reasons for thinking that they will not be able to.

'Ethnicity' and 'Gender' on the Academic Scene

For communist ideology to be successfully introduced into the people's minds, they had to be cut off from their ancestral, social or ethnic roots. The notion that numerous ethnic minorities living in the vast territory of the USSR would gradually give ground to a so-called 'new historical community', the Soviet people, was one of the most vigilantly policed communist myths. With the ideological pressures removed, the area of social research having 'ethnic' and 'ethnicity' as its main objects is going through a challenging recon-ceptualisation of what seemed to be textbook maxims. This situation is typical for the social sciences in a post-totalitarian society. However, rather more dramatic is the fact that even the name of the discipline is under discussion. The Institute of Ethnography has been renamed the Institute of Ethnology and Human Anthropology and the names of the academic disciplines studied there are currently being debated, with proposals ranging from 'Human Studies' to 'Ethnology' and 'Socio-Cultural Anthropology'.

As for the core of the crisis, I quite agree with Tishkov's recent description of it:

> Political and ideological liberalization is an important precondi-tion for changes which have not taken place yet. 'Rebelling' objects of research, especially ethnic violence and rapid politiza-tion of ethnic relations occurring, just threw a light on certain discrepancies of our interpretations of previous realities and challenged the academic community. But what is the nature of the discrepancies? How to take up a challenge? All this is still waiting for adequate comprehension. (Tishkov, 1992)

There are also external factors which hamper ethnological research. Most of these are common to all the humanities in present-day Russia's universities: restructuring of the Academy of Sciences; cuts in state budget funding; the very low salaries of researchers, as well as the economic and political difficulties of conducting fieldwork.

Unlike research on ethnicity, which may derive its strength from rich pre-revolutionary and pre-war academic traditions, gender studies were, and still are to a great extent, a virgin field in Russia. The reasons have already been widely presented in Russian and Western publications on women in the former USSR. To put them succinctly, with all-pervasive Party control over everything in the humanities, there was simply no official demand for looking at social phenomena through the lens of 'gender'. The idea that the 'women's question' was solved under socialism went hand in hand with marked sexism, whether open or veiled, and was at the core of official attitudes in the social sciences and in mass consciousness.

Anastasia Posadskaya, one of the founders of the first Centre for Gender Studies in April 1990, presented her personal experiences of those hard times:

> What I wanted to do was to write a doctorate on women's employment in the USSR ... Everyone said to me that the problem of women's equality with men had been solved long ago in the USSR, and no one was interested in me as a woman researcher, still less as one working on women's questions. (Posadskaya, 1994)

'Perestroika' and later developments have led to a radical transformation of economic, political and social life, but have aggravated women's positions and not brought noticeable changes to official ideologies and public thinking. It is hardly surprising that under this 'male-dominated democratisation' and 'post-socialist patriarchal renaissance' (Posadskaya, 1993), there is still steady opposition within the Academy to gender as an object of social research. To say that the majority of academic staff at all levels do not really understand the meaning of the word 'gender' is not an overstatement. It was only in October 1993 that the first course on Women's Studies was included in the Moscow University curriculum. Although new Centres and Groups of Gender Studies attached to different academic and educational institutions have appeared during the last few years in Moscow, Saint Petersburg and some other towns, a developed network of research units using the concept of gender for exploring sociocultural phenomena is still practically non-existent in Russia.

As for 'gender and ethnicity', it turns out to be an embryo if compared with gender studies in Russia (which is more like a baby learning to walk). There are just a few researchers in different institutions of the Academy working quite separately, without any serious coordination through conferences, seminars or joint projects. There is no question of having courses on gender and ethnicity in the universities. Even at the Moscow Centre for Gender Studies, the oldest one in the country, only economics, politics and culture were among the research priorities, with ethnicity as a 'blank spot' when I joined the Centre in September 1993.

It seems that we are at the very first stage of incorporating gender into this branch of social research. What we have is not, strictly speaking, 'gender and ethnicity', but 'women and ethnicity', since women's problems and attitudes are the only focus, without any analysis of men's attitudes or conceptualisation of previous, male-centred approaches.

Moreover, due to the political sensitivity of ethnic problems on the one hand, and there appearing to be a 'veil of fashion' over mentioning women's problems on the other (unfortunately the latter is a more tangible result of following the Western example than the introduction of gender-variables into social research and policy making), very general and politicised discourses usually dominate at the rare conference and in the rare media publications relevant to gender and ethnicity. A Federal Migration Service official or a leader of settlers' communities may speak about women migrants; a journalist or politician about the hardships of women refugees, etc. However, the urgent need for systematic and professional research cannot be further ignored. The more so since the lack of reliable research findings substantially impedes the working out of gender-specific policies on migration and other ethnically-based issues.

State Response

'We are lacking conceptually-based policies on diaspora, with a differentiated approach to regions and priorities.' 'For almost four years the State has been demonstrating its helplessness in the face of the *"impasse"* migration problem.' These statements, with which I completely agree, were made in autumn 1993 by a number of well-known experts, leaders of migrants' communities, charities and other non-governmental organisations reviewing a draft of a new Federal Migration Programme (*Literaturnaya Gazeta*, 1993).

The importance of the issue of Russian-speaking minorities for Russia is proclaimed every now and then by officials in high positions. Russia is very interested, not only in enhancing its external democratic image, but, even more vitally, in preventing what is constructed as avalanche migration to the 'Motherland'. Nonetheless, tangible results are lagging far behind the problems and needs.

For example, the introduction of dual citizenship could be one important civil rights guarantee for Russian-speakers in the 'near abroad', contributing to the 'fading' of migrational expectations. Property rights of the people moving to Russia is another burning problem. Its solution could enormously release the state budget. Migrants allowed to sell their properties freely and to take the money to Russia would rely far less on public funds for housing and building up their own businesses. Unfortunately, with negotiations at different stages, only one bilateral agreement of this type has so far been concluded, that is between the Russian Federation and Turkmenistan.

Not much is being done to set up cultural and humanitarian links with the Russian diaspora. Language and educational problems related to this are particularly relevant to women. According to my field observations in Kirghizia, a new Central Asian state, and in the resettlers' communities in the Oryol region, women are often the first in their families to think about migration. One of their main fears, *caeteris paribus*, concerns the prospects of children's education and employment while outside Russia. So any diplomatic, cultural and organisational activities to support the status of the Russian language in the former Soviet republics and to promote the peaceful introduction of the newly national languages might be important steps for the better adaptation of Russians to their new role as an ethnic minority.

This brief examination of official policies concerning Russians outside Russia makes it quite clear that gender-specific approaches, including measures preventing discrimination against women, should not be expected. As for migration policies, the situation is very similar. In response to the increasing inflow of migrants from the 'near abroad' and the rapidly growing territorial population mobility within Russia, the government programme 'Migration' was adopted in May 1992, followed by the establishment of the Federal Migration Service as the main state body in charge of resettlement problems. A network of local services is being developed. The Laws on Refugees and Forced Migrants passed by the Parliament in February 1993 created a necessary base for building up legislation concerning people 'on the move'. The laws provide for legal status to be granted to resettlers, together with sizeable, though differentiated, material support and social security measures. However, legislators seem to be completely unaware of the women's problems which inevitably arise when it comes to the practical implementation of the laws.

A striking example concerns legal migration status. Women migrants who find themselves in the position of 'heads of family' because of their husbands' unwillingness to migrate, are not usually automatically granted legal migration status. Instead, they are obliged to go through the rather humiliating procedure of having their cases heard by a special migration control commission, with a number of documents and other evidence being required to prove that the spouses are really separated. Russian-speaking women with husbands of 'titular' ethnic origin, especially those from Central Asia, are most vulnerable. They are left to the mercy of the prejudiced attitudes of local officials. Male partners left in the 'near abroad' can easily be treated as 'agents of Islamic fundamentalism', with only two options for women: divorce or return to the former place of residence.

The gap between theory and practice also manifests itself in the lack of money, jobs and housing at the disposal of the Federal Migration Service and its local branches. Many officials of different levels, when interviewed, openly admit their helplessness because 'the laws do not work', 'funds do not arrive', etc. For example, with the planned resettlement funding as 240 billion roubles in 1993, only 30 billion were received from the state budget. Only a few can rely on the interest-free housing loans of 700 thousand roubles provided by law (the real cost of a moderately sized house in Russia was, at that period, spring 1994, about 6–7 million roubles). An allowance was granted by law to all migrants and refugees, but because of poor funding only a few special groups of people have a real chance of getting this small sum (which is equal to official minimum wages). Among these are single mothers, mothers of many children, together with the disabled and pensioners living alone. There are no grounds for considering this amount of money to be real material support, because it is paid only on one occasion and is very small (the minimum wage was 20.5 thousand roubles in the summer of 1994 in Russia compared with about 5 thousand roubles for one kilogram of meat). What deserves our attention is that women considered to be in need of special support are traditionally selected mainly on the basis of their reproductive roles. Nothing is planned, for example, to protect women's employment rights.

Economic restructuring in Russia is leading to massive unemployment, and about 70–80 per cent of those who have already lost their jobs in present-day Russia are women. The problem is more acute for migrants. Most of them were educationally well-qualified city-dwellers, with long experience of employment in industry, health and education, culture and services. Because of the housing and employment crises in overpopulated towns they are often obliged to settle in rural areas and to work in agriculture. Women seem to be more adversely affected.

Men who have been engineers and industrial workers often become tractor drivers, but there is also a lot of engineering work in the collective and state farms, whereas the social distance between women's former and later occupations is much greater. The list of the professions most dominated by women in the former Soviet Union is headed by librarians (91 per cent were women in 1989), followed by bookkeepers (89 per cent), economists (87 per cent), teachers (70 per cent) and physicians (67 per cent) (Rimashevskaia, 1992). Urban women who have to settle in rural areas are often pushed to move from being doctors, teachers and other 'white' and 'pink collar' workers to low status and low paid agricultural work as milkmaids or pig-tenders.

Moreover, women are often not provided with jobs on an equal footing with their husbands and are told that 'with their lack of jobs it is better to turn fully to maternity and housekeeping obligations'. So, although existing legislation on migrants implies formal gender equality in the sphere of employment, the existence of laws on the statute books cannot prevent discrimination in practice. This is quite natural in a country where, in 1993, women's inferiority in the labour market could be proclaimed at a conference by a minister of labour (*Moscow Times*, 1993). Women are, in fact, gradually being pushed to the margins of the market economy.

Case Studies: Implications for Future Research

Some of my field observations in the Northern Issyk-Kul littoral, Kirghizia, and in the Oryol region of Central Russia can both help to substantiate the above points and to indicate areas where further research is necessary. This fieldwork, part of a larger project entitled 'Ethnic conflicts and the rise of ethnic consciousness in the former USSR', allowed me to develop some working hypotheses about the position of women but, more encouragingly, demonstrated many of the gaps in research on women and ethnicity. One of these gaps is in knowledge of how migration affects the family itself, the balance of gender roles within it and women's lives. Retrospective reconstruction of women's migration experiences through the collection of their oral histories seems to be the most effective method of seeking answers to the following questions.

How far may *de facto* and/or *de jure* separation of spouses be a direct result of: (1) the hardships of resettlement? (2) the decision of only one partner to migrate (with inter-ethnic marriage perhaps being a special case)? (3) family strain caused by the social status deprivation experienced by one or both spouses? Do women from the former USSR demonstrate the 'greater resilience and adaptability than men' reported for women's migration experiences in other parts of the world? Is this 'because they have the responsibilities for maintaining household routines' (Buijs, 1993), or are these parallels not valid for Russian women?

Furthermore, according to my observations in two villages of the Issyk-Kul region, where Russians have been living in large numbers, the core of Russian women's adaptive strategies is in self-isolation from the local Kirghiz community. Yet, with the rise of Kirghiz aspirations to national independence, openness to communication, willingness to assimilate local languages, culture and traditions are of vital importance for those Russian-speakers who do not cherish any plans to migrate. This is even more necessary in the villages where much is in women's hands, not only due to their 'visibility' (discussed above), but also because of the specific village atmosphere, with people's lives usually being open to public scrutiny. The worrying tendency towards self-isolation on the part of Russian women living in Kirghizia manifests itself both at the level of consciousness (in perceptions of the native language and culture) and in behaviour (in the narrowing of everyday and professional contacts). Prejudiced stereotyping (most of the Russian women interviewed constructed their Kirghiz counterparts in negative terms) is the reverse side of this self-isolation 'coin' (Kosmarskaya, 1994, 1995).

As for the roots of this syndrome, ambitions to superiority – the 'eldest brother complex' (all the indigenous ethnic collectivities of

Central Asia were assumed to be 'junior' brothers under the Soviet regime) – are most often mentioned in academic debate. My explanation is that the Russians in the 'near abroad' are lacking a strong sense of belonging to an ethnic or sub-ethnic collectivity. As my respondents put it 'we do not know who we are but we are not the true Russians'; 'we are different from the Russians in Russia'; 'we are mankurts' (heroes of the famous novel, *The Day Longer than the Century*, written by the Kirghiz writer Chingiz Aitmatov, who were deprived of ethno-historical memories). Russian speakers outside Russia seem to shape their identities not on ethnic but rather on ideological lines, considering themselves 'Soviet people' and relying heavily on Moscow as an imperial centre in charge of solving their problems.

These findings support the idea of the high potential for migration of the Russian-speaking population, even in those parts of the former Soviet Union which have been enjoying relative ethno-political stability. But how and to what extent do the imperial ambitions of the Russians contribute to their decision to migrate? As for women, are they driven mainly by the 'natural' women's responsibilities for protecting their children's future, or by ideological motivations? To put it in other terms, what is the specific structure of women's discontent with the rapidly changing ethno-social environment, and is it greater than that of men? Gender-differentiated representations of 'Russianness' is another intriguing area of research, together with the 'anatomy' of national self-images. For example, how are political-patriotic aspects of the latter, and so-called 'Soviet values' in particular, articulating with cultural and historical factors? In-depth analysis of the national identities of Russians as they are currently being created, together with their gender-specific differences, is crucial for evaluating the adaptive versus migration potential of diaspora.

Turning to the situation of resettlement, tensions arise every now and then between the migrants from 'near abroad' and the resident population in different parts of Russia. The fact that the newcomers are sometimes labelled '*nierusy*' in the receiving communities of Central Russia (a colloquial disapproving word deriving from the ancient name of the country and implying 'non-Russianness') adds a new layer of ethnic complexity to these tensions, which are usually explained only in terms of competition for scarce resources.

However, there is a social-psychological dimension to the problem. One of the women migrants that I interviewed in the Oryol region generalised it in the following way: 'They do not like us because here, in Russia, only the poor, sick and worthless are good guests.' With all this in mind, the question arises as to whether the social-psychological experiences of women migrants will facilitate interaction with the local community, or exacerbate the tensions. The answer might be one of the key parameters in estimating the socially destabilising potential of the massive inflow of forced migrants to Russia.

Notes

I would like to thank the British Council for its support of my research at the University of Greenwich, London, which contributed greatly to my better knowledge of gender and ethnicity in the European context. I also wish to thank Helma Lutz, Ann Phoenix and Nira Yuval-Davis for their helpful suggestions on earlier drafts of this chapter.

1. 'Forced migrants' are mainly Russian-speaking people, the citizens of the Russian Federation (or entitled to apply for such citizenship), driven by ethno-political and social instability in the 'near abroad', or within Russia and seeking new, permanent, residence. 'Refugees' are the citizens of the newly independent states, i.e. the former republics of the USSR, seeking temporary asylum in the Russian Federation on the grounds of special refugee status.
2. The Oryol region is one of the traditionally agricultural zones of Central Russia. Underpopulated during the last decade, it is now planned that it should receive migrants from the 'near abroad'.

References

Buijs, G. (ed.) (1993) *Migrant Women. Crossing Boundaries and Changing Identities* (Oxford: Berg).

Kosmarskaya, N. (1994) 'Inter-ethnic Relations on the Northern Issyk-Kul: Socio-psychological Aspects'. In *Ethno-Social Processes in Kirghizia*, pp. 49–74 (Moscow: Institute of Oriental Studies, Russian Academy of Sciences).

Kosmarskaya, N. (1995) 'Russian Women in Kirghizia: Coping with New Realities', *Women's Studies International Forum* vol. 18, nos 4–5, summer.

Literaturnaya Gazeta (1993), 'How to Subdue the Migration Elements in Russia?', 28 August.

Nezavisimaya Gazeta (1993), '*The Russians in the Near Abroad*', Gorbachev Foundation Report, 7 September.

Ostapenko, L. and Subbotina, J. (1992) 'Some Problems of the Russians in the "Near Abroad": Migration, Employment, Conflicts', *Russian Ethnographer*, vol. 2, p. 286. (Moscow: Institute of Ethnology and Human Anthropology, Russian Academy of Sciences).

Posadskaya, A. (1993) 'The Women's Dimension of the Social Transformation – from Problems to Strategy'. Materials from the Second Independent Women's Forum, Dubna, 27–29 November 1992 (Moscow/Hilversum: Moscow Centre for Gender Studies/Ariadne Europe Fund).

Posadskaya, A. (ed.) (1994) *Women in Russia: A New Era in Russian Feminism* p. 187 (London: Verso).

Rimashevskaia, N. (1992) 'Perestroika and the Status of Women in the Soviet Union', In Sh. Rai, H. Pilkington and A. Phizacklea (eds) *Women in the Face of Change* pp. 11–13 (London: Routledge).

Rossiyskaya Gazeta, 16 November 1993.

Statistical Reference Book (1992) *Women: Conditions of Labour and Everyday Life* (Moscow: State Statistical Committee of the Russian Federation).

Tishkov, V. (1992) 'Soviet Ethnography: Overcoming the Crisis', *Ethnographic Review*, no. 1, p. 5 (Moscow).

Urban, J. (1994) 'Ethnic Prejudice and Today's Russian Democrats', *Russia and the Modern World*, vol. 1, p. 39 (Moscow: Institute of International Economic and Political Studies, Russian Academy of Sciences).

Vishnevsky, A. (1994) 'Is the Return Inevitable?' *Znamya*. A journal of Fiction and Publicity, no. 1 (Moscow).

Volkov, A. (1991) 'Ethnically Mixed Families and Inter-ethnic Marriages', *Family and Family Policies* (Moscow: Institute of Socio-Economic Population Problems, Russian Academy of Sciences) pp. 82–4.

8 Nationalism and Gender in West Europe: the German Case

Nora Räthzel

A focus on nationalism and gender in Western Europe brings together two areas with which I have been concerned over the last eight years. On the one hand, I have concentrated on the way in which consent is managed in the majority of the population. On the other hand, I have also studied the way in which men and women position themselves within structures of domination, and whether they go along with or rebel against these structures.

Paul Willis's (1977) ethnographic study demonstrated how resistance to school rules did not mean that working-class boys positioned themselves outside social structures. Instead, it served to fit them for the types of jobs available to them. In similar ways, resistance to particular constructions of nation may not constitute resistance to nationalism. This chapter argues that one way in which consent is organised is in the construction of certain images of the nation, certain images of belonging. It examines the construction and reconstruction of notions of nation in Nazi Germany, in former West Germany before unification and in re-unified Germany – the German Democratic Republic and the Federal Republic of Germany. It also examines a particular construction of homeland (*Heimat*) and the way in which it relates to subordination to the nation state. This is to indicate that constructions of the nation that are articulated in the public domain can serve as raw material used by individuals in their everyday life to construct images of Self and Other.

The first part of the chapter considers definitions of the nation, since there is no general agreement on what it is. The second part of the chapter considers the complex ways in which the nation is constructed. It does this by examining definitions of the nation at two key historical moments in the construction of the German nation. The first is German fascism. The second historical period is in the beginning of the 1980s in West Germany when construc-

tions of the German nation and of '*Ausländer*' (foreigners) were re-
formulated. The third part of the chapter moves to another dimension:
it is about how the images provided by and discussed in the public
space are transformed and lived in everyday life. Since the theori-
sation of the nation is far from easy, it is important not to foreclose
discussion; and in the final section of the chapter I want to formulate
a hypothesis and a question about constructions of the nation and
of '*Ausländer*' in Germany today, after unification.

What is a Nation?

A focus on historical context helps to elucidate the intersections of
national and gender processes. Hobsbawm (1990) argues that, in spite
of many highly seminal efforts to define the nation, there remains
an uncertainty about what it is really about, and how nationalism
functions and becomes powerful (although many serious scholars have
already buried it several times).

So what problems have those who have attempted to define the
nation encountered and how can the debate on the nation be moved
forward? Attempts to define the nation by objective characteristics
such as language, territory, cultural traits, etc. are well known but
so are the problems they pose. They do not, for example, account
for all nation states. Taking the example of language, some states
like Switzerland have different languages but one nation, while in
other states only one language is spoken, although there are different
nations (e.g. English in Britain).

Subjective definitions based on opting into the nation, as one of
Renan's (1882) famous quotations states (through the daily plebiscite),
have also been criticised for their voluntarism (Hobsbawm, 1990)
and for being naive, as many people have been and are forced into
a nation state without wanting to be, while some who want to be
part of one are excluded. In addition to those more specific criticisms
the main challenge for definitions of the nation has come from the
assessment that nations, as well as national identities, are not 'given',
and, therefore, cannot be 'objective'. They are rather social constructions, and historically very new constructions (Hobsbawm,
1990; Gellner, 1991; Anderson, 1988). While the social construc-
tionist paradigm has provided us with fruitful historical and
contemporary analysis, it also poses some problems. Some of the
scholars working within this paradigm treat the fact that nations (and

therefore national identities as well) are historical social constructions as if this makes them 'false' (this is for instance a criticism made
by Anderson [1988] against Gellner and Hobsbawm). It follows
logically from this position that if one could only convince people
that their image of the nation is a recent historical construction, they
would abstain from nationalism. However, what this overlooks is
the power of national constructions and the specific ways in which
they are reproduced. The question posed by Althusser: 'How are
the power relations reproduced?' could be fruitfully posed in relation
to the nation. Equally, Gramsci's question, asked from an opposing
point of view: 'How can the subordinated classes gain hegemony,
that is construct a "national unity"?', is a seminal question for studies
of the nation. These two questions can be integrated into a concept
in which the nation (no difference is made here between nation and
nation state) is viewed as a form of 'societalisation'.

The Nation as a Form of 'Societalisation'

Societalisation can be seen as a double process, taking place as societalisation from above (imposed from outside/strange;
Fremdvergesellschaftung in German) and societalisation from below
(practised by the subject; *Selbstvergesellschaftung* in German). It is the
way in which individuals become, are formed and constitute
themselves as active members in a given society. By using the word
'societalisation' instead of the more common socialisation I want to
stress the active nature of this process for individuals. Socialisation
is often used in a way that suggests that it is a passive process with
individuals being made, for instance, through education, into a
certain social person (a woman, or a member of a social class, ethnic
group, nation, etc.).

   If the nation is defined as a specific form of societalisation (instead
of as its political characteristic, from liberal to fascist) we can analyse
it as a process of balancing the relation between domination (societalisation from above) and self-determination (societalisation from
below). Self-determination in this case is not used in the strictly
political sense, but rather as an attempt to gain control over all
aspects of one's life.

   While in feudal systems there are concrete personal dependencies through mutual obligations between the dependant and the one
depended on, nationality transgresses these direct relationships. It is
constructed as a personal status, independent of social class or any

other social group (see Grawert, 1973). As Poulantzas (1978) has pointed out, the construction of separate individuals, without any affiliation to a collective or group, is a condition for forging them into the new unities (nation, public opinion, etc.) which are necessary to organise consent to the power bloc within the modern nation state.

From the beginning women were not part of this newly forged collectivity. Their voting rights took decades of struggle and real equality (not just formal equality) has not been realised yet. In a different way, those who are not defined as belonging to the nation (whose unification is always in process, never achieved once and for all) are not granted the rights of independent individuals in the nation state (see the discussion below).

What does the construction of the nation mean for the relations of power? On the one hand, individuals are liberated from immediate dependencies, they gain possibilities of self-determination. The limitations of region and state are transgressed. On the other hand, the way in which society works becomes more complex. Concrete experiences are no longer sufficient to the understanding of social phenomena that are relevant to every individual's life. (In fact, concrete experiences were never really enough, but it was felt that they were and the rest was explained through religion.) This relation of gaining some control over one's life – at the same time losing a more limited, but well known, control as well as losing the security that was also part of the relations of personal interdependencies – poses problems for the developing nation state. To organise consent and legitimation the nation state has to engage with the everyday experience of its subjects. Those experiences, the elements of life into which people invest their emotions, the ways in which they develop control of their lives and gain elements of self-determination, have to be 'nationalised'.

The nation state does not do away with dependencies, relations of domination and social contradictions. It tries to reconcile them, by organising the way in which individuals live their relation to social conditions, for instance in constructing the relation between capital and class as one of equal partners. (To avoid misunderstandings: this is a construction, which is 'real' as it is inscribed in social institutions within which representatives of the classes act as opposed, but equal partners.) One way of reorganising the relation of the individuals to their social conditions (and the one that is relevant to this chapter) is to 'bridge' the social antagonisms through constructing a superordinate belonging to the nation that is articulated against the background of a threatening Other. It is mainly against this Other, constructed as not belonging to the nation and yet living inside it, that horizontal differences and vertical antagonisms can be transformed into an unstable unity. Because of the constant instability of this unity, the image of an 'enemy within' who threatens to undermine the social order is always lurking in the background, ready to come on to the scene in times of crisis. The 'enemy within' is often a racialised Other who is excluded from the unity of the nation state. The contradiction between the promise of the modern nation state and what it actually delivers provides a further reason for the inscription of racialisation into the heart of the nation state. It promises comprehensive self-determination of the individual, freedom and democracy and yet only provides possibilities of intervention in restricted forms (within certain political institutions). In certain areas almost no self-determination is possible. We still read the famous sign, quoted by Marx, saying: 'No admittance, except on business.' This contradiction, and the social result of it – the contradiction between the widespread acceptance of the concept of equality, together with actual social inequality – has, as some scholars have pointed out (e.g. Verena Stolcke, 1987), engendered theories and ideologies of natural (or cultural) superiority/inferiority in justification of this contradiction. As it is the specific social position that marks the differences and contradictions between social groups, their unity (homogeneity) can only be derived from the assumption of natural features or characteristics. There are several reasons why the concept of the nation, once established in the nation state, is so powerful. For the questions I am posing, one reason is of particular importance. It is the ability of the nation to articulate itself with practically all practices in which individuals try to gain control over their lives, from body practices, sexuality, family, up to culture, philosophy and politics. To say it in other words: the ability to act on all levels of everyday life exists only in a specific historical form. There is no human ability 'as such'. This specific form is shaped by the traditions, rituals, ideologies and cultures of the respective nation (or nations) within which individuals have developed. Their competence is always a competence within a realm of incompetence, that is set by the structures of the society (or societies) in which they developed their social abilities. This does not imply by any means that there is only one national culture or one national ideology. However, the diverse cultures within a given nation, shaped by class, social strata, gender, age, professions, etc., have certain elements in common when compared with cultures within other nations or with so-called 'foreign cultures' within the same nation. These comparisons and constructions produce the homogenising effect which is no less real because it is the result of such comparisons.

It is because the nation is inextricably linked with state practices that subordination and consent to the nation state can be experienced as a form of securing social facilitation and competences. On a more material level the nation state provides social security (Balibar, 1990). According to the historical and political conjuncture, the forms of power relations operating in the nation state, the different types of nation that are operationalised, the elements that define its unity, and also define the Other that is constructed as threatening it, vary historically and with the political systems in which they occur.

Constructions of the German Nation

I will now consider some recent events in German history and examine the ways in which the German nation was constructed politically and 'biologically'. I started to look at this more closely because of the widespread notion that the German nation is defined as *'voelkisch'* – which means to say that the German nation is constructed purely by descent or 'blood', and that, therefore, there is a specific form of racism in Germany related to exclusions of those who are not biologically linked with the nation. While, of course, this is not incorrect, it is not the whole story.

It is also often said that the German construction of the nation, as opposed to the French one for instance, is based on a romantic notion of an ethnic unity or a unity by blood, instead of being based on the political will of the people and on universal human rights. This dichotomy was originally developed by Hans Kohn (1945), who ascribed the political definition of the nation to the West, the cultural one to the East. However, Heinrich August Winkler (1985) is critical of this position. He argues that both definitions of the nation coexist. Moreover, the political definition of the plebiscite always included elements of force from above and not all cultural definitions of the nation are undemocratic (see Winkler, 1985: 8). In his latest book, Silverman (1992) has shown that romantic and cultural or even naturalising definitions of the nation have always accompanied the political ones, including Renan's (1882).

The following section of the chapter argues that even in fascism we find a relation between the construction of the nation by descent, and a political construction of the nation. These two elements have to come together in order to organise the consent of the dominant groups.

The Concept of the German Nation in Fascism

It is very well known that the fascist conception of the German nation was of a nation as a race, whereby race was defined by the mythical notion of 'blood'. But, on closer examination, there is a second aspect to be found, for instance in the second paragraph of the Nürnberger Reichsgesetzgebung. This says that only those who are German by blood, or by kindred blood, and who show that they serve the German people, can be members of the German Reich (*Reichsbürger*).[1]

In the same paragraph, belonging to the nation is constructed in two ways: through blood and through politically correct behaviour. This behaviour serves as proof of having the 'right blood'. So there was, clearly, a relation between a political definition and an apparently biological definition of those who belong to the nation.

Such a combination is useful from the point of view of the dominating power. The problem for the power bloc, even in dictatorships, is that it has to organise subordination and activity simultaneously in order for society to function. People have to be 'subjects' in this double sense: subordinated and self-active. One way of organising this in fascism was to insist that the nationals had to show by their activity that they had the 'right blood', in order to be accepted as part of the nation. Thus the dual concept of subordination and activity could be organised at the same time. This had consequences for the image of the so-called 'Other' – in the fascist case, for the image of the Jews. The Jews were not only seen as another 'race', but as those who were responsible for the main social conflicts. They were seen as capitalists *and* as socialists, those who undermined the society by exploitation and by revolution. These images provided the possibility of homogenising the nation, of forging together two very different, opposing groups within society: those who were capitalists and exploiters, and those who were exploited. Both groups could see themselves as allies against the foreign forces which they could think of as being the source of their fears: the danger of revolution (for the capitalists) and the sufferings caused by exploitation or unemployment. In addition, if Jews were the capitalists and the socialists, then German capitalists and workers with revolutionary ambitions were no longer in the line of fire.[2] These constructed inclusions and exclusions as part of nation-building were part of a very conscious political programme. One can quote Hitler on this: 'I knew perfectly well, just as well as those tremendously clever intellectuals, that in the scientific sense there is no such thing as race.' But 'I have to fuse those nations into a higher order if I want to get rid of the chaos of an historic past that has become an absurdity. And for this purpose the concept of race serves me well' (quoted in Louis L. Snyder, 1978: 215: from Rauschning, 1939).

And women? They were the breeders of the 'proper race'. The quasi-biological concept of the nation meant that women in fascism came into the concept of the nation as the breeders of the 'proper race'. Where you have a biological, a dominant biological construction of the nation, the construction of women is that of being the breeders of that race. Women, as well as 'races' were identified mainly in terms of their assumed biological features. As with 'blood', women's 'nature' was assumed to be both 'given' and a result of efforts by women to meet the expectations with which they were confronted. Claudia Koonz (1991) analysed how women's organisations and party politics worked to get women to fulfil their 'natural roles' of reproducing the 'Aryan race' and the ideological values and norms necessary to secure consent.

When the fascist war machine needed women in production as factory workers they came into conflict with women's images of themselves as mothers and wives. A new ideological offensive had to be launched in order to transform loyalty to the family and to husbands into loyalty for '*Führer und Vaterland*'. It is important to recognise that, although in Western societies the family can be seen as a cornerstone of the stability of the nation state and, hence, supportive of state domination (see Donzelot, 1977), it can also be a site of resistance against the state. Anti-war and peace-movements have tried to articulate women's loyalty to their husbands and children with resistance against war. Although this politics can be seen as problematic because it reinforces the essentialist image of women as natural caretakers, it shows the contradictory relation between women's attachment to their families and their loyalty to the nation and/or the state.

Therefore I disagree in part with the way in which Anthias and Yuval-Davis (1992) locate women's participation in the processes of 'nationalisation' and 'ethnisation'. They point out five major ways of participation: (1) as biological reproducers of members of ethnic collectivities; (2) as reproducers of the boundaries of ethnic or national groups; (3) as participating centrally in the ideological reproduction of the collectivity and as transmitters of its culture; (4) as signifiers of ethnic or national differences, as a focus and symbol in ideological discourses used in the construction, reproduction and transformation of ethnic or national categories; and (5) as participants in national, economic, political and military struggles. In point three, there is an elision between ideology and culture, which is not helpful in elucidating processes of nationalism and ethnicity. There are, of course, many definitions of ideology and culture. I find it useful to differentiate between the two and to define ideology as societalisation from above and culture as societalisation from below. For the purpose of analysis ideological societalisation would be the way in which individuals are subordinated and subordinate themselves to the state-order, whereas culture is the way in which people attempt to exercise what they regard as meaningful action in their own interests. However, in the empirical practices of individuals we always find both aspects intertwined. Yet, it is important to differentiate them analytically in order to be able to understand the ways in which resistance is articulated with subordination. This is particularly the case since these forms of articulation are at the same time the points of intervention for a radical democratic politics.

If we make a crucial difference between cultural and ideological practices, women's 'transmission of culture' cannot be automatically equated with the 'ideological reproduction' of the collectivity. Instead, the relation between the two would be an open question. Empirical research would have to concentrate on the conditions under which cultural practices as practices of resistance or at least of self-determination become articulated with the 'ideological reproduction' of the nation as a collectivity. I will return to this discussion in the section on 'Images of *Heimat*' in order to exemplify this.

Constructions of the German Nation and Images of 'Ausländer' *at the Beginning of the 1980s*

The period of the 1980s seems a large historical leap from the 1940s in West Germany. However, an examination of this period in Germany, in comparison with the Nazi period, helps to illuminate the intersection of biology and politics. My thesis is that from the

1980s onwards (although this is now changing a little for some groups) the dominant way of constructing the German nation was political. The biological dimension existed only under the surface.

I have examined the press-cuttings from five national newspapers, between 1980 and 1982, reading their articles about '*die deutsche Nation*', '*Deutschland*', '*Deutsche*' (the German nation, Germany, Germans). In analysing this material, I tried to examine the main ways in which the German nation was constructed. All the articles I read about Germany, and the German nation, dealt with the question, 'Can we be one nation when we have two nation states?' This was the main question for the right-wing, the liberals, and for the more-or-less left-wing (there was no national newspaper that was really on the Left). This question had to be posed against the background of the major bulk of theories of the nation that equate the nation with the state or see a necessary relation between both. One quotation is representative of the viewpoint of many scholars: 'It [the nation] is a social entity only insofar as it relates to a certain kind of modern territorial state, the "nation-state", and it is pointless to discuss nation and nationality except insofar as both relate to it' (Hobsbawm, 1990: 9–10). This view is one commonly propounded by theorists (with the exception of Otto Bauer, 1924). He proposed the separation of the nation from the state as a strategy to solve the conflicts within a multi-national state. Then the nations could have cultural autonomy and only specific political questions (for instance international politics) would be decided by the state (see Bauer, 1924, and, for a contemporary account of this position, Nimni, 1991).

But since the general view is that a nation becomes a nation because it is represented by one (nation) state, the fact that there were two German nation states after the war posed the constant question of whether there could be one German nation, or, since there were two nation states, did one have to speak of two nations as well?

The answer to this question was unanimous: there is only one German nation. The differences in the answers lay in the reasons given for its existence and in the ways in which this 'unified nation' was defined. In an analysis of the construction of a united German nation, I explored the two main and interrelated difficulties faced in the construction of a German nation (Räthzel, 1992):

1. As the nation means the unity of nation and state, how can there be one nation, when there are two states defining themselves as German?

2. As national identity has to be constructed as existing and remaining static over time, how can a homogeneous national identity be constructed against a historical background which has been rejected and condemned, German fascism?

The next section concentrates on the discourses of the nation which existed in Germany at the beginning of the 1980s. In order to do this, I will focus on three articles published in *Die Zeit* and written by two historians and a journalist. While three articles published in the same issue of a newspaper cannot be claimed to be representative, I am interested in examining the discourses about the nation which existed at the time. For these purposes, the articles I have chosen are ideal in that they present a range of discourses which indicate the different ways in which the unified nation was being constructed. Furthermore, they represent the main themes which emerged in other short articles at the time. The articles I concentrate on are by Hans Mommsen (1981), Karl-Heinz Janssen (1981) and Hermann Rudolph (1981).

The unified nation. Two of the three authors deny that there must be one state in order for one nation to exist. They argue that the nation is not defined by the state. All three authors agree that the unity of a nation is formed in everyday social experiences, that is, through the character of the political and economic system. As these have been different for East Germany and West Germany, on what grounds can unity be claimed? The rationale for this constructed unity differs, being variously 'solidarity', 'unity in diversity', and common historical experience. Hans Mommsen (1981) argues in *Die Zeit* that the nation is defined by 'solidarity'. The historical existence of a German nation, says Mommsen, transcends West Germany and East Germany: it includes German-speaking Swiss, Austrians and other minorities scattered all over the world who are not even aware that they are part of a historical–ethnic unity and have no political loyalty to the divided Germany.[3] What then are the criteria defining this 'historical–ethnic unity'. We are not told. We may guess that the unity has something to do with the German language, as German-speaking Swiss are part of it, but not French or Italian-speaking Swiss. Mommsen also writes of national–cultural solidarity. So unity might also have something to do with culture, but this is not made explicit. However, Mommsen argues that it is because this unity is so widespread that it is wrong for any state to claim to represent all who belong to this ethnic group. His rejection of the need for a united state is directed against the claim of the West German government to represent the inhabitants of East Germany as well. In addition it could be read as at least expressing reservations about reunification.

In the same issue of *Die Zeit* Karl-Heinz Janssen, in trying to define the German nation, presents the opposite case from Mommsen's. He argues that the West German state should not extend its power beyond its present borders. In his view neither culture nor language can be a criterion for defining the German nation because they bear the connotation of 'blood'. According to Janssen, these criteria would apply to Austrians, German-speaking Swiss, people in the Netherlands, in Alsace-Lorraine, and 'even to those minorities living far away in Russia' which would, for him, be absurd. So maybe Janssen does not think there is a unified German nation after all? Far from it: 'The German nation', we learn, 'has survived Particularism, Pluralism, Separatism. It has always been bigger than the form of state it assumed; it assumes many shapes; it is open to the future.' In short, the goal is a German nation not in the form of an indispensable 'united state', but as the 'development of German diversity'.[4] What is it, then, that allows us to call this diversity 'German' and what is this 'nation' that has survived all these particularisms? That remains the author's secret, since it is never discussed.

The third author, Hermann Rudolph, does see a necessary link between a united nation and a united state. He supports the unification of West and East Germany, although he does not suggest any measures which could be taken to achieve this goal. For him, too, there is a German nation in spite of its division into two states. This unity, according to him, is rooted in history, though not, however, in a historical consciousness as this is far too vague. Unity is based on a common historical experience, that has formed 'common values, norms, ways of feeling' (Rudolph, 1981).[5]

This definition, of course, confronts the author with a contradiction: if the unity is formed through common everyday experience, what about the different everyday experiences that have formed the lives of East Germans and West Germans for the previous thirty-odd years? The author's answer is that the nation is still united, but will not be so forever if two different nation states continue to exist. How can this unity be proved? In a discussion of the elements that prove that there is unity of the nation, the author describes the differences between West Germans and East Germans. East Germans – because they cannot identify with their state – are more 'German', more oriented towards unification. West Germans are described as being less in favour of the national, but they are not yet completely lost. This pre-unification description of the differences between East Germans and West Germans is indeed crucial. Here we find defi-nitions of German characteristics and features, that allow the author to speak about the nature of the German nation. But it is precisely here, where definitions are given, that we find not unity but opposition between the 'two Germanies' similar to those con-structed in the other articles of *Die Zeit*. The descriptions of West Germans and East Germans fit into a dualistic framework (as in Table 8.1).

Table 8.1: The Relation between West Germans and East Germans

FRG	GDR
Freedom	Repression
Identification with the state	Resistance to the state
Wealth	Poverty
Technically developed	Technically backward
Democracy	Socialism
Modernity	Old-fashioned values
Orientation towards the West	Depending on the East
Arrogance	Humbleness
Americanisation of culture	Sticking to German values
Individualism	True family life

We are familiar with this dualistic structure from constructions of the Self and the Other, where the Other is usually of non-western origin. On one side we find mostly positive self-images, on the other the corresponding negative mirror-images of the Other. Sometimes, when images of the East are used to criticise West German society, the structure of the images parallel the dichotomy of 'modern' and 'non-modern' or of 'developed' and 'under-developed'. This gives an indication that descriptions of Others have nothing or very little to do with their characteristics, features, behaviours. Rather, there seems to be a of 'logic of Self and Otherness' in Western capitalist societies. The contents and the target group can vary, but the structure seems pretty invariable.

It is perhaps not surprising, therefore, that as soon as German identity is described we find that the West German and East German populations are placed in opposition to each other. In West German liberal discourse, the East German is the negative Other (except at times of self-criticism, when the East German is constructed as the positive Other). This is equally true of conservative discourse, but not of far Right discourse.

Thus, although there are differences between the three articles, each shares a construction of German national identity where East Germans are constructed as the Other against which the Self can be defined. Because the unified German nation is constructed mainly as the unity between West Germans and East Germans, this Other is, at the same time, also the Self. A paradox thus occurs: the unity of the Self (German national identity) has to be constructed against an Other that, at the same time, has to be included because it is also the Self. When the definition of the national identity is opposed to this East German Other, it is described in various concrete ways; but when construction of the German identity requires a definition of the unity between East and West Germans, there is a void.

Janssen (1981) and Rudolph (1981) refer to the past to articulate their proposal for the way in which the German nation should be organised in the future. Janssen sees the time of '*Kleinstaaterei*' (when Germany was divided into many small states) as a model. Rudolph refers to the time of Bismarck as the heyday which defined what it is to be German. Fascism is absent from both accounts.

Only Mommsen mentions and in fact stresses fascism as a decisive period for the construction of the German nation. For him, unity between East Germans and West Germans can only lie in the fact that they have both experienced fascism. Therefore, he argues, they can only construct their common identity by addressing that history.

However, in general, constructions of the German nation only mention the German history of fascism in order to assert that the new Germany has overcome this tradition. German national identity is not only constructed against the East German Other, but also based on the suppression of an historical Other, in the form of the fascist past. However, the German of the fascist past is unconsciously articulated with the East German Other, for only West Germans are seen to have 'overcome' fascism. This is clear in a phrase used by Theo Waigel, the then General Secretary of the Bavarian CSU (Chisrtlich Soziale Union), who in 1987 spoke in favour of creating a 'natural national identity'. This should be done, he said, by not thinking only about the past for, in so doing, one tends to suppress what above all the Federal Republic has achieved for the democratic West in the way of stability, solidarity, freedom and human rights.[6] Though he was trying to speak in favour of creating a German national identity, Waigel talked only about West Germany having the right (more or less) to forget its fascist past. In implicitly denying East Germany this right (because it did not enjoy 40 years of Western history) Waigel implicitly identified it with this past.

This constructed association of East Germany with fascism has become even more obvious since unification. The Stalinist practices of the East German authorities, especially those of the '*Stasi*' (Intelligence Agency), are always equated with fascist practices and the East German populations are said to have lived under dictatorship since 1933. It is therefore no surprise that the most common feature referred to when people speak about German identity is its insecurity. If there is one thing that can definitely be said about the Germans, writes one author, it is that they are constantly asking themselves: 'Who are we? Where do we come from?' But, in my opinion, this insecurity is not the whole story: underlying it there is another, very secure, though hardly ever mentioned, taken-for-granted notion of the German nation as genetically defined, by 'blood'.

This account has, so far, not discussed the ways in which non-Germans were represented in the discourses of the German nation in the 1980s. The reason for this is simply that they were not represented at all. Once we have shown that the Other for German identity in West Germany is the East German and the fascist German, the absence of so-called foreigners in this discourse seems almost logical. In order to discover, however, if there is any relation between the way in which the nation is constructed and the way in which 'foreigners' are constructed, I shall examine articles from *Die Zeit* on the theme of '*Ausländer*' in Germany.

Discourses about '*Ausländer*'. In *Die Zeit* the articles on '*Ausländer*' are (with one exception) mainly sympathetic. They discuss the origins of 'hostility to foreigners', they criticise the government for wanting to restrict the right to asylum, and they comment on individual cases, where refugees have suffered unjust treatment at the hands of courts or other authorities. Yet the assumptions in these articles do not differ fundamentally from those voiced in the conservative press. The main assumption is that there is a 'threshold of tolerance', the existence of which means that, once a certain percentage of '*Ausländer*' are in the country, the 'natural reaction' of the indigenous people is fear, and that this fear leads to rejection and hatred (see, for instance, Schueler, 1982). The presence of '*Ausländer*' is seen as a source of 'conflicts'.

The threshold of tolerance – the need for control. If we look at how these conflicts are described, we find that the 'problems' are identified as being in the shortage of housing, schools that have to deal with 'too many foreign children' or the high rate of unemployment amongst 'foreigners', which is a burden on the social security system. In short, the number of '*Ausländer*' is constructed as a 'social time bomb'.

For those studying racism, these images are not new. Moreover, they are in no way specific to West Germany. Sadly, we find the same images to a greater or lesser degree in all West European countries. Usually, the strategy deployed against the use of such images is to explain that 'foreigners' are not a greater burden on the social security system than are Germans, that they do not take away 'our' jobs, because Germans would not want to do these jobs anyway, and so on. These explanations stay within the logic of the fears expressed because they imply that if '*Ausländer*' were to take 'our' jobs then they would constitute a problem. Moreover, they do not recognise the role that the construction of negative images plays in the organisation of social consent.

For our purpose it is interesting to note that, in the same way in which 'foreigners' are absent from the discourse of German national identity, the German nation is absent from the discourse of the 'foreigner' (I am referring to liberal discourse at the beginning of the 1980s). Indeed, if we compare the discourse of the nation with the discourse of '*Ausländer*' we find contrasting articulations. The discourse of the nation describes it as a haven of sweetness and light, a realm of harmony, where the positive elements of the national Self – democracy, modernity, economic prosperity, etc. – are described and ensured. Those values are disconnected from everyday experiences and conflicts. This is not totally surprising, as the aim of constructing a national identity is precisely to form a unity that bridges horizontal differences and vertical antagonisms. The construction of this unity – which includes rulers and ruled, capital and labour – necessarily requires silence about the relations of dominance and the social conflicts which derive from these antagonisms. It is in connection with '*Ausländer*' that conflicts – unemployment, housing, schooling, social order, social security – are discussed. They are discussed, however, not as internal social conflicts but as conflicts between the 'internal' and the 'external'. Conflicts appear to be imported from the outside. That is, the discourses of the nation and of '*Ausländer*' are opposite, but complementary. Those problems that are allegedly the result of the 'threshold of tolerance' can be viewed as problems which stem from the inability to ensure a proper relation between production and reproduction. If, for example, housing, especially in workers' areas, and schooling become a problem, this tells us that workers' wages are too low to include the costs of reproduction (e.g. housing and schooling) and that the state would have to provide these facilities (themselves paid for out of taxes). Problems of housing and schooling also indicate that there is an imbalance between the number of workers used and the facilities provided to secure the reproduction of workers. In other words, economic and social developments are not under the sole control of either the members or of the state.

By discussing this lack of balance between production and reproduction as a 'problem of foreigners', the focus is shifted from the inability to control social and economic developments to the inability to control 'human nature' (i.e. the natural reactions against a given number of '*Ausländer*'). And as human nature cannot be controlled, the number of '*Ausländer*' must be controlled. In so far as this transformation succeeds, the image of a national identity is preserved (without it even having to be mentioned) with the construction of unity between rulers and ruled. Both government and people are faced with the 'problem of foreigners'. The only difference is that the government is held responsible for doing something to solve this problem. But questions regarding the functioning of the market economy and the general inability to organise social well-being are eliminated.

The solution proposed to the 'problem' of '*Ausländer*' is control: control of the movement of people, and of access to work, to certain residential areas, and to the resources of the welfare state. This control is only applied to '*Ausländer*' or control of their numbers within the country. This is not simply a process of 'scapegoating'. The notion of 'scapegoats' overlooks the effects of this transformation, which is first, to secure loyalty to the nation of those considered as insiders. In addition, demands that the number of '*Ausländer*' be controlled, and debates about how to do this, place people and politicians in the role of imaginary managers of social processes. The sense of powerlessness and helplessness with regard to social developments is thus transformed into an imaginary competence and a capacity for action.

While there is no direct relation between this discourse about '*Ausländer*' and the discourse about the German nation, the function of both is to secure the borders between each. One effect of this is to suppress social conflicts which might call into question the existence of a unified nation. This is because, insofar as discourses of '*Ausländer*' can be identified as conflicts between the internal and the external, people will identify with the state as the social agent that can put an end to these conflicts. Moreover, the reduction of the presence of '*Ausländer*' to a question of their number suggests that their presence is not the result of complex national and international developments, but a fact for which there are simple, mechanistic explanations and solutions. The image of the flood (or the wave) of foreigners not only produces fear but also, at the same time, a 'solution': the idea that a dyke can be built to keep out the flood. Thus, the persuasive strength of this image lies not so much in the fear it produces but in the relief that accompanies the apparently simple 'solution' it proposes.

We see similarities and differences in relation to the image of the Jews in fascism. The similarity is that conflicts derive from 'outside' or 'outsiders'. The difference is that '*Ausländer*' are depicted as an underclass that threatens the social system. There is no anti-capitalist orientation in those images, as there was in the image of the Jews as capitalists. In West Germany in the 1980s it was not necessary to forge a large socialist, revolutionary working class into the concept of the nation. The few groups on the Left could be excluded as being part of the Eastern Other.

The Gendered Nation?

I have not worked explicitly on the way in which the images of the nation and of '*Ausländer*' are gendered. Therefore, I can only pose some questions in relation to it: Why is it that in all these discussions about what the German nation is, women or gender relations are not directly mentioned? Indirectly, though, there are references to images of women. For instance in the image that 'they', the '*Ausländer*', have too many children, and therefore they are overcrowding 'our' schools. This image implicitly also accuses German women, who, by contrast, fail to have enough children, so that 'our race' is going to die out.

One reason that images of women did not play a decisive part in images of the German nation in the 1980s might be that the counter-image in the bipolar construction of that nation is the East German 'Other'. The elements which are used to depict the more powerful West Germany, the 'true Germany', are those of capitalism, democracy, human rights and individual freedom: elements which could be used to represent the advantages of the West in comparison to the East. Women's freedom, and their equal rights, was not exactly something the West could have boasted of in comparison with the East. Perhaps that is the reason why women's emancipation was not stressed at all in the concept of the progressive, Western German nation. This is quite the opposite now, when the German nation is redefined in relation to people from Turkey, or more generally to Islam. Here the progressive nature of 'the West' is exemplified by stressing the equality it grants women (see Lutz, 1991).

Women's Images of 'Heimat' and 'Ausländer' and Their Articulation with the Nation State

In opposition to the concept of the nation, the notion of '*Heimat*' (homeland) is a concept of everyday life. It is a way in which men and women articulate elements of self-determination: '*Heimat*' is the space which one has appropriated, which is 'one's own' – at least symbolically. But '*Heimat*' is also a political category: the degree to which the ruling forces manage to merge the meaning of 'nation'and '*Heimat*' can serve as an indicator of the degree to which they have managed to win consent, that is, to win the 'minds and hearts' of their subjects. However, the merging of '*Heimat*' and nation can also be a process done by the subjects of the nation state themselves. In articulating '*Heimat*' with nation, individuals can subordinate themselves to the dominating constructions of the nation and reproduce the respective notions of Self and Other. To find out more about these processes I asked men and women in seminars across Germany, Austria and German-speaking Switzerland about their images of '*Heimat*' and '*Ausländer*'.[7]

In the following I am concentrating on the answers given by women. I shall try to make my point by giving just one example of what they said (for a fuller analysis see Räthzel, 1994). My sample was composed of the students and social workers, teachers, youth workers, etc. who came to my seminars because they wanted to learn about racism. I want to show how '*Heimat*' is constructed by some of these middle-class women, and to address the question of how this concept of '*Heimat*' is related to the concept of the nation, and leads to consensus from below. This happens with women who are normally very critical, very political, and left-wing, and not at all in harmony with the politics of the nation state.

In images of '*Heimat*', about feeling at home, especially in women, there are no conflicts and contradictions. '*Heimat*', they write, 'is the place where I can feel secure, where I am loved by others, accepted the way I am – I can act authentically.'

If you ask the same women about their images or connotations of '*Ausländer*' you find just the opposite. Surprisingly, these women, who were often active in anti-racist groups, reproduced the image of '*Ausländer*' as the source of social conflicts: from famine to the drug-dealer around the corner. A range of possible evils came up when the women wrote down what they thought of in relation to '*Ausländer*'.

Very few of the women placed '*Ausländer*' in their '*Heimat*'. The places where they felt at home and the places where they saw '*Ausländer*' were conceptualised as completely different. Only one woman, let's call her Berta, made a direct connection by saying that the cafe she used to go to was now populated by so many 'foreign' men that she did not like to go there any more. When I discussed this finding with a feminist group that had formed a campaign group against sexism and racism, one of the women expressed her solidarity with Berta. She could feel how awful it must have been to find your favourite public place occupied by men. Men, she said, are always a threat, always dangerous for women. This is also true of 'foreign' men. She did concede that those men were also weaker than she was, because they had fewer rights than she had. 'But as they are a threat', she said, 'I'm prepared to use my rights against them. And if that had happened to me, I would rather have them expelled.'

What can we make of such sentiments? Condemnation and shock are clearly not useful to the understanding of these reactions. What seems to be happening here is that different forms of subordination are clashing – in this case sexism and racism. Or to say it more specifically: racism becomes a means through which sexism is fought. It appears to become very difficult – for some people impossible – to realise that the group that dominates them can also be the object of domination by the same forces against which they themselves are struggling. In struggling against sexism, or rather expectations of sexism, from a group that is defined as 'the Other', suddenly the secure space of '*Heimat*' can only be safeguarded by defining it in national terms. The nation state becomes the caretaker of '*Heimat*'. The nation state is seen as the institution that protects against the danger from outside.

During the weekend discussions these women had been saying that they were anti-nationalists and against the nation state. Yet suddenly one of them expressed the desire for the state to police a group in a way they have always struggled against, because they perceived that group to pose a threat to their own group or at other groups constructed as 'insiders'.

Of course, these women (and others) do not have the power to expel anybody. But they are (at least partly, because, luckily in this case, people are contradictory) able to deny those groups constructed as '*Ausländer*' their support. Thus, they might struggle less vigorously against the violation of human rights; they might discriminate against people of migrant origin in everyday life, when it comes to jobs, or to participation and representation in political or other groups.

Therefore, in order to elaborate anti-racist strategies, we have to concentrate on those moments where there is a relation between different kinds of power and powerlessness. It is not that one group has power and the other does not. Both groups have certain sorts of power – and certain sorts of powerlessness and the complexities of these need to be recognised. It is only the 'indigenous' women, though, who can 'solve' their problem of powerlessness by referring to the state – a way of gaining power which at the same time keeps them in their position of powerlessness.

In order to develop anti-racist strategies, it is not enough to be anti-nationalist. It is also necessary to try to work out solutions for these kinds of conflicts, where different power structures work together in such a way as to reproduce and stabilise exactly those dominant power structures (e.g. of the state) against which the subordinated groups usually want to fight. This paradoxical situation may already be a starting point for the elaboration of anti-racist strategies that account for the complexities of these relations of power: it leads to the conclusion that anti-racism is not something one does only or even mainly for those subjected to racism, but for oneself. Anti-racism is one of the ways out of the daily mechanisms of self-subordination by which individuals reproduce the structures of domination.

One possible reason for this transformation of anti-sexism into racism emerged in one seminar I held while discussions about the statement of 'expulsion' proceeded. The woman who had made that statement then for the first time expressed her problems with being in the group. As a feminist working in a group that helped abused and violated women and girls she was more committed to questions of sexual violence than the other women. Therefore she often felt isolated (and the other members of the group then said that they often found her to be quite a radical feminist). This feeling had gained strength when an instance of sexual abuse in which a non-German man had been one of the perpetrators had not been taken up by the group (despite its commitment to act against racism and sexism) for fear of inciting racism.

Therefore, one possible explanation for this woman's referring to the state for help and security could be the failure of the self-organised group simultaneously to tackle the different forms of oppression. This is, of course, a very difficult undertaking. But keeping the sites of intervention separate from each other leads to separated forms of identities, where self-determination in one sphere is paralleled by self-subordination in another. Moreover, these separations correspond to the separation of discourses and of state-apparatuses that help to provide the stability of structures of domination. We have seen how this happens in discourses of the nation and of 'foreigners' and how this is reproduced by the way in which individuals conceive their lives and their possibilities to intervene. It is important to note that the ways in which these two structures support each other cannot be understood as some form of manipulation, or as individuals just aping what is said in the media. The problem is with the way in which cultural practices and practices of self-determination and/or resistance are intertwined with dominant social structures. They form part of the individual's identities and are taken for granted. It would take tremendous effort to transgress these taken-for-granted separate spheres, whereas it is a comparatively easy task to produce constructions of how society works which do not challenge the logic of these separations.

In the discussion above, I have tried to show how constructions of the nation emerge almost unconsciously to safeguard the image of a secure '*Heimat*' in everyday life. In what follows I want to discuss how images of '*Ausländer*' serve to construct specific images of the nation. Here, inclusion and exclusion of certain groups of '*Ausländer*' produce different notions of what the German nation is meant to be. The considerations described below are derived from political experiences and public debates. They are more hypothetical and should be read as suggestions for further reflections.

Reorganisation of German National Identity and Images of the Other

What happened to images of the German nation and the 'Other' after unification? The usual idea is that, after unification, a new image of the German nation had to be invented and, as a result, nationalism was strengthened. But this explanation underplays the increasing complexity of the situation. A short example may shed light on what I mean.

One response to increasing demonstrations of strength by nationalists has been what were called '*Lichterketten*', chains-of-light, because processions of anti-nationalist people carried candles. In Munich, about 300,000 people took part. In Frankfurt, where about 200,000 demonstrated against violence against '*Ausländer*', an incident occurred afterwards in the underground. Somebody, apparently from East Germany, recognisable by his Saxonian accent, said, 'Well, I don't know what this fuss is all about – just for those few "Kanaken"'. A West German man retorted, 'You shut up, or you leave this place, after all you are the reason why we have to do all this nonsense.'

The form of anti-racism that was produced by the West German man was not so much in favour of '*Ausländer*', but rather it was constructed against East Germans in a context where West Germans had to prove that Germany is a democratic, liberal country, 'friendly to foreigners' (as Chancellor Kohl likes to call it), and had to assert their opposition to the bad behaviour of the East Germans, who were spoiling the image of the German nation abroad. In reality, however, the '*Lichterketten*' took place after the death of Turkish women whose house had been burned by neo-fascists in West Germany, in Mölln.

If we look at the different ways in which anti-racism is nowadays articulated in Germany, we can see that every anti-racist group has its '*Ausländer*' whom they like and want to protect. They thus reject other Germans who don't want to protect the same group. For the West Germans, the asylum-seekers are the group they reject most. For the East Germans, it is Gypsies and people coming from Eastern Europe. For many West Germans, the Turks are fine, because they work hard and, therefore, are sometimes even more acceptable than the East Germans. But 'the West' is not a homogeneous group either. There are yuppies who especially love black people (because they stereotype them as great musicians) and people on the Left who are committed to the rights of the Kurds because they consider them revolutionary.

While these processes of liking and protecting particular groups of 'Others' can be patronising, my argument is that the new form of constructing the nation and the 'Other' is no longer about con-structing a uniform, absolute homogeneity, as, for instance, during fascism. In tune with the needs of the flexible work process where flexible people with ever changing abilities and identities are needed, we find attempts to construct notions of the nation that include diversity, but are nevertheless exclusive of certain (differing) groups of so-called foreigners. In competing with each other, the different attempts to construct what is to be the new German nation use different images of 'foreigners' in different ways. The more liberal tend to define the new Germany by including certain groups of 'foreigners' (for instance those who have been living in Germany for a long time and do useful work) and supporting immigration laws that would allow a quota of 'foreigners' to immigrate into the country. More conservative and right-wing groups declare that no more 'foreigners' should enter the country, although they are still in favour of the 'ethnic Germans' (the '*Aussiedler*') entering the country. Neo-fascist groups do not want any non-Germans in Germany, and their attacks are oriented against '*Aussiedler*' as well.

Rethinking the Nation

For the reasons discussed above, I think we have to rethink and recon-ceptualise our concept of multiplicity as a means to challenge homogeneous concepts of the nation. Multiplicity can also become a means of stabilising structures of dominance. In the German tradition of nation-building, for instance, diversity, was (and is) often seen as characteristic of the German nation (see Janssen, 1981, above). This has to do with German history. Until 1871 there was no German nation state, but many small states that called themselves German. Therefore, the notion of multiplicity has always been an important part of the definition of the German nation. The principle of federalism in the constitution is valued by all political parties. The different '*Länder*' (states) and their populations define themselves to different degrees by their belonging to a '*Land*'. In this situation images of the Other play an even greater role in securing some kind of homogeneity that articulates multiplicity without denying it. This notion of diversity is also promoted by the far-Right, for instance by the historian Helmut Diwald, who is known for questioning the existence of the gas-chambers in concentration camps, on the assumption that they were technically impossible: 'Die Gliederung in Stämme ist dem Reich der Deutschen in die Wiege gelegt worden. Sie ist eine unserer Besonderheiten. Ihre Vielfalt und Eigensinnigkeit spiegeln sich sogar noch in den rücksichtslosen Kämpfen der politischen Parteien bei uns. Dieses Merkmal ist bei den Deutschen so ausgeprägt wie bei keinem anderen Volk Europas' (Diwald, 1982). This translates as 'The German Reich was born structured into different tribes. It is one of our peculiarities. Its multiplicity and stubbornness are even reflected in the thoughtless struggles of the different political parties today. No other people in Europe is characterised by this feature in such a distinctive way.'

Multiplicity, in this account, serves as a basis for the exclusion of those who do not belong to the specific diversity defined as typical for Germany (for instance through language, but more importantly through notions of modernity and democracy). In our day this old notion of multiplicity is articulated with post-modern notions of diversity and multiplicity. But this does not necessarily mean that the country or its population is more open towards 'foreigners' and their differences. On the contrary, (post-)modern forms of living plurality can themselves become means of exclusion. Preserving a (minority) culture against the attacks of a dominant culture can, for example, be defined as backwardness. And indeed we have seen and see examples of the essentialising of cultural identities as a reaction (though not exclusively) to discrimination by a majority. That is to say, the notion of multiplicity and diversity does not stand automatically on the side of progress and anti-racist inclusion. Similarly, the notion of unity is not automatically backward or racist. We have to analyse more deeply how these concepts articulate or fail to articulate power relations against self-determination.

Important problems to be addressed remain: how can we develop forms of belonging that give people the necessary security to intervene politically, and are not exclusive? Concerning the relation between sexism and racism I referred to above: how can we develop forms of fighting structures of domination (e.g. sexism) without constructing them as absolute? How can we learn to articulate different structures of domination and thereby form alliances between the groups that are affected by those structures in different ways? How can we learn to negotiate conflicts between individuals and groups who form part of different structures of domination in a horizontal way, that is, without retreating to state-powers? Difficult as these questions are, they must be addressed in order to further understand how nationalism is produced and reproduced in everyday practices and in order to find points of intervention against the articulations of nationalism, sexism and racism.

Notes

I am very grateful to Andy Godfrey and Ann Phoenix who transformed this text into proper English.

1. Reichsbürger ist nur der Staatsangehörige deutschen oder artverwandten Blutes, der durch sein Verhalten beweist, dass er gewillt und geeignet ist, in Treue dem deutschen Volk und Reich zu dienen. (Die Nürnberger Gesetze über das Reichsbürgerrecht und den Schutz des deutschen Blutes und der deutschen Ehre nebst Durchführungsverordnung, 15 September 1935).

2. Just to make sure that I am not misunderstood: the production of these images was not enough to organise consent. Violence was part of these 'persuasive' methods. But they are a part of the explanation for the large support Hitler had before and after power was handed over to him.

3. 'Die geschichtliche Existenz der deutschen Nation als historisch-ethnische Einheit greift über die beiden deutschen Staaten weit hinaus und umschließt auch diejenigen Minderheiten in aller Welt, die sich einer politischen Loyalität gegenüber dem zweigeteilten Deutschland in keiner Weise bewusst sind' (Mommsen, *Die Zeit*, 7, 6 February 1981).

4. 'Die deutsche Nation hat Partikularismus, Pluralismus, Separatismus Überlebt. Sie war allzeit grösser als die staatliche Form, sie passt in viele Gefässe, sie ist offen zur Zukunft.' Das Ziel ist

'eine Nation nicht als unabdingbare staatliche Einheit', sondern als 'Entfaltung der deutschen Vielfalt' (Janssen, *Die Zeit*, 7, 6 February 1981).

5. Es sind die 'Prägungen, Verhaltensmuster und Überlieferungen, mit denen sich die Vergangenheit im Unterbau der Deutschen niedergeschlagen hat' (Rudolph, *Die Zeit*, 11, 6 March 1981).

6. Man solle nicht 'zu sehr rückwärts denken', denn dabei werde verdrängt, 'was gerade die Bundesrepublik Deutschland in den 40 jahren an Aufbauarbeit, an Solidarität und Stabilität für den demokratischen Westen geleistet hat, wie groß ihre Beiträge zur Aufrechterhaltung der Freiheit und der Gewährleistung der Menschenrechte waren' (*Die Welt*, 12, 15 January 1987).

7. A more detailed account can be found in Räthzel (1994).

References

Althusser, L. (1977) *Ideologie und Ideologische Staatsapparate* (Hamburg: Westberlin VSA).

Anderson, B. (1988) *Die Erfindung der Nation* (Frankfurt: Reihe Campus).

Anthias, F. and Yuval-Davis, N. (1992) *Racialized Boundaries. Race, Nation, Gender, Colour and Class and the Anti-Racist Struggle* (London: Routledge).

Balibar, E. (1990) 'Die Nation-Form. Geschichte und Ideologie'. In E. Balibar and I. Wallerstein, *Rasse, Klasse, Nation* (Berlin/Hamburg: Argument-Verlag).

Bauer, O. (1924) *Die Nationalitätenfrage und die Sozialdemokratie* (Wien).

Brubaker, R. (1992) *Citizenship and Nationhood in France and Germany* (Cambridge, Massachusetts/London: Harvard University Press).

Cohen, P. (1988) 'The Perversions of Inheritance: Studies in the Making of Multi-Racist Britain'. In P. Cohen and S. Bains (eds) *Multi-Racist Britain* (London: Macmillan) pp. 9–120.

Diwald, H. (1982) 'Die Deutsche Einheit kommt bestimmt ...', *Die Welt*, 6 March.

Donzelot, J. (1977) *La Police des Familles* (Paris: Les Editions de Minuit).

Gellner, E. (1991) *Nationalismus und Moderne* (Berlin: Rotbuch).

Gramsci, A. (1971) *Selections from Prison Notebooks* (London: Lawrence and Wishart).

Gramsci, A. (1991) *Gefängnishefte 1 bis 6* (Berlin/Hamburg: Argument-Verlag).

Grawert, R. (1973) *Staat und Staatsangehörigkeit. Verfassungsgeschichtliche Untersuchung zur Entstehung der Staatsangehörigkeit* (Berlin: Duncker und Humblot).

Hall, S. (1989) *Ausgewählte Schriften. Ideologie, Kultur, Medien, Neue Rechte, Rassismus* (Berlin: Argument-Verlag).

Haug, W.F. (1979) 'Umrisse zu einer Theorie des Ideologischen'. In *Projekt Ideolgie Theorie: Theorien über Ideologie* (Berlin: Argument-Verlag). pp. 178–204

Hobsbawm, E.J. (1990) *Nations and Nationalisms since 1780* (Cambridge: Cambridge University Press).

Janssen, K.-H. (1981) 'Deutsche Einheit – ein langer Seufzer? (Der Begriff der Nation: zu schade für Parteirituale)', *Die Zeit*, 7, 6 February.

Kohn, Hans (1945) *The Idea of Nationalism* (New York: The Macmillan Company).

Koontz, C. (1991) *Mütter im Vaterland* (Freiburg im Breisgau: Kore).

Lutz, H. (1991) *Welten verbinden – Türkische Sozialarbeiterinnen in den Niederlanden und der Bundesrepublik Deutschland* (Frankfurt aM: Verlag für interkulturelle Kommunikation [IKO]).

Mommsen, H. (1981) *Die Zeit*, 7, 6 February.

Nimni, E. (1991) *Marxism and Nationalism. Theoretical Origins of a Political Crisis* (London: Pluto Press).

Poulantzas, N. (1978) *Staatstheorie* (Hamburg: VSA-Verlag).

Räthzel, N. (1992) 'Nationale Identität und Bilder von "Ausländern"'. In *Osnabrücker Beiträge zur Sprachtheorie*, vol. 46. Der Diskurs des Rassismus. Herausgegeben von Siegfried Jäger und Franz Januschek. März 1992. S.194–209.

Räthzel, N. (1994) 'Harmonious Heimat and Disturbing "Ausländer"', *Feminism and Psychology*, vol. 4, no. 1, pp. 81–98.

Rauschning, H. (1939) 'Hitler Speaks. London. German: 1973'. In *Gespräche mit Hitler* (Zürich/New York: Europa-Verlag).

Renan, E. (1882) 'Qu'est-ce-qu'une nation? Paris. German: 1993: Was ist eine Nation'?. In M. Jeismann and H. Ritter (eds) *Grenzfälle. Über neuen und alten Nationalismus* (Leipzig: Reclam).

Rudolph, H. (1981) 'Wovor wir nicht fortlaufen können. Die Nation: kein unversiegbares Kapital, aber mehr als Gefühl und Wellenschlag', *Die Zeit*, 11, 6 March.

Schueler, H. (1982) *Die Zeit*, 1, 1 January.

Silverman, M. (1992) *Deconstructing the Nation* (London: Routledge).

Snyder, L.L. (1978) *Roots of German Nationalism* (Bloomington/ London: Indiana University Press).

Stolcke, V. (1987) 'Das Erbe sichern', *Das Argument*, vol. 29, no. 163, May/June.

Winkler, H.A. (1985) 'Der Nationalismus und seine Funktion'. In H.A.Winkler (ed.) *Nationalismus* (Königstein/Ts: Athenäum) pp. 8–34.

Willis, Paul (1977) *Learning to Labour. How Working Class Kids Get Working Class Jobs* (London: Saxon House).

Index

abortion, in former Yugoslavia 132
academia
   minority women within 73–4,
      75–6
   position of women in former
      Yugoslavia 133
   research on gender and ethnicity
      in former USSR 151–2, 153
   see also education
All my friends are exiles (poem) 83–4
Anderson, Benedict 3, 4
Anthias, Floya 91, 169
anti-nationalism 71, 134
anti-racism 71, 182, 183–4
asylum seekers *see* refugees
Ausländer ('foreigners'), German
   discourses of 176–8, 180–1,
   183–4

Bakic-Hayden, M. 105
Balibar, Etienne 7
Balkans, Orientalist discourse of
   105–6, 108–9, 110–11
Bannerji, Himani 75–6
Bayramova, Fauzia 150
belonging
   and racist violence in Germany 98
   social construction of 91
Billig, M. 34, 44
black consciousness, and challenges
   to racism 75
'blood and soil' arguments 3–4, 110
body, women as symbol of social
   body 91–2
Bosnians, ethnic identity of 106
Bovenkerk, F. 71
Brah, A. 70
British immigration law 12–13
British national identity
   and European Union 42

and gender of young people 30,
   40, 41–2, 45
and patriotism 35–8, 45
and race 27, 29
and race of young people 30–2,
   33–4, 42
British National Party (BNP) 29
Busia, Abena 83

Carty, Linda 76
Caucasians, migration of and
   prejudice against 145–6, 150
'Central Park rape' 89
community (*Gemeinschaft*), women
   as symbol of continuity 91–2,
   96–7, 99
consciousness raising 15–16, 75
Crenshaw, Kimberlé 90
Croatia, use of Orientalist discourse
   105
culture, as explanation of social
   inequality 79

decentralisation, in former
   Yugoslavia 123–5
descent
   and 'blood and soil' arguments
      3–4, 110
   and constructions of German
      nation 166, 167
   and young people's national
      identity 31, 32, 33
Die Zeit 171, 176
Diwald, Helmut 185

Eastern Europe, new nationalism in
   6
economy
   current problems and deprivation
      in former Yugoslavia 132–3